DANGEROUS

IAN PROBERT

DANGEROUS

AN INTIMATE JOURNEY INTO THE HEART OF BOXING

First published by Pitch Publishing, 2016

Pitch Publishing
A2 Yeoman Gate
Yeoman Way
Worthing
Sussex
BN13 3QZ
www.pitchpublishing.co.uk
info@pitchpublishing.co.uk

ISBN 978-1-78531-199-4

Typesetting and origination by Pitch Publishing
Printed by Bell & Bain, Glasgow, Scotland

Contents

For Laura and Sofia,
how lucky I am.

Acknowledgements

I T'S safe to say that this is the first time that I've ever even considered writing acknowledgements for any of my books. But in this case I really do not have a choice.

During the past eight or so months I have been completely overwhelmed by the kindness and – dare I say it – *love* that has been extended towards me from the boxing community. As such I have to thank, from the very bottom of my wallet, all those people who gave their time to me in what was very much a selfish, self-indulgent project. Legends all of them:

Ben Doughty, for giving me the confidence to write about boxing again.

Herol Graham, for unorthodoxy.

Karen Neville, for being wise and beautiful and changing my perspective on life.

Michael Watson, for allowing me to begin to make amends for past mistakes.

Lennard Ballack, for being a true friend to Michael Watson and making things happen.

Frank Buglioni, for giving me back my appetite.

Clinton McKenzie, kindness and gentleness personified.

Leon McKenzie, for making me realise what I had to do next.

Alan Minter, for being there at the beginning and at the end.

ACKNOWLEDGEMENTS

Ross Minter, for laughter and love.

Mark Prince, for opening up his giant heart.

Glenn McCrory, for opening up his even bigger heart.

Ed Robinson, for his kindness and generosity.

Colin McMillan, for his innate decency.

Kellie Maloney, for allowing me to witness her bravery at first-hand.

Ambrose Mendy, for leading me a merry dance.

Derek Williams, for proving that it's always better late than never.

John Wharton, for asking me.

Steve Collins, for advising me to cry it out.

Anthony Leaver, for letting me come back to play.

Richard Maynard, for a ticket to the circus.

Steve Lillis, for that good word.

Sabrina and Tayla.

Sedat Sag, for loyalty.

Natasha Graham, a force to be reckoned with.

To Glyn Leach, dearly wish we'd had that drink.

All the staff of the Whittington Hospital, for saving my daughter's life.

And to an unnamed Chinese therapist, for sitting and listening to me witter on about myself.

Prologue

FOR anyone out there who is interested (and I'm not entirely sure that even I'm *that* interested) I visited my therapist for the second time this week (although I don't know why I'm calling her 'my' therapist; she certainly doesn't belong to me).

Once again I didn't learn very much from her (does one go to therapists to learn stuff?) except for one very small, minor thing: I'm really not very good at going to therapists.

Being someone who is pathologically punctual (she said we'd address this issue at some point in the future if we had time), I was early. She was late. And all of this set my mind off, not necessarily into a panic, but it got me to thinking as I sat there in a shabby NHS waiting room next to real sick people. *Why was she late? Was it my fault or was it hers?* Last time I saw her she had told me to wait in a specific location at 10.00am sharp and she would be there to meet me. Had she not shown up yet because I hadn't announced my arrival at reception? Yes, that was probably it.

My knuckles began to sweat. I waited until 10.05am and with still no sign of her I decided to be proactive. I would go and look for her.

I had only been there once before but somehow my radar managed to locate her office in the subterranean rabbit warren of identical rooms. But as I went to tentatively knock on her door it suddenly sprang open leaving us standing face to face. If I hadn't been paying attention and able to stop myself it's highly likely that I could have ended up punching her on the nose three times. I don't know what Freud says about hitting therapists. He probably wouldn't encourage it.

There was a shocked silence. It was as if by coming to look for my tardy therapist (she's not mine, by the way) I had broken some kind of fundamental brain-malaise house rule. She looked at me for several long moments, like a granny eyeballing a mugger, and then she sort of said something like, 'Oh…' I couldn't be sure. She's got a very strong Chinese accent.

I broke the silence by apologising for being early and for her being late. I told that there was nothing suspicious about my coming to look for her. Really there wasn't. I was quite normal actually and I was going to try and prove it. Then she asked me to go away and sit back in the waiting room which I said I would but didn't because – let's face it – who likes waiting in waiting rooms? Instead I loitered on the stairs outside her office. If I was still smoking I would have lit up a fag.

All of this meant that a few minutes later when she came to collect me from the waiting room I wasn't there, I was standing on the stairs. And once again there was an awkward silence as she blundered into me, almost falling over in the process, and gave me another shocked look followed by another 'oh'.

It wasn't going well.

We went into her office and I politely asked if I could take a seat. She gave me a shrug, which I quickly translated as meaning, '*Why are you asking me if you can sit down you moron? What a ridiculous question…*' Or perhaps she thought I was actually going to take a seat, pick it up and exit the building with it under my arm. I apologised for being polite and her lack of response seemed to indicate that there was obviously something uniquely absurd about somebody being polite. I told her I was always polite on account of being well brought up. And as the words left my lips I couldn't help but wonder that if I was so well brought up why, at the age of 53, was I seeing a therapist about my nasty and abusive recently deceased father? Then I apologised for apologising.

There was a silence. Then another silence. And then, finally, the silence was broken by a further period of silence.

We stared into each other's eyes. It was very intimate. One of those occasions when you know that if you break the stare the other person has won.

She won. I looked down at my feet and then gathered my senses for another bout of protracted staring. I'd get the bitch this time. Then she finally spoke. 'What would you like to talk about?' she asked.

What would I like to talk about? 'Nothing,' I replied.

Of course I don't want to talk about anything, I explained. Why would I? I've only met you once before and you're expecting me to launch into *when-I-was-a-kid-my-dad-was-horrid-to-me* mode. When I talked intimately, I explained, it was usually with someone whom I knew intimately. Or there was alcohol involved. Perhaps, I suggested, we could both retire to the nearest boozer and after three or four pints of Guinness I'd talk about anything she wanted. Liberally. Honestly. Candidly. And in comfort.

She demurred. Then it was back to the silence. And the staring match.

I talked about Chinese people. It seemed somehow appropriate. Of how I've actually known very few of them in my life. And of how their seemingly innate impassivity always made me feel clumsy and unsophisticated around them. She didn't offer any reaction to these observations but simply continued staring deep into my eyes. Didn't the woman ever blink?

I talked about my illness. About being an undiagnosed hypothyroid disease sufferer for several decades and how it fucked up my life in so many ways. I spoke about this at length, as I'm prone to do. I even managed to bore myself. And finally she showed a reaction. She frowned and in so many words told me to stop 'telling stories' about myself and instead try to articulate my real feelings. She said that my illness was undoubtably a direct result of my childhood.

Now it was my turn to frown: such a comment seemed to me like a monumentally simplistic cliché. But I didn't get time to tell her this because instead I was launching into a description of phatic communion – a form of communication in which words were used not to transmit information but to fill empty spaces. She said she'd never heard of it but that I was doing it now. Of course I was, I agreed. Of course I was.

I told her a few jokes, which she didn't find funny. I told her the same jokes, slower this time, having decided that I was talking too fast for her the first time. They still weren't funny. Fortunately, I wasn't paying for any of this. David Cameron was.

And then for some reason I accidentally-on-purpose started talking about boxing. About how I used to be involved in the sport. About how, many moons ago, I wrote about it for newspapers and edited magazines about it. About how a friend was injured during a fight and this led me to withdraw from the sport and write a book about why I was never going to write about boxing again. I do this a lot. I seem to slip boxing into the conversation more than is healthy or coincidental.

'It seems to excite you,' she announced. 'You should write about it again.'

'Don't be silly,' I replied. 'I haven't done that for…for… for 20-odd years.'

And then the silence returned with a vengeance

When she wasn't staring at me she was shooting sneaky glances at the clock on the wall, whose fingers stubbornly refused to move and then abruptly decided to hurtle around the clock face at supersonic speed. And all of a sudden, just as

I was getting around to telling her about how my father never allowed me to have friends as a child, it was over before it had begun. An object lesson in how to waste an hour of your life in the most unenjoyable, awkward way imaginable.

I climbed to my feet and held out my hand. Once again she looked appalled. In therapist world shaking hands was obviously another monumental faux pas. I apologised for attempting to shake her hand, telling her it was because I was well brought up.

Then I apologised for apologising. Better luck next time, I thought, as I headed for the pub and the pint of cold, frothy Guinness that awaited my arrival

Three hours later another therapist was listening patiently to my life story, gently pouring me placative pints and offering me the occasional sachet of Nobby's Nuts.

Scars

IT was 23 years ago when I last saw him. His eyes were closed and an oxygen mask was strapped to his mouth. His magnificent muscular torso was a tangle of tubes and sensors. He lay on the bed like a sleeping baby. The slightest of frowns pinched his forehead as if he were dreaming the longest dream: a dream that would last for a biblical 40 days and 40 nights before he would awaken to discover that his life had been ripped apart. That he could never again be the person that he used to be.

In a windswept hotel on the outskirts of Essex I sit at the rear of a vast banqueting hall and wait to see his face once more. I'm wearing the suit that I wore at my wedding and for the last three funerals that I attended. You could say that I'm not a suit person. It hangs loose on my body on account of the large amount of weight I've lost in the past couple of years.

'You've put some pounds on,' says a cor blimey voice, 'You used to be a skinny fella.'

The voice takes a seat across from me at the table and I recognise its source. It's also been more than two decades since I last saw him and his hair has waved goodbye – although I'm not one to talk – and he's something like twice the size that he used to be.

'You look like you've lost weight,' I lie.

The other man caresses his beer gut and stares at the floor. 'Yeah… I've been working out,' he says without a trace of irony.

The stranger from my past withdraws to the bar leaving me alone at the dinner table to scrutinise other faces. In the far distance an ex-boxer named Nigel Benn[1] is charging £20 a shot to be photographed with time-ravaged fans. The former world champion looks trim and wears a stylish striped jacket that would probably look ridiculous on anybody else. He grins earnestly and waves a weary fist at the camera. The middle-aged car salesman standing next to him follows his lead for posterity.

On the table closest to me I spot Alan Minter[2] in a dickie bow. A lifetime ago I'd been a 17-year-old waiter serving wine at an event not unlike this one to a bashed-up Minter, who had just lost his undisputed world middleweight title. Back then he was one of the most famous people I'd ever met and I'd been in awe of him. Total awe. But now it's only sorrow. His position at the outskirts of the hall – almost as remote and desolate as my own location – serves as a barometer for just how many people have forgotten his achievements. He's at the back of the queue now and others have moved forward to take his place.

The speeches begin. On a long table at the front of the hall a smiling Nigel Benn is surrounded by other refugees from days gone by. A retired boxer named Rod Douglas[3] sits close to another ex-fighter named Herol Graham[4], the man whose punches put an end to Douglas' career. The two seem unaware of one another's presence and I wonder if this is no accident. To Graham's right is former world featherweight

....

1   **Nigel Benn** born 22 January 1964, Ilford, England. Former Commonwealth and WBO middleweight champion; WBC super-middleweight champion of the world.

2   **Alan Minter** born 17 August 1951, Crawley, England. Former undisputed middleweight champion of the world.

3   **Rod Douglas** born 20 October 1964, London, England.

4   **Herol Graham** born 13 September 1959, Nottingham, England. Former British middleweight champion and EBU middleweight champion.

champion Colin McMillan[5] and an assortment of other former prizefighters' whose blurred features remain hidden in the shadows.

But I'm not here to see these people. Although they all in one way or another belong to my past I'm here to see only one person. I know he's coming because the organiser of this tribute to Nigel Benn tipped me off before generously inviting me along. Everybody else seems to know he's coming, too. It has to be the worst kept secret since someone let it slip that smoking is bad for you.

A whisper from the table, 'Michael's[6] here.' And suddenly I can stand it no longer. I climb to my feet and quietly exit the hall. Standing listlessly at the foot of a smartly decorated staircase are two disinterested looking bouncers. I ask them if they've seen Michael and they gesture towards a small corridor to the left of the staircase.

I find myself standing outside a disabled toilet. I try the handle. It's locked. But just as I'm leaving, the door swings open and a large middle-aged black man with glasses and greying temples appears. We look at each other for a long time and disjointed words tumble from my lips, 'Michael... It's so nice to see you.' It's all I can think of saying. My voice is trembling and already I'm weak with emotion.

The man in front of me is slightly taller than I and wearing a freshly-pressed grey suit. He stretches out a huge hand in my direction and gives me the thumbs-up.

'It's *so* nice to see you,' I repeat. I take hold of that giant hand and gently stroke it like a fragile flower.

'It's good to see you, too,' says Michael. 'Listen, I gotta go now... We'll talk later.'

....

5   **Colin McMillan** born 12 February 1966, London, England. Former British featherweight champion and WBO featherweight champion of the world.
6   **Michael Watson** born 15 March 1964, London, England. Former Commonwealth middleweight champion.

He shuffles past me with obvious difficulty into the darkness of the banqueting hall. Heads begin to turn as Michael rests his hand on somebody's shoulder and is slowly guided towards the top table. The man with the microphone stops talking. It takes several seconds before people begin to understand what is happening.

Back in my seat I watch as Nigel Benn leaves his chair and wraps his arms around Michael. Vanquished and victor reunited. A quarter of a century ago Michael had bludgeoned Benn's exhausted body to the canvas on a memorable evening in Finsbury Park with Benn's Commonwealth middleweight title at stake. But now the pair are locked in a lovers' embrace. The sight is surreal and invigorating and life affirming. I'm breathless and dizzy. Our brief reunion was so simple. So straightforward. So nondescript. In the days leading up to that moment I had been nervous, restless, full of questions. Would Michael remember me? Would he want to see me again after all this time? But it had all seemed so natural. It was more than I could ever have hoped for.

Still more speeches. Food is served: simple but edible and I make decorative chit-chat with the strangers at my table. But I'm yearning to tell somebody about the miracle that has just occurred. About how Michael and I were once friends. About how he was a young boxer and I was a young writer and somehow we formed a partnership that meant something. About how I went to visit Michael on the night of the injury he sustained during a world title clash with Chris Eubank[7] and was received less than warmly by his overprotective friends: even though they should have known better they saw me as nothing more than just another journo, come to get his pound of flesh from the stricken figure in intensive care. About how I decided that the best thing I could do was keep away from him,

7   **Chris Eubank** born 8 August 1966, London, England. Former WBO middleweight champion of the world and WBO super-middleweight champion of the world.

let the ones who loved him do what they could. About how I stopped writing about boxing from that day and tried – really tried – never to return.

At last a break in the proceedings and I find myself walking up to where Michael sits alone for a moment or two. We look into each other's eyes and once again he extends his fist and once more all I can say is, 'Michael… It's so nice to see you.'

Michael looks at me. His face is fatter than it used to be. Ancient scars run like dried up riverbeds above his left eye and across his chin. His hair is dusted at the edges with white, like fake snow.

And I'm choking up again, 'Michael,' I say. 'I just want to thank you. You've made such a difference to my life.'

And it's true. When I first met Michael I was penniless and struggling. Because he *believed* I was able to make a small mark in sports journalism and later as a writer. I owe him a debt that I can never repay.

Michael looks at me curiously. As if he feels a little sorry for me. 'You're too emotional,' he says, his speech slightly blurred. 'You shouldn't worry about things so much.'

'I know,' I agree. 'The older I get, the more emotional I become.'

Then Michael moves his head a little closer to mine. He says, 'I can see that you have the spirit in you.'

Alarm bells ring. I remember that Michael and his family were always very religious. I interrupt him. 'I'm sorry,' I awkwardly stutter, 'but I'm an atheist. I don't believe in God.'

'Neither do I,' says Michael, either lying or de-converted by his near death experience. 'But I can see you have the spirit in you.'

'I'm not so sure about that,' I say.

'I love you,' says Michael.

Did he just say that? Did he just say he loved me? My shoulders droop and I think about all the wasted years. I think about the contribution I could have made to Michael's rehabilitation. I think about what I could have done to assist his slow, painful progress towards a kind of recovery, to repay just a little of what he had given to me all those years ago. The regret overpowers me. The sense of betrayal sickens me.

'I love you, too,' I say. And suddenly everything is all right. We've taken two wildly different routes to arrive here at this hotel in Chigwell on a sticky October night but here we are. I've watched him live out his life in the media. Seen him on the news collecting his MBE. Listened to the crowds cheer as he completed a marathon that took him six tortuous days of walking. But we're here now. I'm 53 and he's 50. There's still time to rekindle our friendship. There's still time.

Michael frowns at me as I gently hold that once violent fist of his in my hand. 'What's your name?' he asks.

Whisky

W HAT am I doing here among the broken noses and bulging scar tissue and calloused hands and knotted brows? The East End accents and shaven heads and bow ties and plunging necklines? I said goodbye to this a long time ago and I tried not to look behind me. But I can't kid myself. I'm no better than the people I used to write about. Deep down I can't keep away. I'm drawn to it. I'm sucked in. The pain and honour and pride and joy and love and hate. Truth and lies. And just like them I suppose a comeback of sorts was always going to inevitable. I'm older, of course, not remotely wiser and my stamina is shot to pieces. Sounds like an ideal time to try and do something that you used to do years ago but abandoned because you couldn't handle it any more. Ring any bells anyone?

* * * * *

Like the fool that I am I decide to walk from the tube to the hotel. It takes about half an hour all in all, give or take the occasional wrong turn and the fact that my shoes just aren't up to the job; I'm not really allowed to wear proper dress shoes like normal people do, I know that. Inevitably my damaged hip begins to play up, as it always does. By the time I arrive I am noticeably limping and the effort of making my good leg do twice as much work has left me dripping with sweat. Steam is coming off me as if I've just stepped out from the shower. When I finally hobble into the foyer and awkwardly shake a few hands it is all too obvious that I don't fit in.

I retreat to the bar. Tonight I'm sticking to shandy. It's important that I don't misbehave. But it goes down too quickly and I order another straightaway. It could just be my own paranoia but I sense that people are staring at me so I find the toilets and look for something I can use to mop away the sweat. I end up using toilet paper but it sticks comically to my forehead like soggy chewing gum. I'm just about to put my freshly-papered head under the hand dryer when a boxer, or maybe an ex-boxer, walks in. The expression on his face is either amused or full of pity. I shuffle away awkwardly.

Everybody seems to be heading upstairs as I'm absorbed into a crowd of around 200 or so 'boxing people'. I can put a name to many of their faces but I'm fairly sure that nobody recognises me. As I climb the stairs I find myself standing beside a well-known boxing trainer named Jimmy Tibbs. I complement him on his recent biography, even though I haven't read it and likely never will. He seems vaguely pleased but suspiciously eyes the toilet paper stuck to my forehead.

My third shandy and I strike up a conversation with Rod Douglas. He and I used to know each other a little many years ago. I remind him that he came to my 30th birthday party when I lived in Bayswater. 'Did I really?' he says, genuinely surprised.

We talk about his son, Tyson. About how I once came to his house when he lived in Bow and Tyson was just a toddler walking around wearing giant boxing gloves and aiming punches at my ankles. In those days I was working for the *Sunday Sport* – a fact that I tend to keep hidden towards the bottom of my CV – and we did a story involving Rod along the lines of 'Nigel Benn Stole My Haircut'. Needless to say it didn't win many Pulitzer Prizes. I tell him about how I recently bumped into the grown-up version of Tyson in a gym, that's Tyson Douglas – not the American Mike Tyson[8] or the English Tyson Fury[9] – and was shocked to discover that he had become a man. A large, muscular, hairy man with a deep voice.

Rod tells me how pleased he is to have been invited to this event. And about how people are being so nice to him. There was always an innate decency about Rod. He looks good. Slim with a well-fitting suit. Unlike myself.

Nigel Benn enters the room and stands close to Rod without ever acknowledging him. Douglas beat Benn many years ago when they were both amateurs and I wonder if the silent treatment has anything to do with that. Surely not after all these years? The pugnacious ex-middleweight boxer is obviously freebasing on adrenaline, clearly enjoying all the attention. He talks mockingly about ex-heavyweight champion Frank Bruno's[10] inability to respond to a punch, about how when he took a hard shot he would just loll about on the ropes with his hands by his sides like a zombie until he was knocked out. I have a pretty clear recollection of Benn doing something just like that from time to time but I wisely decide not to bring it up.

I have it at the back of my mind to try and spend a little time alone with Benn. Maybe get him to talk about those days, way back in the late-80s. It would be nice to discover that there was more to him than the aggressive, truculent persona that he still appears to maintain. 'You're living in Australia now?' I ask, hoping that a little bit of aimless banter might defrost him a little.

....

8 **Mike Tyson** born 30 June 30 1966, New York, USA. Former undisputed heavyweight champion of the world.

9 **Tyson Fury** born 12 August 1988, Manchester, England. Undisputed heavyweight champion of the world at time of writing.

10 **Frank Bruno** born 16 November 1961, London, England. Former EBU heavyweight champion and WBC heavyweight champion of the world.

'Yeah,' he mumbles, without appearing to even notice me before quickly moving off. For a moment I think about following him but decide against it. I watch as he photobombs a group of smiling middle-aged men in shaven heads. He has a huge grin on his face.

He can't possibly remember me, can he? I'm fairly certain that he hasn't a clue who I am even though I was present at a great many of his pre- and post-fight press conferences in the early part of his career and did not attempt to hide the fact that I wasn't exactly president of his fan club. Is that the reason why he just blanked me? Is his memory really that good or is his brusqueness something more congenital? A well-known boxing promoter once described Benn as 'a black man with a chip on his shoulder'. If this is true then it looks to me as though that chip's still there.

But I'm not the only one who's just been blanked. Rod is still standing next to me and Benn didn't say a word to him either. Rod is either pretending that he didn't notice or genuinely doesn't care about this slight. I suspect the former is the case: when I knew Rod all those years ago, like a lot of boxers, he tended to wear his heart on his sleeve.

I ask Rod if he'd mind if I came to see his new gym and maybe interview him and straight away that heart of his leaps into view. For a few moments he looks as if he's in pain. Rod mumbles something about me having already done that and I'm confused. Surely he can't be referring to one of our interviews back in the late 1980s? I don't know how but I suddenly put two and two together. 'You think I'm Ben, don't you?' I frown. That's not a typo you've just read. I'm talking about a writer named Benjamin Calder-Smith, who recently put out a book that had a chapter in it about Rod Douglas.

Rod apologises but his mistake leaves me baffled. I look nothing like Ben. He's taller, broader and infinitely more hirsute than I. It's a difficult mistake to make.

I head over to the bar for my fourth drink and find myself standing beside Herol Graham. They're all here tonight, aren't they? In his heyday Herol was a uniquely talented boxer who had the reputation of being impossible to hit. There are well-worn stories of his loquacious Irish trainer, Brendan Ingle, dragging Herol around the Sheffield clubs offering money to anybody present who could manage to land a blow on him.

It is engrained in urban history that nobody ever could. Somebody, however, has obviously been hitting him. You can see that. In fact, more than many in this room he clearly seems to resemble an ex-boxer. There's a prominent scar across his nose and others above his eyes. This man has certainly been hit. Moreover, there's an incongruous quality to these war wounds. They simply don't seem to belong on Herol's face, which exudes innocence and sensitivity, as well as no small hint of tragedy.

Herol claims to remember me but I don't really believe him. When I was working in boxing I certainly went to a number of his fights and I also attended a fair few press conferences in which he was featured. But I can't recall ever sitting down alone with him for any appreciable amount of time.

In writing this, however, I do remember once receiving a writ from a gentleman by the name of Michael McCartney. Not Paul McCartney's musical sibling I'm afraid, but a rather rapacious Irish lawyer representing Herol's manager of the time, a certain Irish bookmaker named Barney Eastwood. The situation was a frightening mess that concluded with a grovelling apology from the paper I was editing. Maybe that's how Herol remembers me.

The periodical in question had been guilty of printing some quotes by Graham that were mildly critical of Barney Eastwood. At the time I'd thought them fairly innocuous but Eastwood had disagreed and brought in the heavy brigade. It was my first experience of being sued and at the time it scared the shit out of me. Later, I got used to it.

Herol talks to me for a very long time and I'm aware that there's already a common theme developing this evening. Just like Rod, Herol seems to feel a pressing urge to communicate on a deeply personal level. Without any prompting he tells me of his battles with depression and his suicide attempt. 'I drank a bottle of brandy,' he says, 'And then cut my wrists and waited to die.'

It's a slightly awkward conversation to be having with someone who is perhaps only a notch or two above passing acquaintance status but I too share that same desire to forego small-talk. I tell Herol about how the death of my father a year earlier had sent me spiralling into a deep depression – what Douglas Adams would call 'The dark tea-time of the soul'; about how I could not stop myself from crying in the most inappropriate of places, and about how my GP had liberally doled out anti-depressants that had only made things worse.

It's here that we discover further commonality. When Herol attempted suicide he had been taking the same pills that I had been prescribed: a ubiquitous brand called Citalopram. I tell Herol about how I've since discovered that a number of my relatives are long-time users of the drug, about how it's routinely showered over the masses like confetti at a wedding.

We talk about Herol's career; surely the source of the aura of loss that seems to envelop the man in an almost tangible cloud. For Herol was undoubtedly something inordinately special and boxing never really gave him a fair throw of the dice. In the early part of his career Herol was so good, so dazzlingly different in his ring comportment, so insanely great, that the big names on the world scene concluded that he was more trouble than he was worth and simply avoided him. Later on, as Herol approached his 30s, the British middleweight scene

– and to a lesser extent the world scene – became dominated by the Benn-Watson-Eubank triumvirate[11].

And even though on sheer talent alone Herol was more than deserving of a chance to share the stage with these men, he was again excluded. Even more heart-breaking were the three opportunities that Herol did eventually get at winning a version of the world title. The first in 1989 was a highly creditable but grinding split-decision[12] loss to all-time great Mike McCallum[13] of Jamaica. The second, a career-defining and life-transforming loss a year later in Spain. And the final failure came in 1998 after Herol put the defending champion twice on his backside.

We talk about that second loss: always the monkey on Herol's back. On that much lamented occasion Herol was beating his opponent, Julian Jackson[14], hands down; as the old adage says: if it was a boxing match they would have stopped it. At the start of round four, however, with Jackson's right eye swollen into uselessness, the referee indicated that this would be the final round. Herol was told that all he had to do was keep his chin out of harm's way for a further 180 seconds and he would be champion of the world.

Like many, I've watched the video of that fourth round more times than I care to remember. And I kind of suspect

11 Over a four-year period beginning in May 1989 boxers Nigel Benn, Chris Eubank and Michael Watson were involved in a total of five memorable fights against each other. Boxing historians often label this rivalry the 'triumvirate'.

12 When a fight goes the full distance, in championship fights 12 rounds, the winner is decided on points that are recorded by three judges. In a split decision two of the judges rank one fighter the winner, while the third judge scores for the other fighter.

13 **Mike McCallum** born 7 December 1956, Kingston, Jamaica. Former WBA. Light-middleweight and middleweight champion of the world; WBC light-heavyweight champion of the world.

14 **Julian Jackson** born 12 September 1960, St. Thomas, Virgin Islands. Former WBA light-middleweight and WBC middleweight champion of the world.

that Herol has too. Propping up the bar beside him now it's clear that the memory of that night will probably always hurt him more than the punch that seemed to come out of nowhere as he backed Jackson up on the ropes. Whenever you see the fight it's difficult to stop yourself from yelling at Herol to step away, to keep his hands up. But he doesn't. He never does. And all you're left with is an image of Herol lying prone on the canvas for several long, worrying minutes.

I move away from Herol and I'm suddenly standing beside Alan Minter. During his career Minter went one mighty step further than Herol and all of the other boxers here tonight in that for a six-month period in 1980 he actually held the undisputed[15] world middleweight title. My speech is slurring slightly now and Minter looks at me warily as I describe our shared history. Of how I was a purple-suited wine waiter at the Grand Hotel in Bristol shortly after he lost his title to Marvin Hagler and served him at his table. Of how he contacted me in 1990 proposing that he write a column for the magazine I was editing but nothing much ever came of it. We talk about the pre-multi-channel TV era when millions tuned into the BBC – myself included – to watch him fight. When stars really were stars. We talk about his appearance on *Superstars*, the prime time TV programme that pitted elite athlete against elite athlete. Minter got to the final in 1980.

If anything, Minter's dalliance with stardom seems to have had even more of a lasting impact upon him than Herol Graham's. The scent of melancholia that hangs over Herol is matched by an odour of loss that clings to Minter like aftershave. But the talk of days gone by seems to cheer up the ex-boxer and he appears to be warming to me. Minter introduces me to his son. Ross is all smiles and high fives. He

15 In modern boxing it is almost impossible to become an undisputed world champion. Because of the proliferation of governing bodies in the sport (most prominent among these being the WBC, WBA, IBF and WBO) it is possible for there to be an indeterminate number of boxers who hold a version of the 'world' title.

apparently followed in his father's footsteps and took a stab at punching people for a living. Like Minter senior in his heyday, Ross is handsome: his looks not stolen by the punches.

The room begins to thin. People are instructed to move into the dining hall. I spot Colin McMillan and shake his hand. At the risk of even boring myself, he's another fighter that I haven't seen in decades. He hasn't changed much at all. He's personable, intelligent and charming. He wants to talk more about me than himself, which anyone who has anything to do with boxing will agree is a rather unique personal attribute. We head upstairs to eat, agreeing to talk later.

* * * * *

'Ian… Ian Probert.'

Michael Watson's eyes widen and he stares at me, either frowning or wincing. 'Ian Probert?' he says. '*You're* Ian Probert?' The word '*you're*' even sounds like it's pronounced in italics.

I nod my head and Michael repeats my name to himself several times as if I'm not there. Michael's incredulity at my appearance slightly unnerves me. Is he so shocked because I'm unrecognisable from the young man he used to know? Or is it because I haven't changed at all? Unfortunately, my money's on the former.

'Do you remember me?' I ask.

Michael says nothing but continues to stare at me.

'Remember you used to come to my flat in Islington before your fights?'

Michael half-smiles.

'Remember that time before the Benn fight when you came over and I gave you whisky?'

Michael laughs, 'Me? Whisky?'

Now I'm laughing.

He asks where I'm living now and I respond with the same question. People are milling around us and it's difficult to hear anything. A bad time to try to explain why it's been 23 years since we last met but I can't stop myself.

'I came to see you in hospital the night after the fight,' I say. 'I came twice actually. I saw you lying on the bed in intensive care… But I was told… It was made plain to me… That my presence was not welcome.'

'She was very protective,' says Michael, instantly understanding what I'm talking about.

In truth, however, I've never really understood what happened that night. I know that Michael's friends and family were obviously under indescribable stress. And I know that the fact that I made my living as a journalist would have made me an object of suspicion and merely one more face in the hundreds that had laid siege to St. Bartholomew's hospital in the aftermath to the fight. The rejection hurt me but it was not the time to be selfish.

'What about Eric?' I ask, changing the subject. 'Do you still see Eric?'

Now I'm talking about Eric Seccombe, the man who trained Michael as an amateur and was at his side for most of his professional career. In the days when I knew them the pair were inseparable. They really were like father and son.

Michael issues a blunt 'no' and I immediately sense that I may have hit a raw nerve. Then he slowly seems to withdraw from the conversation. His eyes have a distant, faraway look to them. Evidently I shouldn't have mentioned Eric.

Not sure what to do next, I awkwardly shake Michael's hand and move away from him on slightly unsteady feet. A moment ago I'd felt like I could cry, now I'm just confused.

In the corner of my eye I spot Ambrose Mendy[16] sitting at the far edge of the top table. Another face from my past. The last time I saw him was back in the mid-1990s when I

16 **Ambrose Mendy** born 15 August 1954, London, England. Agent and personal advisor to a number of celebrities, including boxers Nigel Benn and James DeGale, footballer Paul Ince and model Kathy Lloyd.

used to visit him when he was an inmate of Woking prison. I move over to him and say hello. Apart from a few white hairs, Ambrose looks pretty much the same as he ever did. He holds out a hand but I refuse it and instead, inhibitions eroded by alcohol, I give him a bear hug, which seems to slightly phase him.

'We must meet for coffee next week,' he says, as if it's something we do all the time. 'I want you to call my office on Monday.'

Later, on the way back from the toilet I bump into Nigel Benn as he's exiting the banqueting hall. I hold the door open for him. He strolls by without registering my presence. No sign of a thank you from Benn. I swear at him under my breath.

* * * * *

More speeches. An auction. Still more speeches. The fingers are crawling towards 11 o'clock and my feet are getting itchy. Sitting across from me at my table is a tall black man, obviously a boxer. Somebody introduces me to him as 'the former editor of *Boxing Monthly*', which is technically true but not really something I'd like carved on my gravestone. The man's name is Mark Prince; he seems genuinely surprised that I've not heard of him. 'You used to be the editor of *Boxing Monthly* and you've never heard of me?' he says, listing his professional credentials. But it's too noisy for me to even consider going into the reasons for – let's call it – my *exile* from the sport of boxing. Instead I chat to his young, pretty wife about babies – something I know far more about these days than boxing.

Mark then surprises me by saying that he recognises me. It takes a while for the pair of us to work out how this can be possible. Bizarrely he seems to remember me from watching videos of the Watson-Benn fight in 1989. I'm a blurry figure at ringside that can be seen joyously pumping the air when Benn hits the canvas. Not the most professional thing to be doing when you're supposed to be covering a fight for the national press. But then I never claimed to be professional.

An interview with Benn is about to start at the top table and I can feel it all getting a bit too much for me. I have a sudden overwhelming urge to escape, to shuffle away from these people from my past. I can't explain it: the evening is just about to enter its most interesting phase and all I want to do is flee. As the lights dim I take advantage of my position at the back of the hall and slope off into the darkness.

Session #3

IN the room there are two chairs facing each other and a small desk in the far corner. The whitewashed walls have long since lost their freshness. There is nothing hanging on them except for that solitary clock.

She sits across from me with a cup of some kind of herbal tea cradled in her palms. She doesn't speak but gives me a forced smile. Then a shrug that says, '*So, you came back?*'

I tell her that I've decided to return after a two-week absence because using my wife as my own personal therapist is simply not fair on her; it's no good for anybody's relationship. I tell her that I'm still randomly bursting into tears, which is a bummer.

And I tell her that the northerner in me couldn't bear to waste free therapy sessions courtesy of this despicable Conservative government.

She frowns at this last comment. 'Only joking,' I reassure her.

'You joke a lot,' she says.

'Well I'm a funny guy,' I reply. '*Funny peculiar.*'

She looks at me blankly, the world's worst audience, and so I fill the gaps by describing my reunion with Michael Watson. I tell her about how I was almost moved to tears.

'You weren't able to cry?' she says, both a question and a statement.

'Well in general I try to avoid crying,' I reply, immediately realising that it's taken me less than a minute to start contradicting myself.

She stares at me with that unreadable expression on her face and the room falls into that familiar silence.

The silence is obviously a means of getting me to talk. I understand that. It's no doubt part of her training. When two strangers are alone together in an enclosed space silence can be very uncomfortable. Hence the need to talk about the weather in lifts. I start to tell her about this but she raises a finger. 'Why return to boxing?' she says.

I sort of laugh a little which causes her to raise an eyebrow. 'Well it was your suggestion,' I say.

She frowns again.

'Don't you remember?' I ask. 'You told me to… You suggested that I write about boxing again.'

More silence.

'Well I don't really know,' I admit finally.

More silence.

'Look… It's a weird thing to be doing. I know that. It's something that was a part of my past. I don't know why. Except… Except… Well, I suppose it has to be linked to the death of my father. I've obviously been thinking about it. I mean, he was the person who got me into boxing in the first place. We didn't really have a lot in common and it was one of the only things we could share, other than alcohol.'

'Alcohol?'

'Yes. Well he used to take me down to the pub with him when I was about 12. He'd always said that he was looking forward to the day when he could take his son *for a pint*. So naturally I tried to please him. We used to go on Sunday mornings, sometimes on Saturdays too, and he'd have seven or eight pints before he drove us home and I'd probably have four or five. I could barely stand up.'

'That is a very young age to be drinking alcohol.'

'Definitely. But they were different times back then. People behaved differently. He'd sit me in the corner with his friends, smoking and playing cards. I didn't really want to be there but I suppose I felt I had to.'

'And boxing?'

'Well he was always into boxing. He bought me gloves when I was very young and one of those punch ball things that you stand on. He used to get *very* excited watching boxing on the television. He'd yell and scream at the screen. You'd feel every punch. It was difficult not to get drawn in.

'There seemed to be a lot of boxing on the telly back in the 1970s. There were lots of stars whom you felt that you knew personally: Alan Minter... Dave 'Boy' Green... John H. Stracey... Funnily enough I spoke about this when I bumped into Alan Minter recently.'

She finishes her tea and places the empty cup between her feet. This forces me to squint a little: her feet look impossibly small and delicate, like a toddler's.

'It was often live on the television on a Saturday night and literally 17 or 18 million people would tune in. It was an enormous audience. My dad would usually combine watching boxing with drinking, the drunker he got the louder he shouted. I suppose I shouted too. I definitely shout nowadays. The cat hides behind the sofa.'

'It's a very violent thing for a father to be sharing with his son?'

'Violent? I don't know. On face value of course it's violent – that's indisputable. It's two people hitting each other until one of them falls over. But the violence is almost incidental. What's interesting – compelling – about it for me is the intellectual contest that one is party to. And by party to what I actually mean is *complicit*. Complicit because to even watch boxing is to be involved in the ritual. Without an audience the fight could not take place. In simple terms without an audience there would be no money to pay the boxers. Therefore, even

35

by watching boxing on a two-dimensional television screen you become an essential part of the food chain. They are fighting because you are paying them to fight, a ritual that goes right back to Ancient Rome and beyond.'

'But it's still violent?'

'Yes but it's a violence that both contestants – although nobody would really call them that – agree to. The violence is but a small part of the dialogue that you are witnessing. It's part of the language they use. It's not like rugby, for example, in which the object is to score points and the violence is there to stop those points being scored.

'In boxing you score points by correctly administering punches to areas of the body that the sport designates as being legal.

'Sometimes those punches hurt but frequently they don't. The ability to avoid being punched is not only felicitous for the boxer but also an essential part of the sport. In boxing, points are awarded not only for punches delivered but also for punches skilfully avoided. Indeed, knowledgeable boxing fans are able to recognise and applaud the defensive skills of a boxer just as much as they enjoy watching his destructive skills.'

She sighs and pauses before telling me that I'm 'telling stories' again, which I don't agree with. But before I can respond she says, 'And what of Michael Watson?'

'Well he's a good case in point,' I reply. 'He's a fighter who's very much admired for his defensive skills. His fight against Nigel Benn was a classic example of brain overcoming brawn. Michael was not an explicitly destructive boxer. He obviously had power but not in same league as Benn, whose power was more readily apparent, even if you were not an experienced observer of the sport.'

'No,' she interrupts. 'What of Michael Watson?'

'Oh… You mean me meeting him?'

She nods her head.

'Well I'm not sure. I'm a little confused. Him not recognising me would have been funny if it wasn't so sad. I've thought about it a lot. Apart from a slight slurring of the speech and his obvious difficulty walking properly it's easy to believe that he's the same person he used to be. But realistically he can't be. I'm hoping to see him again soon. There's a benefit night being held for him just outside London.'

'You want to resume your friendship?'

'Well I don't think that's possible but it might be possible to have some sort of relationship. I feel that I owe him a great deal for all that he did for me when I was younger, I told him that when I saw him. And I also feel that I've let him down badly in essentially abandoning him when the injury happened. Although I don't really think there was anything else I could have done.'

She looks confused.

'I think I told you before,' I say. 'When I went to the hospital after it happened I was warned off... Well not warned off exactly but it was made pretty plain to me that my presence was not appreciated... So I did what I thought was the right thing to do and kept out of the way... Let the family deal with things their own way.'

'But aren't friends worth fighting for?'

She makes a fair point. She's a sneaky one, this one. For a moment I'm lost for words.

Kiss

THE hangover still lingers four days later but my misery is deserved. The pain is fully justified and makes me wonder if I might have a problem. While Laura and Sofia watch TV I Google 'How to know if you're an alcoholic' and take an online test. *How many units do you drink?* I'm asked. I have a think about this and select a lower number from the list of alternatives. *Do you ever drink on your own?* is the next question. I don't do this often enough to click 'Yes' so again it's a 'No'. *Do you lie about how much you drink?* I click 'No'. Lots of questions like this.

I've been secretly thinking that something might be wrong for quite some time actually. It's not that I drink too much, or *have* to drink in the mornings, or see pink elephants if I don't drink. Nothing like that. In fact, most of the time I only ever drink on Fridays and Saturdays. But it's what happens *when* I drink that concerns me. As I get older I seem to lose control more quickly. After a couple of pints of beer or several glasses of wine my inhibitions are definitely let loose on an unsuspecting world and it's never a pretty sight. I can feel myself doing it.

And it's more than just enjoying myself: I can get downright silly and make a complete fool of myself. What's more I can't stop. If a bottle of wine's been opened I'll drink the whole bottle. If two have been opened I have to drink both of them. If I'm in a pub I'll just keep drinking until I get kicked out. Laura jokes that I don't have an off switch. Unfortunately, I couldn't stop myself on Saturday night. In front of people who really shouldn't be present to see me like this.

I whizz through the questions and click the 'send' button. Within moments I'm informed that I might be an alcoholic. There's a number for me to get help. Then I realise that the number has an American prefix so I backtrack in my browser history and append 'UK' to my original search query. More questions. Similar answers. I click 'send' and this time the response comes back that I'm not an alcoholic but that I should be more careful. So I'm an alcoholic whenever I'm in North America but merely borderline back here in old Blighty. Good thing I don't go to America that often.

* * * * *

Somehow the setting seems to epitomise the respective careers of Nigel Benn and Michael Watson. Benn was glitz, glamour and danger; Watson was steady, unspectacular and someone whom you could take home to your mum. Benn's tribute was held in a cavernous hotel on the outskirts of Essex. Watson's is here: a small pub in a place called Ware in Hertfordshire.

I arrive at the venue a good hour or so early and feel a blanket of eyes upon me as I move towards the bar. Before I climbed on to the train that took me here I'd already decided that tonight is going to be a night for sobriety. I need to keep my senses intact. Nothing but Diet Coke for me tonight. I'm going to be respectable. Bright as a button.

There are definite overtones of The Slaughtered Lamb from *An American Werewolf In London*. I feel a wave of hot exasperation wash over me when I ask someone at the bar if I've come to the right place. I am assured that I have, although the response comes with a shake of the head and a poorly disguised tut. This would no doubt be on account of the fact that a large screen has been set up close by with the words 'Michael Watson' emblazoned across it in big red letters. A further hint is provided by the above average quotient of broken to unbroken noses on display.

The minutes tick by as I forlornly wave a £10 note into the air, but there is only one person serving and no matter what I do I cannot attract her attention. Fully ten minutes go by and I'm yet to be served; there are simply too many people here for the barmaid to cope with. I try calling out several times in a pathetic, unconvincing voice but the barmaid pretends not to hear me. The other occupants of the bar turn towards me disapprovingly or mockingly.

Eventually, a girl standing beside me seems to recognise my predicament and takes pity on me. She strikes up a conversation. It turns out that she's been hired as a singer for tonight when the Michael Watson-based festivities are over, although the place is so small I have no idea where they're going to put her. She's smoking an e-cigarette and I question her about it, pretending to be interested. 'I haven't smoked in five years,' I proudly tell her. She makes an impressed noise. Then I go into my usual spiel whenever I meet people who sing, the one about my dad once being a singer.

Relief. It's finally my turn. The girl asks me what I want and I order two pints of Guinness. On face value this looks bad but my logic is that it took so long to get any attention at the bar I might as well have a second lined up to spare me another long wait. The girl beside me raises an eyebrow and joylessly sucks away at her electronic cigarette gadget.

There are just 68 people attending (I know this because I overhear the organiser quoting this figure to somebody who had just handed back two tickets from non-attendants). I can't help but see this as a fairly accurate reflection of Benn and Watson's relative careers: Watson beat Benn and then headed off to relative obscurity (until the injury, that is). Benn lost to Watson but was soon fighting for a world title.

* * * * *

Guinness number two is but a distant memory and the organiser of the event is now over an hour late. Michael Watson is nowhere to be seen and the natives are growing impatient. To ease the tension, the landlord of the pub puts on a DVD of Watson's life story and everyone in the pub stares respectfully at a flat screen TV bolted to the wall.

It is standard fare: images of Michael as an angelic looking schoolboy, interviews with his mother, interviews with former trainers, amateur footage, an interview with a rasping Nigel Benn. Despite the incredibly wooden voiceover (think Alan Partridge voicing The Norfolk Bravery Awards) I find myself sucked into the narrative. The bar thins out a little and I demand my fourth Guinness. Every so often the picture on the screen freezes and there are hoots of disapproval from the room. In the end the flustered landlord stands by the screen holding the Sony Vaio from which the documentary is being streamed at an impossible to maintain angle. The image takes me back to my student days of black and white TVs with coat hanger aerials.

The documentary is about to finish and, sensing an imminent rush to the bar, I get in early and order another Guinness. I am watching the head settle when noises in the room alert me to the fact that Michael has arrived.

As he was the other day Michael looks impeccably dressed in his well-cut suit. Again he's wearing glasses; they bring a statesmanlike quality to the still handsome features that have been softened by time. He's led into the room by someone whom I recognise from years ago but I cannot put a name to. The man rests his hand protectively on Michael's shoulder as the ex-boxer smiles and punches the air triumphantly with a speed and agility that belie his apparent frailty.

Michael takes a seat at a table and receives a round of applause for his efforts. He is joined by Ben Doughty, organiser of both this evening and the Nigel Benn event that

I attended recently. Ben runs a very popular Facebook page, which I joined a couple of months ago. In the short time that I have known him he has been incredibly kind and generous to me: it was at his invitation that I attended that tribute dinner for Nigel. Ben is a well-known face in boxing circles; as an ex-boxer himself, he regularly interviews boxing figures with intelligence and grace.

Ben makes a brief introduction and commences his interview with Michael. I order myself another Guinness as Ben discusses Michael's early days as an amateur. It's plain to see that Michael is enjoying the attention. There is a permanent grin etched upon his face.

The interview moves on to Michael's pro career, his early successes, the impact of his first loss. It's going well: the crowd are clearly enjoying it. Then something strange happens.

I'm leaning against the bar in semi-darkness slobbering into my glass of black liquid and Michael suddenly spots me in the crowd. He stops talking and stares in my direction in bewilderment. 'Is that…? Is that…?' he mumbles.

One by one the crowd of onlookers turn to look at me.

'I'm gonna get all emotional now,' says Michael.

I feel myself smiling as Ben raises the microphone to his lips and tells the audience who I am. It quickly becomes more than a little embarrassing as Ben provides a description of how Michael and I first met. Of how I was a penniless squatter living in north London and Michael was up-and-coming prospect. Of how he became a champion and I became a writer. Of sorts. It's pretty obvious that nobody else present here has a clue who I am. Frankly it would be a minor miracle if they did. But I barge may way through the audience and move closer to Michael. I take hold of his hand and, as before, all I can say is, 'It's so nice to see you Michael.' I've really got to work on my opening lines.

Michael mumbles something in return but his words are too muffled to translate. 'I've got something for you,' I tell him,

referring to a copy of my book *Rope Burns* which I've brought
along to give to him; it extensively name-checks Michael and
I'm pretty sure he's never read it. 'We'll speak later.'

I return to my position at the bar and I'm filled with joy
and confusion. I'm genuinely moved that Michael recognised
me almost straight away this time. I can't remember anything
affecting me quite so much. In fact I could almost cry. However,
it slowly dawns on me that in pointing me out Michael seems
to have no apparent recollection of meeting me just two weeks
earlier. It could simply be that I'm misreading the situation,
or it could be the Guinness. I'm not sure.

The interview draws to a close and Ben invites questions
from the audience. I'm drinking far too quickly now, I know
that I am but I can't stop myself. I seem to be permanently
handing money over to the barmaid. And it's most probably
down to the excitement of the occasion that I do what I do
next. With my back to Michael I am aware of a standard set
of textbook questions being issued in his direction.

'What was your hardest fight?' asks someone.

'Nigel Benn,' replies Michael without hesitation.

'Who punched the hardest?' asks another.

'Nigel Benn,' comes the response.

'Who's the best fighter you ever fought?' says someone else.

'Nigel Benn.'

You get the impression that if somebody were to ask
Michael who made the best cup of tea he's ever tasted the
answer would be Nigel Benn. People laugh good-naturedly
but Michael's responses are interesting from a psychological
standpoint. The ex-boxer's career record tells a very different
story to what Michael is saying. In all he was defeated four
times by three different opponents. Surely it would be
natural to assume that the individuals who beat him should
by definition be better than the person whom he beat?

As I ponder this question it suddenly flashes into my
head how amused Michael was on the last occasion that I

saw him when I had mentioned that we once drank whisky together. He genuinely laughed when I recalled that long lost evening. My mind is beginning to fog over and my inhibitions have evaporated away. Buoyed on by the Guinness and the adrenaline I proceed to do something truly nauseatingly, effortlessly cringeworthy.

Indicating to Ben that I have something to say, a microphone is duly placed at my chin. 'It's not a question I have,' I slur. 'But I'm going to reveal the secret weapon that helped Michael to beat Nigel Benn.'

All heads turn immediately in my direction. People begin to awkwardly shuffle.

'It was whisky!' I proclaim, fully anticipating that Michael and the rest of the room will have no choice but to break down into guffaws of uncontrollable laughter.

There is a silence. A long indescribably uncomfortable silence. Michael looks over at me appalled and horrified. I hand the mike back to Ben and get myself another drink.

* * * * *

More drink. Gallons of drink. I'm on a roll now. I'm buying beers for anybody who comes within a square foot of me. I'm overflowing with bonhomie. I'm slapping backs and declaring undying love to anybody who is not speedy enough to get away from the rotund sweaty apparition that is accosting them. I flirt with two plump middle-aged women who look like grandmothers but in fact are probably younger than I am. I insinuate myself upon a young couple and encourage them to pose for a photograph with Michael whether they want to or not. We go outside and they reveal to me that they are travellers, and I, having just read the *The Diddakoi*[17] to my daughter, reveal myself, obviously, to be an expert on the subject.

17 *The Diddakoi*, a children's novel by Rumer Godden, published in 1972

Outside the pub I bore these poor unfortunates rigid for the best part of an hour while continually bumming cigarettes off them. 'They're so expensive these days,' I cheerfully announce, helping myself to cigarette after cigarette. 'Asking someone for a fag is almost like saying, "Hey mate, can you give me a quid?"' At one point the singer with the e-cigarette comes outside on a break from singing 'I'm Every Woman' and shakes her head at me. So much for me not having smoked for five years.

Back inside, I sidle up to Michael once again and perch myself roughly alongside him. Our thighs rub. Doubtless he can smell the alcohol on my breath as I regale him with stories from our past. For the second time I try to explain why I did not lend him support after the injury. If he forgives me at all he doesn't say so.

Later I'm standing at the bar with the man who had guided Michael into the room earlier, whose face I recognised. He introduces himself as Lennard Ballack, Lennie to his friends. He tells me he remembers me from all those years ago. 'What do you do for a living?' I ask.

'Well, I look after Michael,' says Lennie, a little nonplussed.

Even as my brain goes into shutdown memories of Lennie return to me. He was Michael's childhood friend, somebody who was always there when Michael was fighting. A quiet, dignified figure who stood alone on the outskirts of the gym, content to remain anonymous while his friend garnered all the attention.

I find myself overpowered by admiration for Lennie. I want to grab hold of him and kiss and cuddle him. He's stood by Michael for years and years and years while so many people have abandoned the injured fighter or used their apparent generosity to increase their own celebrity.

Others may have grabbed the headlines over the years with their efforts to help Michael but it is Lennie who has had to sacrifice his life on a minute-by-minute basis. Lord knows what he's had to go through, the things he's had to do for his friend.

I request Lennie's number and tell him that I'm thinking about writing about boxing again. I ask him if it might be possible for me to visit Michael at some point in the near future. But even as he says he'll arrange it, I'm aware that I'm out of control like a driverless truck full of explosives careering down a hillside. My alcohol consumption tonight must have exceeded double figures and I'm talking too much. Far too much. I'm repeating the same things like a needle stuck in a groove. I'm repeating the same things like a needle stuck in a groove. I'm repeating... My breath is toxic enough to poison small furry animals. My damp, overweight torso pins Lennie to the centre of the room. His eyes search for a means of escape.

I move back to Michael once more and suffocate him with my semi-comatose monologues. Michael says nothing and simply stares into the distance as if in another world. I ask him what's wrong and he says, 'I'm tired, Ian.'

'Tired?' I say.

Once again I head outside to find the travellers and purloin yet another cigarette from them. As I prop myself against a wall I notice a number of figures swiftly exiting the pub into the darkness. I can't be sure how many there are but one of them is definitely Lennie and another is Michael. There is an urgency about their movements that momentarily drags me from my drunken haze. I put down my glass and follow them as they head towards the car park. 'We're taking Michael home,' Lennie breathlessly tells me. He has a serious expression on his face.

I reach over to Michael and plant a kiss on his cheek. A big, sloppy, beery kiss.

Session #4

ON the previous occasions I'd recorded her on my phone and she hadn't noticed. Now, because I'm a middle-aged man with a pretty bog-standard gadget fetish, I use a joke spy pen with built-in audio recorder that I've bought from a dodgy Chinese site. It's supposed to look like a real pen but she spots it straight away protruding from the pocket of my t-shirt and gives me a look which I assume must be her version of reproachful. Then as usual silence is to be my punishment.

'Look, I get it,' I say. 'I've seen *The Sopranos*. I know you're not supposed to say very much. I know that's the way it's supposed to work.'

No change in facial expression. She just sits there scratching away at a notepad.

'So I've been thinking I'm just going to use you. I'm going to spend the hour venting… Talk about things that I can't talk to my wife or anybody else about simply because it's too boring for them.'

Silence.

'Is that okay with you?'

'You should do what you feel is right,' she finally responds in an exaggeratedly weak voice.

Silence.

'So I went to see Michael Watson a second time. Remember? Michael Watson? I told you about him last time. He's the boxer I used to know that got badly injured.'

She nods. 'Why did you do this?'

Silence from me. Then, 'I keep telling you. It was *you* who suggested it.'

She shakes her head, impassive as ever.

'Don't you remember? Check your notes. You told me to write about boxing. Well, you didn't actually… You advised… Well… You asked me why I didn't write about boxing anymore, which I suppose was a fair enough question.

'Well, anyway, I thought about it and decided that I'd dip my toe in the water.'

'Dip your toe in the water?'

'Yes,' I say. 'It's an expression. It means, erm, give it a little try; see how you feel about it.'

'And how did *you* feel about it?'

'Well it was weird, obviously it was weird. There were lots of people there I didn't know.'

'No. How did *you* feel about it?'

'Well I felt scared I suppose. I felt very much like an outsider, which I obviously am. The vast majority of people there all knew each other. And I understand that it's completely irrational but I felt that everyone was looking at me. It can't be true, I know it can't but that's the way I felt. I was also pretty emotional. When I saw Michael I had to force myself from crying. It's only the second time I've seen him since 1991 when he had his accident.'

'Accident?'

'Yes. I told you. He was injured in a fight with Chris Eubank.'

'That is an accident?'

I pause for a moment. All of a sudden she's asking too many questions. I think I might actually prefer the silence.

'Well I think that what you're talking about is semantics. Accident. Injury. It's the same thing.'

Now she pauses.

'All right, I know what you're saying,' I continue. 'An accident and an injury are obviously two entirely different things. I get that. You might say that one is an inevitable by-product of the other. You're implying that I shouldn't be using the word "accident" because boxing is all about trying to hurt your opponent. That's true. Obviously it's true. But the aim of boxing is not to *seriously* injure anybody.'

She fidgets in her seat and continues to fiddle with her notebook. 'Is not injury unavoidable?' she asks.

I want to tell her no but I decide to think about it before I respond. She's right, of course: injury is unavoidable in boxing. I can't think of a boxer alive who is entirely untouched by the sport. Even so-called defensive masters such as 'Sugar' Ray Leonard and Floyd Mayweather carry their war wounds. Both of these boxers have scars above their eyes and most probably other things that aren't apparent in photographs. Less elusive boxers carry more obvious mementoes: broken noses, swollen brows, calcium deposits in their joints, slurred speech, brain damage. The list is actually endless. A small percentage suffer fatal injury.

'I think we're talking about degree of injury,' I say finally. 'There's obviously a line drawn between what is acceptable in terms of damage and what is not.'

'Who draws the line?'

'Well society, I guess. And the sport itself. Although it has to be said that it's largely self-governing and basically run by people with a vested interest in making money from boxing. It's very corrupt. It's always been corrupt. It goes with the territory.'

'And where do *you* draw the line?'

'Me? Well I think that's obvious. Seeing Michael get injured was enough to start me questioning myself and stop me from wanting to write about boxing.'

Except it wasn't really. I did, after all, write an entire book that attempted to rationalise my decision to abandon my involvement in boxing. And even then I didn't entirely keep away from it. There was a piece I did for *Time Out* to promote the book, about a boxer named Kirkland Laing[18]. And there was a feature I did for *The Guardian* about Frank Maloney[19], when I followed him around for a whole weekend. Back then I told myself that these were merely human interest stories that happened to have a boxing theme. But I was probably kidding myself.

'But you're right… There was another guy I knew. His name was Rod Douglas… He got injured in a fight with Herol Graham. I knew him quite well and that wasn't enough to stop me from earning money from boxing.'

'And where do *you* draw the line?'

'I would have to say that the question is just too simplistic. You must understand that boxing has been around in various forms since the ancient Greeks. And nobody's ever been able to manage to find a way of stopping people from doing it – not that anybody's really wanted to – so in order to answer that question it must be on the understanding that boxing is something that is impossible to completely abolish. It's here. It's part of our culture. It fulfils an almost primordial desire that goes way beyond any rules that can ever be imposed.

'If you can accept that boxing will never go away then the only thing that you can really do is try to improve the safety aspects of the sport. And that's why we find boxing in the condition that it is in the 21st century. A very clearly defined set of rules have been established which are constantly evolving to order to ensure that what happened to Michael is avoided as much as it can be.'

'But where do *you* draw the line?'

....

18 **Kirkland Laing** born 20 June 1954, Jamaica. Former British, Commonwealth and EBU welterweight champion
19 **Kellie Maloney**, (formerly known as **Frank Maloney**) born 23 January 1953, London, England. Boxing manager and promoter, notably of Lennox Lewis.

'What I think is not important. But if I must answer I'd have to say that I can't really say where I'd draw the line. My feelings are ambiguous: On the one hand I'm 100 per cent sure that I don't want people to get fatally injured for my enjoyment. But I also know that there are people out there – boxers I mean – who actually see the injuries they sustain as badges of honour; so I suppose it's up to them if they tolerate broken noses and scars and suchlike.

'I understand the boundaries of the line: I know that the spectacle of two men standing before you aiming punches at each other until one of them falls to the floor unconscious can be one of the most exciting things that you will ever bear witness to in life, well in my opinion anyway. But there is no part of me at all that wants to see either of them get hurt in any way. I get no pleasure from seeing these people bleeding, and I get no pleasure in seeing them sustain a broken nose. And I obviously don't get any satisfaction from seeing a person get fatally injured. You'd have to be a psychopath to enjoy that.

'So these are my boundaries: I enjoy watching people fight each other but I don't actually want them to hurt each other. That's what you might call a mutually exclusive statement but it happens to be true. But perversely – and I don't really want to say this – I suppose I do enjoy watching people get knocked out.'

She stared at me in apparent surprise at what is actually a startling admission.

Images broadcast on television simply do not do justice to what you will witness in person when a man – or these days a woman – is hit so hard, and in just the right place, by a punch that is delivered at the precise angle and velocity, as to effectively slam the soft pulp of the brain against the side of the skull and bring about unconsciousness. The sight is always completely shocking to even the most hardened of observers, forcing time to stand still. In boxing the knockout is frequently its most memorable detail.

Moreover, boxing fans will talk about a particular knockout and celebrate its memory in the way that others might commemorate a notable moment in world history. To many – sub-consciously or otherwise – the knockout is more than just the practical climax to the fight; it is imbued with symbolism of an almost mystical significance. It is a fact that seasoned observers of boxing are more likely to eulogise about a knockout than they are the defensive qualities of a particular fighter; and eulogise is an appropriate word. For in boxing the knockout has often been called the symbolic death.

'Do you intend to go and watch more people being knocked out?' she asks suddenly.

'Of course not,' I say. 'That's ridiculous. I've never been to a fight with the sole intention of watching somebody get knocked out.'

'But it happens.'

'Yes it happens. But only in the way that a racing car might crash during a Grand Prix. You don't actually go to a race hoping that somebody will crash but you're always aware that there's a chance it might happen.'

Silence. And I'm conscious that I'm talking myself into a corner. I would be a liar to say that I've never attended a boxing match hoping for a knockout. I certainly wanted Michael Watson to knock out Nigel Benn when they met in 1989. There have been others, too.

'So what will you do next?' she asks.

'Well I have it in the back of my mind to look up a few more people whom I used to know in boxing. I don't know what the purpose of this would be but it's something I'm going to try and do.'

More silence.

'I've been thinking that I might try and write something about it. Sort of use it as a means of getting something out of my system. Whatever that is… You know, as a form of therapy.'

Sweet

S O I try to do it. I try to meet people from boxing whom I used to know many years ago. I have no idea why I want to do this but somehow it seems to me like the right thing to do.

But where do you start? Once you've decided to go back and endeavour to meet up with people for the first time in almost a quarter of a century, how do you actually set about doing this? And even if you do manage to find anyone still around after all these years who will consent to meet with you, what do you tell them? How do you explain it to them when you don't even know the reason yourself?

Well the first bit is relatively straightforward: it helps a great deal that many of the people I have it in mind to revisit are fairly well known and can easily be Googled. It's not as if I'm trying to find a bunch of strangers that I used to hang out with in my teens. It's also good that I bumped into a few of them at the Nigel Benn tribute recently and that some even seemed to remember me from back in the Dark Ages.

As regards the second question, well that's trickier. I can't really contact people and tell them that I want so see them because I've been ill for a very long time, that my dad's just died and I'm having trouble handling it, and that my Chinese therapist has sort of suggested that I start writing about boxing again. Can I?

However, if I was looking for a clue about what to do next, how to begin this thing if I'm going to do it, then it was staring me in the face at that Benn bash the other night. Colin McMillan is the name of that clue.

Boxing fans will remember Colin McMillan as the former WBO featherweight champion of the world but he could have been so much more.

Back in early 1990s 'Sweet C'[20], as he was nicknamed, was well on the way to becoming a household name. He was physically beautiful and the recipient of a university education.

Moreover, when he stepped into the boxing ring he really did appear to have a special kind of talent that set him apart from his peers.

Colin performed like a top American. He was blindingly fast, impossibly slick, inordinately difficult to lay a glove on – always an obvious advantage in boxing. And he gave the impression of being a modern kind of boxer – whatever that means – elegantly hauling the sport into the 21st century with a modesty and charm that made him instantly likeable. In interviews he seemed too innocent to be a fighter; the slight hint of a lisp that he carried imbued him with an air of vulnerability.

If you saw Colin in action, however, his ascent towards stardom seemed almost inevitable.

But it all went wrong one dreadful night in 1992 during what was supposed to be a routine world title defence against a Colombian pressure fighter named Rubén Palacio. Like all of us, boxers will experience the occasional off-night; Colin's off-night came in front of millions of viewers, who watched open-mouthed as his career systematically unraveled. After unexpectedly struggling to cope with his challenger for the first half of the fight, disaster struck when McMillan's left arm

---

20   In boxing the nickname 'Sweet' has a particular kudos. It is usually only bestowed on the sport's finest exponents.

was left dangling uselessly by his side after it was dislocated during a clinch[21].

In boxing one can easily grow hardened to the casual impairments that are an inevitable by-product of the sport. Although injuries such as cuts, swelling and bruises would certainly not be deemed superficial in any other walk of life that is how they are routinely regarded both inside and outside the ring. However, on this occasion the sight of what remains a highly unusual injury in boxing was enough to make veteran ringsiders turn away in horror. It was as if someone had severed the strings which supported the puppet's arm. The contest was immediately halted and Colin, aged only 26, was never to be the same fighter again.

Naturally, the boxer tried to regain what he had lost, as all boxers are wont to do. Almost a year to the day after that calamitous night Colin attempted to take his belt back from his successor, one Steve Robinson of Wales. And although he would have been odds-on to beat Robinson easily prior to the injury Colin was not able to do so on this occasion. Externally Colin may have looked the same as ever but in more ways than one he had lost something that he could never regain. This defeat was followed by a run of victories contested for lesser titles that flattered to deceive until, in 1997, Colin suffered a recurrence of the arm injury and called it a day forever. It was an incredibly sad ending to a career that fizzled out like a malfunctioning firework.

But I remember Colin from a long time before he encountered fame and the tragedy it brought with it. I remember the days when he was a six-round fighter who routinely stood by the entrance to boxing venues and politely shook the hand of any boxing writer who chanced to pass by. It is to his credit that such an obviously contrived gesture never

21 The clinch is a defensive move in which one or more boxer will wrap their arms around an opponent, usually to elicit a pause in the action.

came across as such. As his nickname indicated, Colin was sweetness incarnate in person. Generous with his time and generous with his feelings.

And Colin never seemed to forget. One afternoon, some time in 1995, I happened to be walking down the Hackney Road with some work colleagues. As luck would have it I was talking about boxing – for some reason the subject often seemed to come up in conversation with me – and telling them how I used to work in the business. They were sceptical.

They knew me as a designer/writer and assumed I was probably just making up stories. It was then that a very flash looking car drove by and came to a halt right in front of us. It was driven by Colin McMillan, still famous enough to be recognised in those days, who wound down the window and gave me a friendly wave that silenced my doubters.

And so it is that I decide Colin will be the first person from my past whom I will contact. It doesn't take much to arrange. I send Colin a Facebook friend request which is almost instantly accepted. I then message him politely asking if we could meet up for a chat. Colin doesn't ask why I would want to meet him but immediately sets a date a week from now. And that's Colin McMillan for you. Decent, Sweet C.

* * * * *

We arrange to meet at a Turkish restaurant close to Colin's home in the Redbridge area in the north-east of London. It's a freezing November evening and the rain is lashing down in waves. As usual I'm early – more than an hour, as it happens. In an effort to kill time I trudge up and down the deserted high street before taking refuge in a local library. Finally, I locate the restaurant and sit sipping a beer to calm my nerves. I shouldn't be nervous; it's not as if I'm about to enter a ring or anything.

But I am nervous. With the exception of one other person, it's been a very, very long time since I sat down to formally interview anybody connected with boxing, although I've warned Colin that this will probably not be a normal interview.

Back in the day this was what I did for a living. It seems unbelievable to me that I could ever have done so. And now I'm a bundle of nerves, trying to stop myself from shaking while I wait for the former world champion to arrive.

Colin arrives almost exactly on time and takes a seat across from me at the table. His hair is closely cropped to his skull and for someone who is approaching 50 there is a noticeable absence of wrinkles. We shake hands and it's as if I'm reaching out and grasping my past. I wonder again why I'm doing this. Colin wears a tracksuit and looks as fit as he ever did. When he was boxing Colin fought in the 9st division, a weight that most people will probably have seen the last of in their teens. He tells me that he's only 2.5lb above that weight. The years have obviously been generous to him, although it's clear that he has worked hard to earn that kindness.

'To be honest with you,' I awkwardly begin, 'I'm a really crap interviewer.'

Colin ignores the comment, giving the slightest trace of a frown and smiles back at me. 'How are you? You all right? You good?' he says.

And in an instant I'm proving exactly how inept an interviewer I really am. Colin looks on politely as he gets the full story of how my dad died recently, of how I got depressed and of how I'm using the writing about boxing as a possible form of therapy. In the flick of a coin Colin is actually interviewing me and I won't stop talking. I can't stop talking. It's embarrassing for both of us.

Colin tries to hide his puzzlement and smiles back at me. But his patience is tested as I continue to try to ramble on about my 'comeback', if you can call it that. And when the words soon run dry there are several uncomfortable moments when we don't really know what to say to each other. Fortunately, food is delivered to the table to reduce the discomfort. I find myself staring at his athlete's body, a profound contrast to my own.

'You look like you've been in the gym every day since the day you retired,' I mumble.

'Not really,' he replies. 'What it was is that I made a conscious decision after the shoulder popped out that when I retire I'm going to stay retired. If you start going to the gym, start training, going through the motions I think you always get that temptation to get back in there. I stayed away from a boxing gym for years and years. I've only sparred about two or three times since I retired.'

Colin giggles a lot when he speaks. I've forgotten that he does this. We talk about the problems he's had adjusting to life after boxing, 'Why boxing is so difficult is because in other sports you get a gradual decline. In boxing, one week you can be up there about to fight for a world championship, with people talking about you ruling for a long time, and the very next week you might get beaten and people are saying you should retire. So you have to readjust and ask yourself, "What do I do?"'

I'm shuffling in my seat. Already this is turning into a conventional run-of-the-mill interview. It's not really what I want. Although it might help if I had even a vague idea in my head of what I was hoping to gain from speaking to Colin.

'When you're fighting all you do is eat and sleep boxing,' Colin continues. 'Even when you're on holiday supposed to be resting you can't wait to get training and start again. Your whole focus is on boxing. Then when you stop and you realise boxing is over you've quickly go to find something to redirect your focus and energy to get you on that path.'

I'm thinking about my own depression after my father died, which is all I seem to be able to do at the moment, I ask

Colin he if experienced similar feelings when boxing was over for him. Was it like the loss of a family member?

'Not really. There was a massive void when my career came to an end. It was a hard adjustment to make. I was quite lucky as my retirement party in Legends nightclub in Barking coupled as the start of my stint as the promotions manager for the club – so I had something to focus on and keep me occupied immediately.

I have quite a few things to do these days. I run a boxing training company and a sports agency. I do some of the admin work for my wife's import business. I'm quite happy. I've got a nice life.'

It's obvious that Colin's been asked questions of this nature a thousand times before. And he's well-practised at playing this particular game: he answers my stream of consciousness with more consideration than it deserves.

'I was quite fortunate that the importance of getting an education was always impressed upon me. It made me plan for the future,' he says.

'Somebody once said to me, "Enjoy it while you can – it don't last for long," and that's always stuck with me. Before you know your career has come and gone. You've got to try and maximise your potential.'

'Yes,' I say. 'But having experienced the extreme highs in boxing it must never be far from your mind.'

'I don't think of it very often because I'm quite philosophical in life. People forget that the 1990s was the golden age of boxing and I was riding the crest of a wave. When I came into the ring I had complete confidence in my ability. I wanted to become undefeated champion of the world; that was my original objective. Everything was going towards that until the shoulder popped out.'

In boxing there always seems to be one defining moment in a fighter's career. In Colin's case it will always be the shoulder injury that haunts him.

'If the shoulder hadn't popped out and I'd have won the fight, then I'd I've been paid very, very well for the next fight,' he says. 'I was just about to get into the big money. They were talking about a quarter of a million, which at the time was big money.'

'It's so terribly unlucky,' I tell him. 'An awful thing to happen to anybody.'

'Better it happened after I become world champion than before,' he shrugs. 'But at least boxing's open a few doors for me. Even though my heyday was two decades ago I still get recognised and that kind of stuff now. People do remember who you are. It's nice when people appreciate what you've done.'

'And you don't seem to have changed at all from when I knew you,' I say. 'Either physically or mentally.'

'No matter who you are, you are going to change when things are changing around you. Back then everybody wanted a piece of me. Kind of… Come here… Do that… You've got to train… You've got your family… There's kind of loads of things going on. You can't maintain that forever.'

It is at this point that I pull out a book and ask Colin to sign it. Its title is unusual and its equally unusual author will always be associated with the ex-boxer. Colin and I spoke about this briefly when we met at the Nigel Benn tribute and he doesn't seem unsurprised that I'm bringing the subject up again.

I barely knew the late Jonathan Rendall, although we occasionally sat together at the back of press conferences in the days when you were allowed to smoke cigarettes at such events. However, I felt his loss too deeply when he died in 2013 at the age of 49. It was a terrible shock. Jonathan was a journalist for the broadsheets, writer, as well as occasional television broadcaster. In 1990 he became an unlicensed advisor[22] to Colin.

22 In boxing **advisor** is a term often applied to a manager who does not possess official recognition from the sport's governing body.

At the time Colin did not have a traditional boxing manager, preferring to handle his affairs on his own terms. 'To be fair I had a couple of offers but they weren't really great.' says Colin, 'In those days you couldn't be self-managed straight away. The [British Boxing] Board Of Control[23] stopped you.'

Because of this, Rendall became a close confidante to the fighter, helping him to deal with promoters and negotiate his way through the contractual minefield inherent to the sport. Rendall was one of boxing's many mavericks. His love of alcohol, of tobacco and of gambling undoubtedly played a part in his untimely death.

Prior to meeting Colin I had re-read Rendall's eccentrically titled, Somerset Maugham prize-winning *This Bloody Mary Is The Last Thing I Own*, which outlines the story of the pair's relationship. Colin signs the book without saying a word but when I ask him about his friend his response is guarded.

'I got on very well with Jon,' says Colin. 'I had a lot of time for him because, you know, he was quite young. He was only a couple of years older than me but he was a very knowledgeable, sharp guy. We met years and years ago and he was a boxing nut. We had a great journey. It was terrible when he died but it happens every week now. People are obviously getting older and time is just flying by.'

* * * * *

I leave the restaurant strangely deflated. Colin shakes my hand and efficiently goes through the formalities: he tells me how good it was to see me – which surely cannot be true – and says that I should contact him if there's anything else he can do to help. As I make my way home through the darkness I can't help but conclude that I've fucked up. My first formal

23 **The British Boxing Board of Control** (BBBofC) is the governing body of professional boxing in the United Kingdom. It was formed in 1929 from the old National Sporting Club.

interview with a boxer has been a failure. I ended up talking to Colin about his career when I actually wanted to talk about something else. And I particularly regret bringing up Jonathan Rendall; Colin's curiously empty response suggests that I may have crossed an invisible line.

I exit the tube at Archway and stroll up the hill towards my home. I'm so preoccupied with my thoughts that I don't notice as I walk through a red stop light. Before I know it I'm suddenly standing in the middle of a busy road. Cars swerve to avoid me and slam on their brakes; the noise snaps me back into consciousness. I'm like the swimmer who gets tired halfway across the river: do I turn back or should I go on? In the split second that I spend thinking about what to do next I spot a lone cyclist hurtling towards me. Time slows down as we perform a comical dance. It's like what happens when you find someone blocking your path in the street: he turns left to avoid me and I turn left; he turns right and I turn right. And then he hits me.

I'm not aware of any pain as his front tyre slices into my lower leg. I hear the hollow clatter of metal and I see a figure flying through the air in slow motion to land ten or 15 feet behind me. Cars shine their headlights on me like searchlights. I feel warm liquid soaking into my jeans and a voice calls out, 'What do you think you're fucking doing!?'

'Crossing the road,' is my numbed response.

A sudden calmness descends over me. I move quickly over to the fallen rider and place my arms around his shoulders. I tell him not to move and ask him if he is feeling any localised pain. I really do use the word 'localised', which makes it sound as if I know what I'm talking about. We're both visibly shaking as he slowly climbs to his feet. Amazingly there is nothing broken. I take his fully body weight and help him on to the pavement, where he sits looking blankly into the distance. Then I go back and pick up his bike, which seems impossibly light.

I ask the cyclist his name and put my arm around his shoulder a second time. I hug him like a mother embracing a child and ask him if he is all right. Absurdly, I'm just about to ask him if he fancies going out for a beer one night. It is then that he notices me limping and sees the blood. 'Are you okay?' he asks. Luckily I'm very close to the Whittington Hospital.

I begin my slow hobble up the hill to a place and a set of questions that I'm shortly to become intimately familiar with.

Sour

I TAKE the tube to Farringdon and my thoughts are consumed by death: the idea that at any moment something might happen, that a gentle prod in the back might hurl me into the path of an oncoming train and in the blink of an eye it will all be over. I've been thinking about death a lot recently. Maybe it was talking about the late Jonathan Rendall the other week, re-reading his book. Night after night I lie in bed until the early hours thinking of nothing else. Yesterday morning I toyed with the idea of taking anti-depressants again. The packet is still where I left it on the bookshelf in the bedroom.

I drag myself through the catacombs of the London Underground like an old man. The gash on my purple and yellow leg is slowly healing and the stitches will soon come out. But it still hurts like hell. People rush past me: a blur of arms and legs and faces that take on a comedic quality, moving at twice, three times my speed like characters in a silent movie; speedboats leaving me in their frothy wake.

I'm deeply troubled by something that I don't quite understand. I wonder if writing about boxing again after all this time is at the root of my preoccupation with death; the idea that if I was to stop somehow everything would be done. There'd be no reason to go on. The circle would be complete. Or perhaps it's guilt. Guilt and the hope that what I'm about to do this afternoon might have the remotest chance of righting a wrong that I committed a very long time ago.

More than a quarter of a century ago I did a terrible thing to another person. Something that still fills me with shame: shame at my own weakness and shame at the fact that I deceived another human being for nothing other than money. It still leaves a sour taste in my mouth. That person's name was Derek Williams[24], a heavyweight boxer who went by the nickname 'Sweet D'. I want to make things right today. I need to make things right.

[Is it any coincidence that I seem to be revisiting my boxers in alphabetical order: last time I met with Sweet C, today it's Sweet D. Next time will I be meeting Sweet E? The time after that Sweet F? I laugh out loud at the notion and the pretty young girl sitting beside me on the train nervously edges away from me.]

* * * * *

I exit the tube and hobble up and down Farringdon Road until I finally locate the gym where Derek Williams works. It is strapped to the side of an anonymous tower-block, presumably in an effort to attract office workers and their attendant beer guts. As I enter, a booming bass hits me like a blast of hot air.

A stilted conversation at the reception desk: these days always a stilted conversation with a young woman of eastern European origin. I shout to get myself heard above the din and she motions for me to sit down. The music pounds my brain like a claw hammer as I fidget beside the lift waiting for Derek. He arrives about five minutes later: a giant, megalithic behemoth of a black man, on a totally different scale to all around him. I find myself wondering what it must be like to

24 **Derek Williams** born 11 March 1965, London, England. Former British, Commonwealth and EBU heavyweight champion.

live in a world where everybody else is a midget; everybody, that is, except the people who hit you back.

When I knew him years ago Derek was a strikingly good-looking man with a princely bearing. He hasn't changed much. Aside from a little extra weight and a slight thickening of the features the intervening years have mostly kept their distance. 'How are you, Ian?' he says in a voice as deep as he is tall. 'You're looking good.'

We both know that this isn't true but I'm already learning to tolerate this particular variety of white lie. I shake Derek's mammoth fist, fingers like sausages, and ask if there's somewhere we can go that is more quiet. We head for a nearby Costa and I immediately feel eyes upon us in the street. The older Derek Williams remains such a striking, imposing figure that one cannot help but stare at him. People turn to look at us as we enter the café: the fat balding middle-aged white guy with the limp and the black colossus.

Derek has three phones, which he lays out on our table. I tell him I don't remember meeting anybody else who has three phones. That it suggests to me that he can't be doing too badly for himself. 'This is for the work with Jim Watt[25]'s people,' he cheerfully explains. 'This is for the work I do with all the gangs. And this is personal.'

'Like the Bat Phone,' I say.

'Yeah, yeah, yeah, man,' he replies.

I pull out an iPad Mini from my bag and find the audio recording app that I intend to use. I ask Derek if he'll say something so I can check that it's working.

'Hi!' he says in a cavernous voice that instantly has customers swivelling their heads in our direction. 'This is the former heavyweight champion "Sweet D" Williams. Still tall, dark and handsome. I'm sitting here with Ian now and looking forward to how I can give any information about the fight game.'

25 **Jim Watt** born 18 July 1948, Glasgow, Scotland. Former WBC lightweight champion.

We begin. With little prompting Derek launches into a detailed description of what he's doing with his life. Derek seems to primed to do this, as if it's essential that everyone should accept him as more than just an ex-boxer.

'My day job is running the boxing in Gym Box,' he tells me on autopilot. 'What I do is supervise their boxing team. I also work with challenging kids. I keep myself busy by giving things back to the community. I also train my son, Kered Williams. He had his first amateur fight two years ago and he won in the second round.

'I used to be part of the Kids Company that just closed. They did things for children from broken homes and gangs. My whole thing was to try to empower them to turn around. So I was the director of programming.'

Derek talks so fast that it's difficult to keep up. I ask him if the company in question is the one set up and run by Camila Batmanghelidjh, recently controversially placed into liquidation.

'That's right,' he replies. 'I used to go in there two, three times a week. Camilla was a force of nature. She was amazing. But now it's a case of understanding how to move forward.'

Derek stops talking suddenly and looks at me for a few moments. He asks me my age. 'Guess,' I say, instantly regretting my rashness.

'About the same age as me,' he says, too generously.

'You're being polite,' I say. 'I look knackered and you look good.'

And then it's back to boxing because, after all, Derek is an ex-boxer and I'm an ex-boxing writer. This was our only point of connection whenever we met all those years ago so why break the habit? Derek might be only the third boxer that I've interviewed in a quarter of a century but I'm suddenly beginning to understand something that I overlooked before: they all like talking about boxing. Even when they're no longer doing it, you can't stop them talking about boxing.

'Muhammad Ali was a great influence on me.' Derek continues. 'Now, looking back on it, some of the things that Ali said and done was quite offensive to people. Some of the things he said to Joe Frazier was really hurtful.'

Boxers like talking about boxing. How could I never have realised this? And there was me thinking how lucky I was, how fortunate I was in life, to have met with and had the chance to extract a few words, a few phrases from these unique individuals. In reality is seems that they were just as anxious to offload their stories as I was to listen.

'I had ten amateur fights. I never had an outstanding amateur career whereby I won titles. With me there was no plans.' Derek explores the chronology of his life. 'I fought on a lot of Frank Bruno's undercards. I was getting fair money. I was like getting £5,000… £10,000… It was good money for the time. And I was studying to become a draftsman.'

I tell Derek that we have something in common: my first job when I left school was as a trainee draftsman.

'One time I was fighting on an undercard and I was getting £30,000. And I think the main fighter was fighting for a world title fight and they was getting £25,000. So I thought I'm glad I'm not a small weight.'

I've heard all this before, of course: we all have. And not just from Derek. In his case it's the story of a physically advantaged young man who excels at boxing to such a degree that he takes it up professionally. A run of wins, a couple of losses, a few titles and then a long run of defeats followed by retirement. In Derek's case, however, those particular titles comprised the British, European and Commonwealth heavyweight titles. When you consider that most professional boxers plying their trade in this country can only dream of owning silverware of this nature, these are no minor achievements.

Derek, however, is more interested in telling me what happened when he flew over to the US in the late 1980s to be heavyweight champion Mike Tyson's sparring partner. I have clear recollections of him telling me exactly the same stories 25 years ago.

'Sparring with Mike Tyson really made me,' he remembers. 'He had good sparring partners: Greg Page[26]... Oliver McCall[27]... Outstanding fighters. I was about 21 at the time and I was annoyed because everyone thought I wouldn't last long in the ring with him.

'I said, "What you trying to say? Are you trying to say that Mike is going to knock me out?" I done three good rounds with Mike and afterwards people were clapping. Don King[28] came up to me and said, "Hey! You're a good fighter!" He wanted to manage me.

'Over the weeks me and Mike was sparring and people started to take note of my name. It was a chess match. People was loving it. Mike said to me, "How come I've never heard about you? You're a good fighter."

'That was the funny thing. I was handling this guy who was supposed to be the bee's knees. In my head I knew I got the better of him. One day I was feeling sore. So I went into a sauna and Mike was in there. We started talking and he was nice. In my head I was thinking, "I'm there now."'

Derek reveals that he's writing a book about his life at the moment. 'It's basically looking into the mind of a champion,' he says. 'How champions see things. I boxed at a high level. I was number one in Great Britain for eight years.'

I tell him that if he does that the opening chapter has got to about Tyson. But Derek disagrees. He's more interested in letting people know about the time he feels he was drugged before a fight. This allegedly happened in 1990 when he

....

26 **Greg Page** (25 October 25 1958–27 April 2009) Kentucky, USA. Former WBA heavyweight champion of the world.

27 **Oliver McCall** born 21 April 1965, Illinois, USA. Former WBC heavyweight champion of the world.

28 **Don King** born 20 August 1931, Ohio, USA. Notorious and flamboyant boxing promoter.

defended his European title against Jean-Maurice Chanet in France.

'Somebody came up and said, "You have water?"' he recalls. 'And then soon after I started to feel really hot. I was sweating before the fight started. As I walked towards the ring I felt drained. I was depleted of energy by the second round. All I wanted to do was go home and sleep.

'We don't know what it was but the funny thing was when Chanet later came to England to fight Lennox Lewis he had something on his body. The BBBofC made him wash himself off. And then he went back to France and got banned from boxing.'

I ask Derek if he can recall the moment that he suddenly decided that he would no longer box.

'When I was boxing I used to run all the time.' he says. 'From a young age I set my alarm for five o'clock in the morning to be out the door by 5.30am. I used to run five days a week in all weathers. I was running one morning and reached a hill and I was tired and I said to myself, "You don't need to do this," and so I ran on the flat instead. I realised then that my mindset had changed and that something inside of me had changed. Once you don't have that drive inside of you no more it's time to move on.'

'Were you ever tempted to make a comeback?' I ask.

'No. You have to respect yourself,' he replies. 'I didn't want to be no stepping stone for people. But one time a guy from New York called me and said, "Hey Derek, I hear that you've retired. We want you to fight this young heavyweight. He's just turned pro. He's green." I said, "Who's this guy?" And he said his name's Klitschko, Vitali Klitschko[29]."

'I said, "No. I ain't interested, man." If you're fighting just for the money it's not an incentive. Your focus must be on being the best.

....
29 **Vitali Klitschko** born 19 July 1971, Belovodskoye, Soviet Union. Former WBO and WBC heavyweight champion of the world.

'He said, "Derek, he's slow and clumsy – you'll kick his ass." Later he called me back again and offered me $50,000. I said, "When's the fight?" He said, "In two weeks' time."'

'But didn't you miss the buzz?' I ask. 'That feeling of walking into the ring with thousands cheering? There must be nothing else like it in life.'

'Yeah, the whole thing is a buzz. You like the crowd. You like the thrill of the opponent throwing punches and you throwing them back at him. All that is like a dance. I miss fighting. Not because I want to go back but because of the excitement. We have our time in the sun but we move on.'

'If you could go back and do it all again what would you do differently?' I ask

'I would have moved to the right instead of the left when Lennox Lewis[30] hit me,' says Derek. We both laugh.

'When he knocked me out I was so surprised that I was knocked down. I thought, "Wow! what's happening?!" It was the first time I'd ever been down but it didn't hurt. You don't feel any pain because of the adrenaline. A good shot don't hurt you. The shot that hits you on your jaw detaches you from your senses.'

* * * * *

Derek continues to talk. Another machine gun monologue is on its way. It's no wonder that he's occasionally employed as an after dinner speaker. Some 20 minutes have gone by since I last managed to ask a question and he's barely stopped for breath. However, the sudden seriousness of what I tell him next stops him in his tracks.

'Can I say something to you?' I interrupt.

'Yeah.' The dryness of my tone produces a frown.

....

30 **Lennox Lewis** born 2 September 1965, London, England. Former undisputed heavyweight champion of the world.

'One of the reasons I wanted to see you is that I wanted to apologise.'

'Yeah?' he repeats, obviously confused.

'I wanted to apologise for 25 years ago… Doing that article. Do you remember it?'

Derek shakes his head. 'I can't remember it,' he says.

He may not remember but this is the real reason I'm here. The real reason that I wanted to see Derek 'Sweet D' Williams and try to set the record straight. Back in the late 1980s I somehow managed to find myself in the position of boxing reporter for the one of the worst newspapers of that era. When I tell people about it these days they laugh. They think it's hilarious that I would ever have done such a thing.

But at the time it was certainly no joke. I was young, desperate for money and apparently willing to set aside any principles I thought I had by working for one of the red-top equivalents of *Viz*. A quarter of a century later and I still can't really defend it.

In life we all do things that we don't really want to do, particularly when we're younger. We all jump through hoops on the promise of better things to come. However, on the morning of my first day on the job I did something that I've always been ashamed of.

'So what happened was, I was 24,' I murmur, guiltily. 'It was my first job ever in journalism. The *Sunday Sport*. Remember the *Sunday Sport*?'

'Yeah.'

'I was on the phone to you.'

'I think I remember. Did you do the story about the ladies and stuff?'

'Yes. it was my first morning on the job.'

I cover this pretty shameful episode in great detail in my other book on boxing, *Rope Burns*. But the nub of the story is that under pressure from the newspaper's unscrupulous sports editor I was persuaded to telephone Derek a number of times and get him to admit that his fans regularly performed fellatio on him. I'm not proud of succumbing to this pressure and I'm frankly still surprised that I was able to go through with it, but at the time there was the very real threat that I might lose my job and so I took the coward's way out.

When the newspaper duly appeared on Sunday morning my story came with the headline 'My Gals Call Me Sweet Dick' (Derek's nickname, remember, was 'Sweet D' – *geddit*?). It's probably true that some people may have found the story amusing but I certainly didn't and nor, unless I'm completely missing the point, did the man standing in front of me.

'I felt really bad about it,' I say.

'Yeah?' says Derek, apparently untroubled.

'You didn't want to beat me up or anything like that?'

'No. I don't do that kind of thing. With me, Ian, my whole mindset is to teach people about channelling their aggression and anger into positivity. People do things in life for whatever reasons they do them, right? The important thing is to have control.'

'Were you not angry?'

'No.'

'Did you not feel exploited?'

'No. "This is amazing," I said to myself at the time, "this is amazing." I said, "Don't get mad. Don't get mad. Leave it." I didn't say nothing like it to this dude but this is the way life is. I let it go.'

'That makes me feel even worse,' I say. 'I can't tell you over the years how much it's haunted me. I was young back then but that's no excuse… So the least I can do is say sorry.'

Derek scrutinises me for several moments before speaking. 'I accept your apology, man,' he says. 'I accept it.'

And just like that it's over. I understand that we all perceive things in different ways, of course we do; that one man's malefaction is another's petty crime. But I never expected it to be so easy. For 25 years I've been dreading coming face to face with Derek Williams, not for fear of any physical retribution – in many ways that would have been too easy – but because I just didn't think I'd ever be able to look him in the eye.

And now that I've finally done so he's proven himself to be the bigger man, both physically and morally. As I look at Derek he grows a further couple of inches in stature – as if he needed to be any taller – and I shrink by the same amount.

Back

I T is the morning after a terrorist massacre in Paris has left more than 120 people dead. A fuliginous mist of melancholia hangs over London, throttling the sunlight. The atmosphere on the streets brings to mind that feeling of punch drunk stupefaction to which many people unexpectedly succumbed on the day that Diana Spencer died. The fact that I'm on my way to Bromley to meet a boxing manager whom I haven't spoken to in decades is, of course, completely inappropriate to this sombre occasion. If I had a proper sense of perspective perhaps I would be sitting at home thinking about those who have lost their lives.

The boxing manager in question is not your standard off-the-shelf example of that genre. Indeed, if I were looking for some kind of scale by which to gauge the effect the years have had on myself and the people in boxing whom I used to know the case of Kellie Maloney would almost certainly provide the most extreme example.

The last time I saw Kellie, her name was Frank and *his* appearance was rather more in line with what you might expect your sharp-suited archetypal boxing manager/promoter to look like.

In those days if you were to sum up Frank Maloney in a single sentence you might say that he was a small man with a big personality. He had the stature of the former jockey that he was and the vocal inflections of a seasoned *EastEnders* regular.

Via Twitter DM, Kellie has instructed me to meet her on Bromley High Street, where we plan to have a coffee and chew the cud. But as always I arrive at my destination more than an hour early; I exit a destitute Bromley-by-Bow tube station and pick up a phone message that she left while I was underground. The message crackles with interference but between the pops and hisses I can just about make out the fact that Kellie is apparently suffering from a bad back and is suggesting that we meet at a Costa in Bromley High Street. I type the address into my iPhone but the GPS refuses to recognise it so I decide to ask someone for directions.

I stop a young Asian guy and he cheerfully provides me with over-elaborate instructions that I pretend to understand. As I point my body in the direction that he indicates it gradually begins to dawn on me that he might be following me. I up my pace and so does he. I up it a second time until I'm walking at a very respectable pace for a semi-cripple but he's still there right behind me like Nico Rosberg chasing Lewis Hamilton.

An acute feeling of shame washes over me: because of the events in Paris last night I find myself growing irrationally nervous. I am reminded of similar feelings that people experienced whenever anybody who happened to look vaguely middle-eastern climbed into a tube carriage in aftermath of the 7/7 bombings. In the months after the atrocities such jitters among commuters were almost palpable. And so it is today: the person walking behind me shouldn't be alarming to me but he is.

It's a false alarm, however; obviously it it's a false alarm, and I eventually arrive at Bromley High Street to discover that it looks nothing like the busy high street I'd been expecting. There's a launderette and a newsagent's and a couple of kids aimlessly kicking a ball around but there's no sign of a Costa of any description with a transgender boxing manager ensconced within. I check my phone to see if I've made any mistakes but the GPS is still being uncooperative so I decide to take a stroll around the area.

I wander on to a busier street, hoping that this might be the actual destination but only end up getting even more lost. When I check the time I realise that three quarters of an hour have passed since I arrived in Bromley. I now have only 15 minutes left in which to find Kellie. The prospect of arriving late brings me out into a cold sweat. I really must talk to my therapist about this.

I try calling Kellie but she's not answering. I walk about a bit more and call a second and a third time. Finally Kellie answers. 'Where are you?' she says.

I explain that I am in Bromley High Street but can find hide nor hair of a Costa. She asks me to look around me and describe what I see. There is a long silence, followed by a heavy sigh. 'Which station did you come out of,' she asks. 'North or South?'

I'm confused for a moment before I reply, 'There is no North or South,' I say. 'Just Bromley-On-Bow.'

'I don't live there,' comes the exasperated response. 'I live in Bromley, *Kent*.'

* * * * *

Almost two hours later I'm exiting Bromley South train station. I'm sure that people can actually see traces of egg on my face as I limp by. In transit there have been further exchanges of messages between Kellie and myself. It turns out that her back is now so bad that she is unable to leave her flat. She suggests that I walk there from the train station, something like a 15-minute hobble for me and my dodgy hip.

Kellie is only the second person I have known personally who has undergone gender re-assignment surgery; I'll tell her this later. The first was a guy named Graham whom I worked with back in 1978; only in those days they called it a sex-change and very few people felt the remotest need to be kind or understanding or sensitive about it. The whole thing was one huge Benny Hill-type belly laugh. Naturally, it didn't help that Graham chose the name 'Griselda' as his alter ego (he really did) and that someone from the office spotted him out one night clad in the sort of outfit that Les Dawson might wear to the laundrette.

Reaction in boxing to Kellie's unexpected metamorphosis has, however, been almost entirely supportive and an incandescent credit to the sport. After the initial sniggers had died down and people had overcome their shock at Kellie's transmutation almost everybody who knows her or has even a passing association with Kellie has displayed unreserved kindness and sensitivity. To the uninitiated an apparently macho sport such as boxing might be expected to react to news such as this in an entirely different manner.

But boxing is sympathetic to extremes and might almost be called a gentle sport. Images of a tearful defeated boxer being tenderly held in the arms of a trainer, referee or opponent are actually commonplace. Thus a supreme act of bravery such as the one undertaken by Kellie will always be given the respect it deserves.

In the couple of days leading up to my meeting with Kellie, however, I can feel myself growing more and more agitated. As well as the usual nerves that one might expect to accompany a reunion with a long forgotten acquaintance, there are a number of other issues on my mind; trivial things that less paranoid people than I probably wouldn't be quite so concerned about. Firstly, I'm concerned that I might accidentally slip into calling Kellie by her former name: it's an understandable mistake to make when you've gotten used to calling somebody by a certain moniker (or, in this case, *Monica*). Moreover, there is the fact that I might accidentally get his gender wrong, as I just did then. Indeed, whenever I speak about Kellie in casual conversation at home my 12-year-old daughter is always the first to tell me off when I inevitably mess up. And I do this a lot.

There is another reason for my concern. Being only the second transsexual that I've personally known there is also the issue of correct protocol when we actually come face to face. In the past whenever I bumped into Frank I usually shook his hand. I can't really do this with Kellie, can I? It's a silly thing to be fretting about but there you have it (and funnily enough when I later meet Kellie's former press agent he will confess to having exactly the same concern). In the end I decide that the best thing to do will be to kiss Kellie on both cheeks, as one often does when meeting a woman in a formal situation. In all honesty it says a quite lot about me as a person that the thought of doing this makes me feel uncomfortable. But uncomfortable I am.

* * * * *

Some three hours after setting off I finally arrive *chez* Kellie. The Maloney residence is located in a nondescript, tree-lined avenue, a typical kind of suburban street that mixes opulence – in the form of grandiose multi-level mock-Georgian apartments – with the poverty of shabby council houses stained with efflorescence and featuring listless overweight teenagers smoking in doorways. I check that this really is Kellie's address and ring the doorbell, ready to deliver my self-conscious kisses. After a long period of silence I am gradually aware of weary footsteps descending stairs. The front door opens painfully.

I was always taught to look people in the eye when you meet them and I ready myself to do this but there is no outstretched hand coming from Kellie, nor is a cheek of any description proffered in my general direction. Well actually that's not quite true because instead I am presented at eye level with a pair of unmistakably male buttocks as Kellie turns her back on me before I am able to catch a glimpse of her face and slowly trudges back to whence she came. I am reminded of a memorable scene from Norman Mailer's 1975 book *The Fight*, in which, moments before his classic battle with Muhammad Ali, defending heavyweight champion George Foreman turns his back on his opponent and stretches out his buttocks as if to say, in Mailer's words, 'My farts to you.'

This particular pair of buttocks is enwrapped in loose-fitting tracksuit bottoms of indiscernible colouring. I trail behind them in awkward silence. Kellie's flat is on the third floor of the building and progress up the stairs is woefully slow. Kellie is in so much pain she is barely able to walk. When we eventually reach our destination it is shrouded in darkness and our voices echo in the silence. I make cursory attempts at conversation but my words are met with grunts of pain and displeasure.

Kellie's flat is spacious, sparsely decorated and show-house tidy. The living room is dominated by a large window through which the subdued Kent light gently filters, lending a film noir quality to the setting. As I take a seat Kellie painfully lowers her diminutive figure on to a large *chaise longue* some 20 feet away from me. She lies there drenched in shadow so that I am barely able to make out her features. Already this is the second time that I have been denied access to a glimpse of Kellie's new face. I find myself wondering how much of this is conscious.

Kellie's physical conversion has undoubtedly made her facial appearance one of the focal points of her being; having to continually explicate this radical transmutation to both strangers and non-strangers must be onerous to say the least. There is also the fact that there have been newspaper articles as well as a Channel 5 documentary which chronicle the near disastrous consequences of the facial surgery that Kellie has undertaken in order to become female.

Kellie gasps and groans and struggles to get comfortable and tells me about her back. She thinks it might be sciatica, which I am no stranger to myself. This prompts me to immediately enter lecture mode. As if she needs reminding I grandly inform her that sciatica is an extremely painful and debilitating condition and that people will never appreciate this until they actually experience it. She says that the doctor doesn't really know what it is and I, of course, take the opportunity to tell her about my own hip condition, which went undiagnosed for close to two decades. I advise her not to wait around for doctors and to get an immediate scan, which was how my own condition was eventually diagnosed after years of misery. She tells me she'll get on to it in the morning.

Finally, I ask to see the painkillers that she has been prescribed, which prove to be laughably inadequate. I delve into my wallet where I keep a spare supply of my own painkillers and offer some to her. There. I'm Kellie Maloney's candyman. Somehow, I always thought it would end like this. She declines.

The last time that I saw Kellie's ubiquitous progenitor in person was around 1997 after Herol Graham's win over the American Vinny Pazienza[31] for a meaningless bauble called the 'WBC international super-middleweight title'. On that occasion I had been commissioned by *The Guardian* to profile the then manager of heavyweight champion Lennox Lewis. At the time I optimistically kidded myself that the fact I was writing about a boxing manager was coincidental and actually had nothing whatsoever to do with boxing. It was the first boxing-related piece I had written for a periodical of any description in seven years and my last for a further 17.

....

31 **Vinny Pazienza** born 16 December 1962, Rhode Island, USA. Former IBF lightweight champion of the world; WBO light-welterweight champion of the world; WBA light-middleweight champion of the world.

Since that occasion the erstwhile Frank seems to have gone out of his way to draw attention to himself. There was the gaudy Union Jack suit that he always wore at ringside, the weekly column in the *Daily Sport* ('No Baloney – It's Frank Maloney!'), and there was his doomed attempt to become mayor of London in 2004. It is, however, his alter-ego Kellie that unreservedly trumps any of his previous efforts at self-promotion. Sitting in this peaceful living room in Bromley on a lazy Sunday afternoon, it is, however, surprisingly easy to forget the person she used to be.

* * * * *

'What's this about?' mumbles Kellie, although I'd tried to get across the reason for my desire to see her in the exchange of DMs that preceded our meeting. It is admittedly bizarre to hear Frank Maloney's unequivocally masculine tones coming from Kellie Maloney's remodelled lips. Later, Kellie will tell me that she could choose to do something about this anomaly but she has had her fill of operations.

I pause self-consciously for a few moments, as I will do a lot over the next few months. 'It's a weird one,' I say eventually. 'You're going to think I'm a bit mad.'

I then proceed to detail the events of the last 15 years: about how I fell ill with a seemingly endless collection of symptoms. About how I put on maybe 40lb in weight, about how I would regularly faint, invariably injuring myself as I fell to the floor a dead weight. The broken noses, the facial gashes, the third-degree burns on my back caused by falling unconscious against a boiling hot radiator. The deep, deep, dark depressions.

The continual feelings of imminent death…The bodily rashes and eczema…The inability to concentrate for more than a few minutes… The loss of hearing and sense of taste… No stone is left unturned as Kellie – at what is doubtless the most significantly transformative point in her life – becomes my unwitting unpaid therapist.

The incredible thing is that Kellie seems to be altogether unperturbed by anything I have to say. When I think about this later I'm all the more impressed. I don't know how I would react if someone whom I vaguely knew 20-odd years ago asked to see me out of the blue and suddenly started telling me the most intimate details about themselves. I'd certainly be hard pressed to remain as cool about it as Kellie Maloney appears to be when I move on to the subject of my father.

I tell Kellie all about him. About the beatings I used to receive as a child. About the psychological bullying that turned me into a loner and ultimately a very peculiar adult.

'I never thought you was strange,' says Kellie. 'A bit eccentric maybe.'

I tell her many of the things that I am reluctant to tell my therapist. And Kellie just takes it in, gently processing the information and offering occasional advice when appropriate. It's a completely unexpected situation for both of us, I think. And when I finally finish talking I can feel just a tiny bit of weight slip away from my shoulders.

It may be that I am the first person in a very long time whom Kellie has met that doesn't want to talk about the technicalities of Frank becoming Kellie. That in itself may be a relief for her. I offer to make Kellie a cup of tea but she insists on doing it for herself. We move into the kitchen, me limping and Kellie hobbling in pain. For the second time I offer her some of my personal painkillers. She demurs.

We sit at the kitchen table and I am able for the first time to get a closer look at Kellie's face. There are still traces of Frank there, obviously there are and always will be. To exorcise Frank she's had well-documented surgical procedures that almost cost her life. The make-up is applied less skilfully than, say, my wife's. Nevertheless this is a woman sitting beside me. Unmistakably it's a woman. And I notice that my own behaviour has changed because of this: in a subtle way, probably only recognisable to nobody but myself I am interacting with Kellie as I would any other woman. I'm not yet quite prepared to enter the flirting stage but there's a certain softening of my demeanour.

As we speak, I'm reminded of the last time that I sat alone with the person who used to be Frank Maloney. On that occasion it was in the kitchen of the house that he shared with his wife and kids in east London. It was around the time that Lennox Lewis had lost his heavyweight title and Maloney's millionaire financial backers had gone bust.[32] As we sat together the never anything but earnest boxing manager made no attempt to conceal his depression. It was then that Maloney did something altogether unexpected: in mid-conversation his voice suddenly trailed off and for several long moments he stared blankly into space as if in a trance. I can remember calling his name out several times but it was as if I were no longer in the room, as if time had stood still for Frank Maloney.

Then, as if nothing had happened, the boxing manager suddenly snapped back into consciousness and resumed talking to me again.

This event is an anecdote that I have related to a number of people over the years, without them ever quite believing me. And it is why, when I first heard the news about Kellie's gender re-assignment, I was not quite so surprised as I perhaps should have been. Instead of the streetwise wheeler dealer boxing manager for which Frank always worked hard to be perceived, I always saw him as something more sensitive and fragile. Indeed, in the days after stories of Kellie's transformation hit the headlines I contacted her to tell her just this.

----

32 In order to manage boxer Lennox Lewis, Maloney received financial backing from the Levitt Group financial services empire, which crashed in 1990 owing £34m.

'Yeah... In those days I used to zone out,' says Kellie when I remind her of that afternoon. 'It was my way of coping with things.'

We move on to more trivial matters: Kellie discusses her appearances on the busy celebrity circuit: an early post-transformation appearance on *Celebrity Big Brother* and a Christmas appearance on *Mastermind* (specialist subject: boxing), the Channel 5 documentaries, Katie Hopkins's show, the newspaper exclusives, a best-selling autobiography (the second; the first – as Frank – unsurprisingly did not sell nearly as well the most recent). It seems fairly clear to me that Kellie is enjoying the attention.

We talk about the impact that the arrival of Kellie has had on her married life. And right on cue the sound of a key turning in a lock signifies the arrival of the former Mrs Frank Maloney and their 14-year-old daughter. What's interesting about their entrance is the air of cosy domestic normality they carry with them. It's clear that the former couple still have a great deal of affection for each other. Indeed, the reality of this apparently nondescript domestic situation completely belies a *Daily Mail* story published a year earlier which tells of Tracy's 'total devastation' at her husband's 'bombshell'. Perhaps the couple have learned to live with the situation a little in the interceding months. Certainly, their daughter appears to have done so. Her belligerent teenage attitude towards her father bears striking similarities to my own daughter's treatment of myself.

The two females stay for about half an hour and then I'm alone again with Kellie. She clutches her back more urgently. The pain is intensifying. For the third time I offer her my own painkillers and now she takes them. We sit at the kitchen table and inevitably talk about boxing. Kellie seems genuinely touched by the boxing fraternity's reaction to her unexpected emergence. Although she mentions one or two dissenting names – rival promoters – she tells me that she has been overwhelmed by the kindness and understanding of her peers. We talk about her desire to tell her story at book recitations. She clearly wants to be heard. But then so did Frank.

I stay for about five hours in all and doubtless get a lot more out of the meeting than Kellie probably does. However, before I leave Kellie gives me yet another example of the inherent kindness that can be found at the heart of boxing.

I may not have seen the former Frank Maloney for a very long time but that does not stop her from inviting me up to Birmingham the next weekend to watch one of fighters perform. Like me, Kellie is in the midst of her own boxing comeback. Earlier in the year she was doorstepped by two young fighters who needed her help. Kellie's subsequent decision to return to management surely makes her one of the most unique managers in the history of the sport. I tell Kellie that I'm humbled by her munificence, and that it takes me right back to the very first time I met her alter-ego in the late 1980s when, as a rookie reporter, I was unexpectedly invited to spend Christmas at his pub. I tell Kellie that Frank's unreserved generosity made it difficult for me to trust him back then. My reasoning was that there just had to be some kind of unscrupulous reason for such unexpected altruism. It was boxing, after all. The land of gangsters, Don King and 'Doc' Kearns[33].

'Yes, this is boxing,' Kellie shrugs, wincing at the pain.

....

33 **Jack 'Doc' Kearns** 17 August 1882–7 July 1963. Washington, USA. Boxing manager remember chiefly for managing undisputed world heavyweight champion **Jack Dempsey** 24 June 1895–31 May 1983), Colorado, USA.

Crackers

THERE'S something about the sport of boxing that was always going to attract the world's speediest consumer of cream crackers. And in common with everything else about the owner of such an idiosyncratic title, gaining an audience with him proves to be just about as straightforward as juggling a greased piranha fish.

Many months after initially messaging him via Twitter to request this rendezvous I'm standing outside Stratford tube station hunting for the Pret A Manger in which he claimed he would be waiting. Predictably there's no sign of such an establishment and Westfield in Stratford is one fuck of a big place that happens to look uncannily like Westfield in Shepherd's Bush. It's as if the architects couldn't be arsed to draw up a new set of plans.

To compound matters I've run out of data on my phone until tomorrow – which means that sending him a smiley but slightly concerned emoji is not an option. Moreover, despite the industrial painkillers I've been sucking like smarties my hip is playing up badly. I must look a sight as I stumble up and down the escalators asking anyone who will listen for directions to the nearest Pret.

Eventually – and by eventually I mean a solid 45 minutes of trudging aimlessly around in circles like an extra from *The Walking Dead* in surely the most boring and faceless shopping centre in the entire world – I do manage to locate the eatery in question. Obviously it's nowhere near where he said it would be: it's on the third floor adjacent to a cinema and just as obviously he himself is conspicuous by his absence. So I hobble around some more, sweating like a spit-roasted pig and occasionally checking my impotent mobile, hoping I might catch a glimpse of my quarry.

I eventually criss-cross my way back to the station entrance but by now I'm struggling to keep my cool. In truth I shouldn't really be surprised that I'm wasting my time. In the preceding months we must have exchanged dozens of messages, some answered immediately, some answered weeks later apparently in a form of exclusive cryptic hieroglyph. But the end result as ever is that my position in life is pointed out to me in unequivocal terms: he's the leader and I'm the follower. I want him and he doesn't want me. It's a plain and simple truth. He's doing me a big favour by agreeing to see me and I'm offering very little in return.

This is what life can be like for anybody with aspirations to be a journalist, if you can call it that. The vast majority of time you want them more than they want you. It's something that you have to get used to if you have any ambition of seeing your name sitting beneath a headline. Which I never did and actually still don't.

But by now the evil, nasty, Simon-Cowell-Dick-Dastardly-Voldemort part of me is inexorably crawling to the surface: I'm thinking, *You fucking cunt, I came to visit you in prison I don't know how many fucking times, I gave you sweeties for Christ's sake. And I never asked you for a fucking thing in return.*

I'm thinking shameful things that a normal, civilised person has no right to be thinking.

I look around the crowded entrance to the station for anyone small enough on which to take out my frustration but everyone's too big and my anger quickly dissipates when I finally get a text from him with a 360-degree video attached that has been shot outside a busy Pret A Manger. Evidently there's more than one Pret in Westfield. If you substitute the vowel in the name you'll get a pretty accurate description of how I'm feeling right now.

I text an apology that will never be enough to compensate for my disgraceful thoughts. I feel foolish and humiliated at my inner temper tantrum. From nowhere I receive the enigmatic response, 'My hair is now... Silver!!'

Equally enigmatically, I text back that it's ironic because I'm always pathologically early, which obviously has nothing to do with anybody's hair turning silver, as well being a fact that I'm sure you're becoming mind-numbingly aware of by now.

Another response, 'Happy to come to meet you tomorrow afternoon if you have spare time? Apologies.'

I respond that I can't make tomorrow but can do Thursday or Friday and that I know he must be very busy.

'I will make time!' Comes the grandiose reply.

And that's the last I hear from him for two months. Until then I'm entrenched in radio silence.

* * * * *

I'm half an hour early so I take a stroll around freezing Soho, carefully checking the time on my phone every couple of minutes. After another exchange of Twitter DMs we've arranged to meet at something called Century Members Club on Shaftesbury Avenue. I walk past the door to check it out. Unless you knew it was there you wouldn't know it was there. Sandwiched between one of a million Chinese restaurants in the area and a nondescript souvenir shop, none of the hordes of tourists and their clicking camera phones would have a clue about its existence. It's him all over really.

With five minutes to go to our meeting I press a self consciously unobtrusive doorbell and I'm inside. The interior smells of hard cash and a pinch of lavender. The girl on reception is young and pretty like a Connery-era Bond girl. Her eyes wander over a computer screen and she tells me he's waiting for me on the roof terrace. I unwisely take the stairs rather than the lift. This means that I'm huffing and puffing when I finally locate his table, discreetly hidden away in a comfortable booth by a window. It's taken months to reach the point where I'm finally sitting cheek to jowl with boxing manager without portfolio and long-standing Guinness World Record holder for the fastest time taken to eat three cream crackers, Ambrose Mendy. He grasps my hand breezily, like I'm someone he sees every other weekend and occasionally goes on holiday with.

Sitting opposite Ambrose are two young black men. One of them looks suspiciously like IBF super-middleweight champion James DeGale[34], whom Ambrose advises, but I don't catch his name when he mumbles a polite hello at me and I'm not prepared to risk showing my ignorance by asking if it's really him. I don't recognise the other man but I'm struck by his gentlemanly air of respect. After a few minutes the two men drift away, leaving me alone with Ambrose for the first time in 20-odd years.

I touched upon this during that shameful rant I mentioned a few pages back. On that earlier occasion two decades ago *Friends* was the hottest thing on Friday night TV, people genuinely believed that Ali G was an actual person and I was sitting across from Ambrose at a table in the somewhat less exclusive surroundings of Woking Prison, where he was serving time for fraud – his third protracted stay behind bars if Google isn't telling fibs.

At the time I'd had no contact at all with anyone connected with boxing in some six years but I was prepared to make an exception for Ambrose. I'd always had a soft spot for him.

....

34 **James DeGale** born 3 February 1986, London, England. IBF super-middleweight champion of the world.

Indeed, I can still vividly remember the first time I ever saw him in the flesh. This was in 1989 at the Albert Hall when the boxer he represented, that man Nigel Benn, was fighting a nobody called Mike Chilambe for the commonwealth middleweight title. I watched that one-round cakewalk sitting between Michael Watson and his trainer, Eric Seccombe. It was one of those fights that give boxing an even worse name: Benn seemed to connect with little more than a ludic swipe of his polished red glove for Chilambe to keel over as if struck by a four-be-two. Indeed, the appearance of Ambrose that night was infinitely more memorable than the fight itself.

Shortly before the mismatch began Ambrose's impeccable silhouette could be seen sailing gracefully before the ring lights. The hacks in the press seats were nudging each other at the spectacle. The image for me, however, was striking and symbolised the changing tides in boxing: the expertly-cut suit and immaculately gelled barnet seemed the polar opposite of the spit, sawdust and cigar smoke image of the sport. This is not to suggest that Ambrose was the first person ever to don a smart suit at a boxing match but he seemed to do it with so much more panache than anybody else. Of equal importance was the fact that Ambrose was black: black, icily articulate and fiercely independent in a world where black men fought and white men thought.

Later, at the post-fight press conference I was able to listen to Ambrose speak which he always did with considerable flair. His autodidactic presence usually filled the room, as did the dislike of this upstart that emanated from a conspicuous percentage of the press ranks, the majority of whom were, of course, even whiter than I. This is not to suggest that there was any blatant racism at play there – although I'm unconvinced that Ambrose or any of the black boxers present that day would agree. It was more a case of resentment at the old guard being forcibly usurped by the new. Discomfort and unfamiliarity. That and one's natural indisposition towards anything that happened to be different. At least that was my reading of the situation. Whatever the case, in private very few reporters had a good word to say about Ambrose and his so-called 'black pack'[35]; preferring instead to dwell upon his prison CV as well as other less substantiated insinuations.

So it was that at some point in the mid-1990s I picked up a newspaper and read about Ambrose's latest incarceration and ended up going to visit him in prison.

The man sitting across the table is a twinge heavier now. His hair is thinner and whiter but it's still the same Ambrose Mendy. Two decades have left their mark on him but you'd have to say the cream cracker diet befits him. He asks me what I'm doing with myself and compliments me on a short video of me playing guitar that he'd seen on Facebook. But before I can respond he's into a long rap about Steve Lillis, a presenter on BoxNation[36] whom I used to work with a very long time ago. I tell Ambrose about how Steve took over my job when I left the *Sunday Sport* and he remembers how green Steve used to be and recalls the naivety of the questions he used to ask at press conferences in the early days. All that has changed now, of course, says Ambrose. Steve has more than earned his spurs over the years.

Which leads Ambrose on to his relationship with the boxing promoter Frank Warren, owner of BoxNation. I've heard the stories many time before but they still engage. Ambrose tells me how Warren was the best man at his wedding before they fell out over Nigel Benn, whom Ambrose managed to appropriate and became unlicensed advisor to. Ambrose wistfully remembers those early days, when he apparently owned two Rolls Royces and saw his first live boxing match with Warren. 'We were both "captivated",' he recalls. He talks

35 The **Black Pack** were a group of celebrities who modelled themselves on Frank Sinatra's Rat Pack

36 **BoxNation** is a dedicated boxing pay TV channel, operated by Boxing Channel Media and promoter Frank Warren.

about his battles with the cartel.[37] His battles with the board. His battles with everybody. He tells me he hasn't spoken to Warren for 27 years. Tea is delivered by a waiter with a French accent and then it's on to Ambrose's unprintable theories about who shot his former friend.[38]

It's been such a long time since I've seen him that I've quite forgotten that where Ambrose is concerned you have to be prepared to fight to be heard. The ceaseless stream of conversation that flows from his lips is furnished with negligible punctuation. This means that you have to unceremoniously crash the conversation in order to make any kind of contribution. This is easier said than done.

Ambrose is now talking about his dodgy knee and tells me all about his meeting with a specialist. He talks about how he still plays football every week and regularly races his sons. 'There is only one condition,' he says. 'I have to be the one who says "go".'

Ever eager to discuss my own collection of illnesses, I manage to butt in. I talk about how my avascular necrosis of the hip was only diagnosed after more than ten years of intermittent pain. I tell him about my feckless visits to so-called specialists and advise him to seek a second and third opinion before he ever allows himself to come under the knife.

Then Ambrose reveals to me that he has had prostate cancer and tells me about a successful operation to remove a tumour. He says that there had been no symptoms beforehand and that the lump was only discovered by accident. Nowadays

37 The **cartel** was a secret although legal alliance comprising boxing managers and promoters Mickey Duff, Terry Lawless, Mike Barrett and Jarvis Astaire. During the 1970s and early 1980s the cartel dominated British boxing before being exposed by the *Sunday Times*.

38 On 30 November 1989, Frank Warren was shot outside the Broadway Theatre in Barking by an unknown assailant who was never caught. Former boxer Terry Marsh was accused of the shooting but acquitted by a jury.

he's checked every three months and thank God he's remained clean.

Then it's on to prison: I tell Ambrose that apart from an overnight stay in a police cell when I was in my 20s I'd never been anywhere near anything resembling a prison until I visited him. It was quite a memorable experience for me: prior to my travelling to Woking, Ambrose had given me a list of items that he wanted me to bring. In addition to the obligatory file in the cake, Ambrose was particularly anxious that I bring along a large bag of mixed sweets. When I arrived at the prison, however, I was immediately frisked by a prison guard and the sweets were confiscated. I guessed at the time that the reason for this probably had something to do with the potential to conceal contraband among the sweetie wrappers but it could also have been a reflection of Mendy's relationship with his jailers.

What still surprises me, however, was what Ambrose did next: which was to march up to the prison guard, dip a fist into the bag of sweets and help himself to a generous handful while the guard stood by and did nothing. Ambrose and I laugh at the memory.

The conversation moves on to writing and I finally get the chance to explain why I've made contact with him. I once again go into the well-trodden story and my father and depression and pills and the path that has led me to get back in touch with a tranche of figures from my past. Ambrose frowns as his brain processes this information which allows him to segue nicely to his own writing. The pace of the afternoon is relentless. Subject after subject rattles by like a train rushing through a station.

He tells me about a play he's written and about a book he's started entitled, *Free Dinners Go Last*, which I tell him is a good title. And I mean it. He tells me he's already completed the book while behind bars but the manuscript was destroyed by a 'screw' who 'had it in for me'.

We talk about the kids' book I wrote a couple of years ago, and my efforts to promote it by visiting schools across the country. This somehow leads Ambrose to reveal his great admiration for the children's TV programme *Peppa Pig*. For a surreal moment I find myself sitting in an exclusive Soho members club listening to a notorious boxing iconoclast singing the theme tune to the show. Fellow diners warily frown at us over their copies of the *Financial Times*.

Ambrose invites me to come and see one of his fighters in action. He tells me that it's an unlikely to be James DeGale because the boxer is keen to fight abroad. When I began thinking about writing this book it did cross my mind that sooner or later I might have to attend a boxing show. If I'm going to do this I probably couldn't find a more interesting or eclectic host than Ambrose Mendy. He says we must meet again in a week's time to talk.

But Ambrose has another meeting to go to on a different floor of the same club. Before he leaves he talks about the recent Hatton Garden bank robbery, about how he knows all of the main protagonists and about how stupid they were. And as he does so I remind him of a question I asked him 20-odd years ago during one of my prison visits. 'Why do you do it?' I had asked. Why does he place into jeopardy the obvious wealth of natural talents that he possesses?

Ambrose had thought long and hard before he replied. 'Because I like it,' he'd said.

* * * * *

Later that evening a text from Ambrose arrives while I'm sitting at home bored, 'Many thanks Ian. Enjoyed the convo!!'

And that's the last time I hear from Ambrose Mendy.

Cry

THE first week of January and the New Year's resolutions have kicked in. No more alcohol for me for three months and I've also set myself the target of losing two stones of seal blubber; just like a boxer has to lose weight before a fight. Writers shouldn't be fat, should they? Particularly retired boxing writers in the process of tentatively un-retiring. As well as this I've been cycling 15km every morning.

But my resolve is already weakening: when the alarm goes off at six in the morning suddenly the idea of staying in bed seems like the most sensible thing in the world to do. It's too wet outside and too warm in. I tell myself to text Steve Collins and make an excuse, maybe arrange to meet up with him in a week or so.

But no. Bad sense prevails. I drag myself out of bed and head for the tube. It's been difficult enough arranging to meet the one-time middleweight and super-middleweight world champion and I'd be a complete fool to throw it away for the sake of a couple of extra hours' kip. Steve lives in St Albans and he's currently training a young boxer named Frank Buglioni[39]. The gym is in a place called Cheshunt. I've already been there once before when I went to interview Frank a day or so before

----

39 **Frank Buglioni** born 18 April 1989, London, England.

my father died. Steve was also there on that occasion and, truth be told, I found him rather intimidating.

The first thing he said to me on that morning was, 'I thought you were going to fuckin' kiss me!' which, I guess, was a comment that may have been related to the gormless expression that I must have been wearing on my face at the time. When I telephoned Steve just before Christmas to make this particular appointment he was wary and full of questions. And when I told him that I wasn't looking for a conventional interview but wanted instead to 'hang' for a while he said, 'What do you mean *hang*? No you can't *hang*!' Fair enough.

It takes about an hour and a half to get there and as I walk the streets searching for a cashpoint I'm struck by how waterlogged it is here. We all been hearing all about the floods on the news but London has so far remained largely untouched. Cheshunt, on the other hand, is absolutely wringing with water. Sodden. Wetter than a breakfast TV presenter on *Strictly Come Dancing*. It looks as though Hagrid has been spraying the town with an industrial hosepipe for a couple of decades. Huge freezing ponds block the roadside as I pull my hood ever tighter. Then at some point I reach for my shoulder bag and realise that it isn't there. I've left it on the train. I shake my head, exasperated. I really am getting old: it's the second time in a month that I've mislaid my iPad Mini along with my wallet.

Even when I was earning a full-time living writing about sport I always found stepping into a boxing gym to be more than a little daunting. It's not so much the fact that such a place really does conform to just about every cliché that you've ever been served up in films such as *Rocky* or *Raging Bull* or *Carry On Punching Each Other Indefinitely*. When you enter a boxing gym there really are – *quelle surprise* – sweaty, hairy, heavily muscled boxers aiming punches at punchbags and speedballs. And they really are overseen by authentic grizzled-looking trainers (although, like policeman and doctors, the 'grizzled' trainers seem to be getting younger and younger). For me, it's more about the sense of intrusion that one is acutely aware of in such an environment. I'm unsure if other writers or journalists share this experience, and it's probably due to my own inherent feelings of paranoia, but I've lost count of the number of times I've felt my throat dry up and my fingers start to tingle when I walk through the door.

And so it is when I self-consciously slope into the Target Fitness gym to find Steve Collins and Frank Buglioni busy at the centre of the ring, one throwing, the other receiving punches. I catch Steve's eye and nervously nod before moving to the outskirts of the room, anxious not to intrude. Steve immediately climbs down from his position above me and generously brings over a chair for me. I sit and watch the two men in action; they are evidently concentrating on the young boxer's inside work.[40] Frank manoeuvres Steve against the ropes, throwing uppercuts and hooks at the enormous pads that the older man is wearing for protection. Every now and again Steve will exclaim, 'That fuckin' hurt!' in a sandblasted Irish accent. Apart from the owner of the gym, I am the only one watching this spectacle. I already feel privileged.

During a break in the action Steve ambles over to me. 'Have you seen that fuckin' guy?' he says, beckoning me to follow him, handsome and sandy-haired, very few marks on his face that betray his former occupation. 'He's 80 years old and he's just taken up boxing!'

This, apparently, is Friendly Steve. A different proposition to the last time I met him. He pats his belly and tells me how much food he ate over Christmas. As bellies go it's not that extraordinary. On a normal person it would actually be a more than passable flat belly. I'd love to have a belly like that. But this, after all, is a boxer, albeit an ex-boxer. They have different standards to us mere mortals. Steve hurls me an anecdote: he

40 The art of throwing and defending punches at close range

tells me how he booked the family into a hotel for Christmas dinner and that it was so bad that all they could do is laugh about it. As he talks, the octogenarian boxer in question strolls by and Steve's eyes follow his progress.

I remind Steve that age should really be no barrier to taking up anything. I tell him about a 70-year-old I know who recently took up the piano and is flourishing.

'My wife's starting learning piano,' says Steve, 'The only problem is we've got so many people staying with us that she has no time to practise.'

'Who's staying with you?' I ask.

'I don't know,' replies Steve. 'Just people... They just turn up and stay.'

Frank Buglioni steps into view and gives me a smile and a warm handshake. He's an extremely good looking young man with thick dark hair and refined features that are mainly untouched by his choice of career; he's already done a little modelling, forcing one to wonder why, in allowing other professional boxers to take swipes at it, he would choose to place this cash cow countenance in such jeopardy. But Frank's life is in transition. Last year he lost two fights, the latter for a world title. In days of yore a bout of this stature – win or lose – would have been perceived as a great achievement, a source of celebration. Nowadays, however, there is such a proliferation of world titles available to boxers that they have been rendered practically meaningless.

Some critics are already sniping that Frank may have reached the limits of his ambition. Frank, however, certainly doesn't believe so and nor does his trainer Steve, who, I notice, keeps slipping in words of encouragement such as, 'That's the sort of punch you'll need to throw when you're world champion.' Positive reinforcement and all that.

I stand behind Frank and watch him work out. I'm a little surprised by how much bigger he looks than last time I saw him and whisper this observation into Steve's ear.

'Yeah,' says Steve casually. He's coming back as a light-heavyweight.[41] He's much stronger at that weight. Mind you, at the moment he's a cruiserweight.'

I ask Frank when his next fight is and there's a slight hesitation. Trainer and trainee look at each other for a moment and then Frank shrugs.

'He doesn't know yet because Frank's his own man now,' say Steve, cagily.

I listen as Steve explains how his young charge has now left his manager, Frank Warren, and is self-managing. The repercussions of that admission are manifold and I already find myself wondering whether Frank jumped or was pushed. Perhaps more than any other human endeavour boxing can be an unforgiving business. On the basis of little more than an off-night today's champion can be tomorrow's forgotten man. The margins between success and failure are so slim that even a five per cent reduction in performance can mean the difference between triumph and tragedy.

....

41 There are currently 17 universally recognised weight classes in boxing:

Weight limit (lb/kg/st)	Weight class
Unlimited	Heavyweight
200/90.7/14st 4	Cruiserweight
175/79.4/12.5st	Light-heavyweight
168/76.2/12st	Super-middleweight
160/72.5/11st 6	Middleweight
154/69.9/11st	Light-middleweight
147/66.7/10.5st	Welterweight
140/63.5/10st	Light-welterweight
135/61.2/9st 9	Lightweight
130/59.0/9s 4	Super-featherweight
126/57.2/9st	Featherweight
122/55.3/8st 10	Super-bantamweight
118/53.5/8st 6	Bantamweight
115/52.2/8st 3	Super-flyweight
112/50.8/8st	Flyweight
108/49.0/7st 10	Light-flyweight
105/47.6/7.5st	Strawweight

I put on a positive spin for Frank and tell him what great news this is, about how fantastic it will be to be in control of his own destiny. But inside I'm fearing the worst: it's an undeniable fact that Frank lost two fights last year. He, as well as everybody else in the business, will understand that blemishes of this nature do not generally increase a boxer's marketability.

When I met Frank two years do ago he was the first boxer I had spent time with in over 20 years. Inevitably it did not take me long to fall in love with him, as I always tend to do with boxers that I meet. Indeed, Frank proved to be such a sweetheart that I could not even bring myself to take up his offer of tickets to see him box. I simply did not want to see him run the risk of getting hurt. Now I'm fighting a very strong inclination to put my arms around Frank and cuddle him, as I would my daughter if she had fallen over and scuffed a knee.

Steve heads off for a shower and I watch as the 80-year-old grabs a selfie with Frank. Both men hold their fists up to the camera in a pose that I've been seeing a lot lately. 'How is it that all boxers have to do that?' I smile. 'It would be much more interesting if you stood like this.' I do my best impersonation of a sub-Larry Grayson/John Inman/Alan Carr camp pose and the two men both laugh. Frank even imitates my pose for the camera.

When Steve returns we sit on a bench in the corner of the gym and I tell him how nice Frank is. And I genuinely mean it. How nice all boxers are, in fact.

'I always say the nicest people in boxing are the boxers,' he agrees. 'I feel that schools should have boxing as part of the curriculum. Because if you get a punch in the face it's not a nice thing. So you're aware then of how it feels if you're going to punch somebody else in the face. There's very few bullies who are successful boxers. The boxing gym has saved so many people's lives. Everyone should have one.'

I tell him I have my own theories as to why boxers are so often such personable people. That it's something to do with the burning off of testosterone and the fact that statements concerning who a boxer might think he is are usually made inside the ropes not out. In doing so I happen to let it slip that to my mind there was only really one boxer I met whom I didn't really like. This piques Steve's interest and he's immediately keen to know who it is. I reluctantly tell him. 'Nigel Benn, eh?' he says of the former two-time world champion. 'Nice fella... I've got a lot of time for Nigel. He's a good friend.'

In 2005 Steve and the rival whom he vanquished twice in the ring were the unlikely co-stars of a Channel 5 reality vehicle entitled *Commando VIP*. The show featured the two ex-boxers sharing accommodation in a military style environment, as well as undergoing a number of physical challenges.

'There's an old saying: if you want to get to know someone go and live with them,' says Steve. 'And I've lived with Nigel Benn. It was not long after we retired so it was kind of a bit raw. He was great company. He has his demons but once you get over them he's a nice man. I like him.'

Steve, as it happens, is a member of an exclusive club in the world of boxing. When he retired in 1997 he was still the reigning WBO super-middleweight champion. Unlike so many of his brethren, Steve's title was not violently ripped away from him within the ropes. This puts him in a similar kind of category as the likes of heavyweight legend Rocky Marciano[42], who retired undefeated in 1955 after an unprecedented 49 straight wins; Floyd Mayweather[43], also

----

42 **Rocky Marciano** 1 September 1923–31 August 1969. Iowa, USA. Former undisputed heavyweight champion of the world.

43 **Floyd Mayweather** born 24 February 1977, Michigan, USA. Former WBC super-featherweight champion of the world; WBC lightweight champion of the world; WBC light-welterweight champion of the world; IBF, WBO and WBC welterweight champion of the world; WBC and WBA light-middleweight champion of the world.

unbeaten in 49[44]; and Joe Calzaghe[45] of Wales, who retired in 2008 after 46 straight wins. A select class of prize-fighter who retired from the sport on top and were never tempted back.

In Steve's case however, there is the suggestion that this decision may have been forced upon him. According to press reports of the time, Steve retired after collapsing during a routine sparring session. Following brain scans that could find no cause of the collapse, the boxer apparently decided to call it quits. However, he patently fails to mention this incident when I ask for more information about the last days off his reign career.

'I retired after fighting an American named Craig Cummings because I realised I had nowhere to go,' he remembers. 'I was told that a fight with Roy Jones Jr[46] was out of the question and there was a whole string of young up-and-coming fighters arriving on the scene. They didn't appeal to me because they weren't marquee fighters, I was 33-years-old by then and missed my family. I was comfortable and I thought that the moment you get up and you don't want to go out in the cold and the rain is when you give up the game.

'I was in training camp in LA and I rang my wife and said, "I'm coming home. I miss everybody and I have no desire and it's been going on for two weeks now. I cannot be arsed any more." When I decided to retire I felt a weight fall off my shoulders. I actually felt happy.'

'Can you remember your thoughts on the actual morning that this happened?' I ask.

....

44 In **Floyd Mayweather's** case his retirement is unlikely to be permanent.

45 **Joe Calzaghe** born 23 March 1972, London, England. Former undisputed super-middleweight champion of the world.

46 **Roy Jones Jr** born 16 January 1969. Former IBF middleweight champion of the world; IBF super-middleweight champion of the world; WBC, WBA and IBF light-heavyweight champion of the world; WBA heavyweight champion of the world.

'I was lying in bed thinking, "What am I getting up for?" There was no aim. There was no picture of my opponent on my wall. What's the drive? It's not money, because I had money. There was nobody left, there was only Roy Jones and that was never going to happen.

'I felt I'd been in a locked room and now I could go and enjoy myself. I was young enough then to follow my next ambition.'

It could be said that Steve's desperate desire to fight Jones bordered on obsession. Even when he was well into his 50s, the Irishman was still making noises about coming back to fight his once supremely accomplished but now physically depleted rival. Indeed, this may give us a real insight into Steve's true feelings as to the value of the championship belts he once held.

The period of the 1990s in which Collins campaigned happened to be a stellar era in British boxing. With domestic rivals in abundance of the calibre of Michael Watson, Nigel Benn and Chris Eubank there was never any real financial incentive for Steve to try his luck in the ring with the statistically superior generation of fighters plying their trade across the water. Names which included the likes of Michael Nunn[47], James Toney[48] and arguably the best of the bunch, Jones Jr.

But any hopes of that unlikely contest were finally put to bed late in 2015 when Jones at the age of 47 was brutally relieved of his senses by a faded British fighter named Enzo Maccarinelli[49]. It was Jones's fifth career knockout of a

47 **Michael Nunn** born 14 April 1963, Iowa, USA. Former IBF middleweight champion of the world; WBA super-middleweight champion of the world.

48 **James Toney** born 24 August 1968, California, USA. Former IBF middleweight champion of the world; IBD super-middleweight champion of the world; IBF cruiserweight champion of the world;

49 **Enzo Maccarinelli** born 20 August 1980, Swansea, Wales. Former WBO cruiserweight champion of the world.

decidedly undistinguished latter part of his career. Its nature was of extreme concern to ring observers.[50]

'I saw the knockout,' the Irishman laments. 'I like Roy a lot, he's a gentleman. I like his company. He's a friend, although that's an overused word in boxing. I spoke to him in London recently and told him not to take the fight. I told him Enzo's a very dangerous puncher – you've a better chance of beating me than beating him. Not that you would.'

The sight of a once great fighter's legacy being so violently obliterated by inferior opposition is one of boxing's most distressing yet persistent spectacles. Throughout history there have been far too many boxers who refused to hang up the gloves until a sense of reality was brutally impressed upon them. 'It's sad to see Roy Jones repeat the mistakes that so many others make,' I say. 'I will never understand why fighters insist on going on and on.'

'I think he just enjoys fighting,' sighs Steve. 'I don't think he needs the money. He just likes doing it.'

'Yes but the thing about Roy Jones is that whenever he gets knocked out it's actually frightening,' I say.

'Yeah… When a guy goes down flat on his face there has to be some lasting damage.'

I ask the ex-boxer if he's ever been knocked out himself.

'No. But when I fought Mike McCallum, who wasn't the biggest puncher, he caught me with a combination of four or five shots in a row and it totally disorientated me. I guess I was knocked out on my feet for a short period of time.'

'It's like an out-of-body experience,' I say, explaining that for a long time I regularly suffered fainting spells due to my undiagnosed hypothyroidism.

....

50 Although at the time of writing Jones Jr is still fighting. In March 2016 he fought a boxing fan named Vyron Phillips in a grotesque parody of a fight and stopped him in two rounds. Phillips, who had never before boxed, had been offered a reward of $100,000 if he had somehow found a way to win.

'I know what you mean. When he hit me I could actually see the next day's newspapers in my head and they were commenting on what had happened, saying, "Collins was stopped in seven rounds". But I said, "No!" and came back into my senses.'

And thankfully sense is what Steve appears to have in abundance. In contrast to so many of his brethren, Steve is financially secure in his retirement years. He tells me about the farm he runs in St Albans, and of his plans to stage events there as a money-making scheme.

'And yet here you are,' I say. 'Covered in sweat in a dingy boxing gym with a boxer throwing punches at you. Why do you do it?'

'Well I call it the fellowship of boxing,' he says conspiratorially. 'It's like family. There's camaraderie. But listen, I've never had any interest in getting involved with any fighters. I don't have the time and I don't have the dedication. But Frank approached me and I just liked him as a person.'

'So this is the first person you've trained?'

'Well… I've trained my son. He's now an active professional. He's a well-educated young man but at the age of 23 with no amateur experience he decided to become a boxer. I thought this was a bit mad because he definitely had a future as a rugby player. He was huge – over 16st but with the boxing training his whole physique's changed. He's become leaner.

'He's dropped down to cruiserweight and now he's contemplating light-heavyweight. But he's had so many setbacks due to rugby.'

'Rugby is a dangerous game,' I tell him. 'Even more so than boxing.'

'Yes, he's had horrific shoulder injuries because of rugby.'

'If he manages to get down to light-heavyweight people are inevitably going to start talking about him fighting Benn and Eubank's sons,' I say.

'Well Nigel Benn's son and my son are very good friends. They met on Facebook and then met in person. Nigel Benn's son is a lovely, lovely boy.'

During the 1990s Benn, along with Michael Watson and Chris Eubank, enjoyed a celebrated five-fight rivalry which boxing aficionados often refer to as the 'triumvirate'. However, it is Steve himself, I remind him, who holds multiple victories over Eubank and Benn. Of that generation Steve, in fact, has the superior head-to-head record. Does it irritate him that people tend to forget this?

'Not really. When I was fighting I was very intense,' he says. 'A lot of guys had more ability than me so I really had to work hard to succeed in the ring. I consciously didn't like my opponents because it made me train harder. But I never hate them because you can't hate someone.'

I ask Steve to guess what my favourite performance of his was. He offers a few suggestions before giving in.

'It's your second fight against Eubank,' I say. 'Your performance was completely nutty. You were all elbows and and shoulders – and you never stopped going forward for a second. Your energy levels were off the scale.'

'Well that was part of my plan. The first fight we played the mind games[51], which was great but you won't get away with that twice. So I had to change my approach.'

'You must have trained like a madman to keep up that sort of intensity?'

'And it was totally drug-free. No steroids needed or whatever rubbish they take nowadays. That was the fittest and hardest I've ever been in my life. And if you looked at me I never stopped punching.'

Intensity is a word that can be easily associated with Steve Collins. Listening to him talk it is easy to perceive the single-mindedness that prompted him as a young man to move from

51 Collins unsettled Eubank by claiming to have been hypnotised prior to their fight so that he would feel no pain.

Dublin to join the gym of boxing great Marvin Hagler[52] in Brockton, Massachusetts.

'At eight I wanted to be a boxer,' he tells me. 'I knew I was going to be a world champion. My parents thought I was mad. They used to laugh at me. But I just knew this was for me.

'Marvin Hagler was my idol. He was middleweight champion of the world. I could relate to his style. So I said I'm going to find out where is he is and go to his gym. Because I want to fight like him.'

'How old were you?'

'Twenty-one.'

'That's an amazing thing to do.'

'I was working in the Guinness brewery. It was a very good job. I was an apprentice electrician. I had a very good future. I was representing my country at amateur level and I was picked to box in America. I'd always intended to go over but now that I was going to go with the boxing team I decided once I was in the country I wasn't coming back.

'I popped on the bus to Boston. Found a job, an apartment, and then found the Petronellis'[53] gym.'

'You just walked in and asked to box?'

'No. I attended a Petronelli boxing show and asked a mutual friend to introduce me to Goody Petronelli. He said, "Come on down to the gym."

'Course when I got there I think he put me in with Robbie Sims.[54] He tried to beat me up and couldn't. So then they asked me to join the gym.

'You'd see Marvin Hagler there all the time. It was very, very exciting for a young man.'

....

52 **Marvin Hagler** born 23 May 1954, New Jersey, USA. Former undisputed middleweight champion of the world.

53 **Goody and Pat Petronelli** Massachusetts-based boxing managers and trainers.

54 **Robbie Sims** born 5 November 1959, Massacheusetts, USA.

'So when you train Frank Buglioni, do you ever think back and feel that the lessons you learned from the Petronelli brothers and Hagler are being passed on through time?'

'Sometimes. But I educated myself in boxing. I educated myself in how to train to fight. The knowledge I have now that I can pass on to Frank I wish I'd had at the time.

'You've got to love fighters and you've got put them first in boxing. When I boxed some people said I was a selfish guy who thought only about himself. And I said, "Yes, I did!" A lot of guys are loyal to the wrong people. I was loyal to me and my family.'

'Do you wish you could go back to the early days?'

'Oh yes. They were the best days of my career. I was young and the world was my oyster. But I'm very happy now. To me every day is better than the one previous.'

'I wish I could say that.'

'You *can* say it. It's your mindset. I can give you loads of reasons why I would say it. My kids are the best things that happened to me but the worst is losing people you love. That's the only thing in my life that I dread.

'My dad died when I was a teenager, which broke my heart. I never got over it. But it made me who I am. You never get over it. It's 35 years on and I still can't talk about it. Because I loved him.'

I tell Steve about my father. About how he died a year earlier and about the difficulty I've had coming to terms with it.

'Anti-depressants are not good,' he declares. 'Just cry it out. Talk about it and cry it out. Time heals. You're lucky because you had him that long. I was a teenager.'

'Well the thing is we didn't get on,' I say. 'I saw him maybe five or six times in the last 15 years. And he refused to see me on his deathbed.'

'Really? That's sad… That's harder. I'm glad I lost my dad as a teenager and loved him. What you have is not the loss of life, it's the loss of time. I feel sorry for him.'

Lung

BUT Steve Collins has no reason to feel sorry for my father. And neither do I. Because right now somebody else close to me is suddenly in far greater need of support.

* * * * *

The first symptoms were flu-like. She had fevers, chills and was exhausted most of the time. It seemed prudent to keep her off school, believing that after a day or two's rest she'd be right as rain. However, she didn't get any better. Day after day went by and all she could do was lie on the sofa and sleep. The fevers intensified and she refused to eat a thing, despite my sometimes over-enthusiastic and clumsy attempts to compel her to do so. After five days of this I finally called the doctor who suggested I bring her into the clinic. 'She's too ill to travel even short distances,' I said. At which, he mumbled something about Calpol and giving her food and that was that. This was my first mistake, well second actually: I should have insisted that something was done straight away.

By day eight my wife and I were getting *really* worried. All of a sudden meeting boxers that I have not seen for 25 years seemed even more irrelevant than ever. Aside from a little bit of fruit she'd still not eaten at all and was shedding weight faster than a supermodel preparing for a Vogue shoot. I called the GP again and this time insisted that she see her. When we got into the doctor's surgery Sofia was looking so ill that no one could deny she needed urgent attention. The doctor very efficiently filled in a few forms and sent us immediately to A&E. There, she was seen within minutes and given a variety of tests. Later, a consultant spoke to me in private and told me that they didn't know what was causing the illness but that Sofia needed a drip and at the very least an overnight stay.

Here comes mistake number two – or three, depending how you look at it. That afternoon, having not eaten all day myself, I dragged myself to the nearest eaterie, which happened to be a McDonald's, leaving Sofia with my wife. While I was hastily swilling down a coffee, I got a call from Laura, who told me that Sofia had just been discharged and would not, after all, be staying overnight. I was understandably confused by this latest development, but my brain was numb due to lack of sleep. For the second time I should have insisted that something be done immediately. Instead we simply took our daughter home.

This left us looking after Sofia for a second long and increasingly anxious weekend. Her condition continued to deteriorate. On Monday I called the doctor again, who was able to log on to the hospital computer and check out Sofia's test results. 'Inconclusive' was the word he used before advising me to give it one more day and if there was no improvement to take her back to A&E. At 5.00am the following day I was awoken by Sofia coughing. The cough was unremittingly constant and achingly painful. It was a frightening sound. I tried to fill her up with cough medicine and hot lemon, the usual things that you're supposed to do, but these were hopelessly inadequate, rather like throwing rice at a machine gun turret.

Later that morning I told my wife to get ready to take Sofia to hospital but as luck would have it the fever suddenly disappeared, as did the cough. I didn't think it would do us much good to take Sofia to A&E saying, 'She was really ill this morning but she's improved since then. Can you take a look at her?' With this in mind I packed my wife off to work and waited to see if Sofia's cough and temperature would return.

By midday they were back with a vengeance and I had to do something. So I literally dragged Sofia to A&E. This time round they didn't mess about. Within ten minutes she'd had her heart rate measured and declared dangerously high. Next came a speedy X-ray and a very difficult conversation. Sofia, it was explained, had a very rare condition. She had developed what appeared to be a 4cm x 6cm cyst or abscess on her lung that was half-filled with liquid. She was dehydrated and had lost a lot of weight (by now she'd eaten only a little bit of fruit in ten days). And she also had pneumonia.

From there on the wheels were set swiftly into motion. Sofia was immediately put on to a drip, feeding her nutrients and very powerful antibiotics five times a day. My wife and I took turns sleeping on a camp bed by her bedside. It was *Carry On Camping* with the canned laughter replaced by aching joints and the snores of other displaced parents.

For the first couple of days I stupidly attempted to try to write by Sofia's bedside while she slept. But I wasn't able to concentrate – who would be? As a parent, of course, you end up blaming yourself. And the more I thought about it the more I realised that there had been definite warning signs in recent months. In December, for instance, I had taken her to the doctor after she had continually complained of shortness of breath. He had examined her heart, taken her blood pressure and asked whether she was stressed at school before declaring her fit as a fiddle. After she left that doctor's room that afternoon, Sofia had burst into tears. I had then returned to speak to the doctor only to be very curtly told that he could find nothing wrong with her and that he had other patients to attend to.

My numbering system is falling to pieces right now but that was quite possibly Mistake 0.5. I should have been more assertive. I should have insisted that Sofia have an X-ray. I should have demanded a magic pill that would have restored my little girl back to rude health. But such is the benefit of hindsight and all that. Whatever the case, on the afternoon of Sofia's diagnosis I fired off an angry email to that doctor and promptly received three very nervous, apologetic phone calls from the health centre in question. Needless to say, this didn't make me feel remotely better about anything.

From then on it was a waiting game. Thankfully Sofia's recovery, although not rapid, was definitely in the right direction. And as I sat by her bedside over a ten-day period I had a lot of spare time on my hands. Most of it was spent aimlessly tinkering with my iPad while simultaneously fretting about my daughter.

Inevitably I began to form relationships with other patients and their anxious parents, as well as the doctors and nurses who were in attendance day and – sometimes annoyingly – night. There was the little girl named Talya who had been there for two months after an innocuous fall at school had left her with a badly infected foot and the prospect that she might never walk again. She is a picture of cuteness and grim intelligence; if I could take her home with me now I would.

Yesterday was the best and worst day: by the far the biggest cross that Sofia has had to bear has been the cannula (a word I didn't know until last week) that has been put into her arm in order to administer her drugs. It seems she has inherited my sensitive skin which means that the needle has been regularly rejected. Eight times in seven days actually. Listening to her tiny voice whimper at night as they tried to find a new vein in which to torture her a little bit more has been impossible to take. As a parent it is sometimes your responsibility to provide reassurance just at that time when you are most in need of reassurance yourself.

As a solution to this awful situation Sofia was put to sleep yesterday and something more permanent called a PICC line was inserted into her arm. As I held her hand outside the operating theatre and watched the morphine send her instantly to sleep I finally let the tears go. The next hour and a half was too painful. While I sat sipping coffee by her empty bed my mind began to play tricks on me. I wondered how I would break it to her mother if things went wrong. I wondered how our relationship could possibly survive the death of our only child. I selfishly toyed with the idea of killing myself if I had to do this. And then I thought about the effect it would have on Laura to lose both members of her family.

But now, less than 24 hours later, things have changed considerably. I'm sitting here at the dining room table typing away as Sofia and three friends sit playing together on the Wii. Screams and shouts of delight fill the room. Sitting beside Sofia is a community nurse, who is administering the second of two doses of antibiotics that she must have at home every day for very possibly the next six weeks. In the evening Sofia and I must return to stay the night at the hospital because community nurses do not work at night and she needs six doses of drugs per day. It's going to be a tough month and a bit but already it's not quite as tough as it was yesterday.

This morning, after being given the good news about Sofia being allowed to go home during the day, I was shown a recent X-ray of the lung abscess. In little more than a week the drugs have exceeded all expectations. The object, whatever it is, has considerably reduced in size. The outlook suddenly looks a little less bleak. Lots of Ts need to be crossed before Sofia gets a clean bill of health, and the holiday we had planned is off due to the fact that Sofia is not allowed to fly for six months, but she's alive; I'm alive; Laura's alive. And I'm suddenly left with whole new appreciation of normality. Boring dumb stupid normality. What bliss.

Alarm

WHEN I was younger I got drunk one night end ended up in a police cell. As I lay on the solitary piss-stained bunk I looked up at the ceiling of the cell and felt a tremendous feeling of placidity wash over me. *This isn't so bad*, I reasoned. *If this is what prison is like I can handle it.*

The reality was, however, that unless I killed one of the guards with a sharpened lollipop stick I would most likely be going home in the morning and the little bit of notoriety that this experience might afford me would be healthily repaid in beers and possibly women. I knew plenty of girls back then who liked a bad boy. Perhaps I could be a bad boy once I'd done my tiny dribble of porridge.

That happened 35 years ago and truth be told I never quite made it to bad boy status. The last guy I actually fought with is now dead of cancer, and the reason that we fought was because he accused me of plagiarism. It was a distinctly middle-class difference of opinion and an equally flocculent variety of skirmish: he aimed a punch at me and I sort of wrestled him to the floor, where we rolled about in the Xerox dust like a couple of wrinkled teenagers. But isn't that what Christmas parties are all about?

I never quite earned bad boy status but I'm getting to know what it's like to do my time. Because life for me at the moment is all about living in a prison cell. Lights out is around 9.30pm and my prison wardens are all young and beautiful. From there on in its the sounds of silence that fill my head. The noises made by anguished, frightened children crying for their mothers (never their fathers) which, without fail and usually in exactly the same order, elicit from me feelings of abject sorrow followed by selfless pity followed by aching sadness followed by mild irritation followed by red hot anger followed by if-you-don't-shut-that-whining-fucking-brat-up-so-I-can-get-some-sleep-I'm-going-to-chuck-the-fucking-whinging-parent-out-of-the-fucking-window-and-really-become-a-fucking-bad-boy. Sleep deprivation is a very successful torture method and has been known to start wars.

As I wrote that last sentence an electronic alarm sounded from a machine by my daughter's bedside from a gadget that looks a little like the one used by Bones to examine unconscious Klingons. It keeps doing that. It's letting the whole ward know that the drug being pumped into my daughter's arm via a thin plastic cable is not reaching its target. It's a bit like what happens when the hose pipe bends while you're watering the garden (oh, to stand in the sunshine watering the garden). And amid the farts and burps and snores and slurps of the rest of the ward I am aware of a murmur of irritation. Some other sleep-starved parent wants to throw me out of the window and earn themselves a slice of bad boy status.

But none of us can do this. Because we're in a hospital for sick kids and whatever feelings you have about your lot in the world you have no choice but to make like an erstwhile Page Three model: grin and bear it. And this is actually no bad analogy because when you're the parent of a sick child in hospital you are naked. Every routine, every ritual, every secret practise that makes you who you are is cast aside and laid open to the universe.

It's 7.34am and the lights have just come on. I've already been up for two hours. At least we don't have to slop out. In the beds around me anxious parents are already talking in not quite so hushed tones about their own concerns, their own damaged children. Soon a damp mop will be dragged around the ward and my daughter will be offered a breakfast menu which she'll refuse to choose from. Interesting the speed in which new rituals worm their way into your life. In two hours' time Sofia and I can go home for the day. Compared to many here we're the lucky ones. But it's not really home because it's a home that is invaded twice daily by yet more elegant prison wardens as they refill my daughter with drugs. There goes that alarm again.

Each time that alarm goes off you're aware of an on-rush of footsteps. This is followed by the bustling image of an impossibly pristine young woman in a sparkling pressed nurses uniform, a mere child of flawless skin and glossy hair. We're all destined to get to know nurses in one way or another and I can tell you that they have very little in common with the old Benny Hill version of a nurse. While they can occasionally be seen to move at Benny Hill double-quick herky-jerky speed it is there that any similarity ends. It is the nurses – my stoic, uncomplaining, smiling prison wardens – that I find most interesting of all.

Each one is my daughter and each my mother. Because even though my own mother was actually a nurse I never really had any understanding of what she actually was. I don't remember her having that driven look in her eyes of the girls who surround me here. And she never struck me as someone who was prepared to sacrifice herself for others. But she must have been.

This is the long haul for me. Life has temporarily ground to a halt. My days are spent waiting for the nights and my nights are spent longing for the days. And already I'm finding out more about myself than I'd really like to know. More than any person would really like to know.

Pain

HEROL Graham is in pain and can barely walk. I have one hand on his shoulder, supporting him in an embarrassing, awkward kind of way, scared that he might tumble and I won't be able to carry his weight. At his other shoulder is a fresh-faced young nurse holding a canister of oxygen connected to the ex-boxer by a thin plastic umbilical cord that terminates at his nostrils. The three of us negotiate the corridor together in slow motion. From a transparent catheter Herol's blood can clearly be seen. Red and runny like cheap tomato ketchup. I make a joke about this being the first time that I've ever been faster than him and he weakly attempts to raise a fist in mock outrage.

Before I know it I'm back at the hospital once again. The same hospital where they stitched up my damaged leg. The same hospital that my daughter left only a day ago. The same floor in fact. The adjacent ward even. I'm recognised by a couple of nurses who pass me in the corridor; they give me a business-like nod. 'Want a fight?' Herol mumbles weakly at a bewildered hospital porter.

* * * * *

Last night I received a text from Herol's partner, Karen Neville, explaining that he had undergone emergency surgery on a ruptured appendix. I was supposed to have met him to talk over a month ago, but inevitably life kept getting in the way. First he couldn't make it because of a prior engagement that he'd forgotten about. Then I couldn't make it because of my daughter's illness. And now here he is: a ten-minute walk from where I live. In the ward next door to the one that housed my daughter for two worrying weeks, his muscled body lying prone and helpless on the less than white starched sheets of a hospital bed. Looking weak and green. My captive boxer.

I'm a past master at this hospital business now. Having spent the best part of a fortnight sleeping on that camp bed by my daughter's side I know the ropes, as it were. Before heading up to see Herol on the fourth floor I go down to the first and visit the newsagent's. The walk up and down these stairs has become my daily form of exercise. I skim the magazine racks looking for something suitable. There are no boxing magazines, although I suspect that Herol isn't really one for reading such titles. I consider buying him a motoring mag or a fitness magazine. The choices are limited. In the end I get him a science magazine, a book of puzzles to pass the time, a pen to do those puzzles with, some fruit juice and a chicken Caesar wrap. For the other hospital inmate I'm going to see after I've finished with Herol, the little girl named Talya with the injured foot, I purchase a couple of comics.

Herol is in Mercer's Ward. When I later mention this to my daughter's consultant she shakes her head grimly and says, 'That's not good news.' When I get there I self-consciously ask after Herol's whereabouts at reception. Karen had told me that Herol would be glad of some company but even so I can't help but read into the suspicious look on the male attendant's face when I ask after the once famous boxer. Although deep down I wonder if he knows who Herol used to be. I wonder if anyone knows who Herol used to be.

The attendant leads me to Herol's bed. The one-time British and European champion's head is propped up by a couple of pillows. His expression is rigid, as if he's not really here. At the other side of the bed is a good looking white woman of about my age. We shake hands rather too formally. 'You must be Karen,' I say.

We sit down beside each at Herol's bedside and I delve into the carrier bag I'm holding and pull out a Jacqueline Wilson comic that I've brought for Talya. 'I've got you something for you to read,' I say to Herol. 'Only joking.'

There is weak laughter and Karen explains that Herol is currently nil by mouth. So we guiltily split the food I brought for her stricken partner, hunger easily triumphing over valour. Karen says she hasn't eaten all day. The ward is smaller than the one that my daughter was in. There are only four beds in total. The others are occupied by people in their 70s or 80s, making the already youthful-looking former star seem ridiculously baby-faced.

There is an atmosphere of doom in here. I feel eyes upon us. Word has apparently gotten around the ward that a famous ex-boxer is here; his presence is adding a little interest to the dull, monotonous hours that patients and visitors have no choice but to try to fill.

Karen and Herol are clearly decent people: they listen patiently while I serve up my well-rehearsed spiel about getting ill and being unable to work for years and years. Karen interrupts me with questions about levothyroxine[55] and TSH[56]. She obviously knows her stuff. I ask her if she herself is hypothyroid[57], at which she lowers her voice and tells me

55 **Levothyroxine** is a drug commonly given to sufferers of hypothyroidism.

56 **Thyroid Stimulating Hormone** (TSH) a pituitary hormone that stimulates the thyroid gland to produce thyroxine, and then triiodothyronine which stimulates the metabolism of almost every tissue in the body.

57 **Hypothyroidism**, also known as under active thyroid, is a common disorder of the endocrine system in which the thyroid gland does not produce enough thyroid hormone.

about her cancer. She reveals that she is in remission. She tells me about the myriad operations she has endured, about her facial reconstitution surgery. And then she tells me about how she has recently lost her job.

My protracted and uncomfortable recent sojourn at my daughter's hospital bedside taught me one important thing that I currently cannot stop repeating to myself: there is always someone worse off than yourself. It's such an oft-repeated cliché that one actually feels a little ridiculous saying it. But it's so grindingly, relentlessly true. There was I allowing the relief that I felt at my daughter's recovery to be replaced by selfish but inevitable feelings of panic at looming deadlines, dissatisfaction at the meagre sales of the kids' book I put out a year ago and trivial worries about my own health.

When in fact there are so many people in my immediate vicinity who would leap at the chance to replace their very real concerns with my inconsequential own. I don't really know what to say to Karen and her sick partner. I mumble something about life getting harder and harder the older you get; hardly front-page news.

Then Karen tells me about her numerous misdiagnoses and her continuing efforts to get some form of justice for the pain she has been through. And all the while Herol, the guy I used to watch on the telly when I was still living at home with my parents, lies there on his bed saying nothing. In spite of myself I am drawn to the scars on his face, each one having its own story to tell. Each one a curious survivor in its own right.

There is a smile on Karen's face as she tells me that the doctors have told Herol that he needs to start farting if he's to get his bowels working correctly. I enquire as to Herol's prowess in that particular discipline. 'Oh Herol can fart all right,' she laughs. The ex-boxer's appendix operation had apparently been more complicated than is usual. Instead of the anticipated half-an-hour, Herol had been under the knife for five hours. Karen is obviously someone who enjoys detail. She tells me all about how the pus inside him had hardened and wrapped itself around his internal organs. I absent-mindedly find myself thinking about my wife's cooking. In an attempt to cheer him up, I tell Herol the story of Muhammad Ali's appendix operation, of how it delayed this return fight with Sonny Liston[58] in 1965 and of how his doctor had admitted that he hated to cut into Ali's perfect, beautiful torso. The anecdote does its job. Herol's face breaks into the mildest of grins.

Karen does most of the talking. And whenever she pauses for a break I do the rest. Herol just lies there staring into the distance. It is only later that I remember how he told me that he still takes anti-depressants; the vacant look on his face has clear undertones of the one that I used to see in the mirror when I was taking those little white pills.

A nurse arrives to run some tests on the ex-boxer. Her young face seems to ignite a touchpaper somewhere inside Herol. He suddenly comes to life, offering up a few feeble jokes which she awkwardly laughs at. It occurs to me that Herol must still expect to be recognised as a celebrity wherever he goes; he must be used to people treating him in a certain way. But there isn't even the slightest glimmer of recognition coming from the nurse. All she sees is a middle-aged black man whose weak witticisms are getting in the way of her doing her job.

* * * * *

Tests over, the nurse encourages Herol to go for his first walk since the operation. I try to help out as he attempts to raise himself from the bed, his intelligent face grimacing in pain. And then we go for our little stroll around the ward: former

---

58 **Charles 'Sonny' Liston** early 1930s–30 December 1970) Arkansas, USA. Former undisputed heavyweight champion of the world.

boxer and former boxing writer. Me, as always, limping. Him stumbling like a geriatric.

When we return to Herol's bed almost an hour later there is somebody waiting for him – a young man with Turkish features. He introduces himself to me as Sedat – 'Like the president?' I ask – and explains that he runs a gym which Herol often frequents.

Nobody says anything but I am suddenly aware that I am overstaying my welcome. I make my excuses. As I am leaving, however, Karen takes me to one side. 'Come back tomorrow and interview him,' she says softly, a serious look in her eyes.

'I couldn't really do that,' I say, squirming a little. 'It doesn't feel right with him in bed and all.'

'No come back tomorrow and do it,' she repeats, friendly but firm. 'It will help him. Herol needs to keep his brain active.'

* * * * *

There is nothing that I can tell you about Herol Graham that a Google search will not provide in immediate and poignant detail. There are pictures of Herol as a young fighter, his face boyish, his smile more Victorian guttersnipe than prizefighter. There are images of him and Karen joyfully enwrapped in each other's arms in younger, happier, more carefree days. There are stories of failed suicides. And there is a disgracefully mocking article in *The Sun* that gloatingly describes how Herol is now working stacking boxes in an ASDA warehouse ('BOXING great Herol Graham shows he still has stacks of talent — by lifting boxes in his job at an Asda warehouse'). A photograph of Herol in overalls accompanies the article in question; one wonders how many pieces of silver the ex-boxing great must have received in order to encourage him to compromise his legacy to such a degree. I'm also reminded that even now, even in his September years, Herol Graham remains a mere commodity in the eyes of many people. Why should this surprise me at all?

There are also pictures of his fist comedically flattening the face of the Jamaican fighter Mike McCallum, whom Herol fought in 1989 for the WBA world middleweight title. Like so many boxers when frozen in time by a fast camera shutter, McCallum's face resembles Popeye's rubberised visage during a pummelling by Bluto – or, for younger viewers, Scratchy pulverised by Itchy – leaving one to wonder how a person's delicate facial structure could possible survive such abuse. I was wearing my reporter's hat that night and watching from ringside at the Albert Hall.

In retrospect it was probably one of Herol's best performances. However, it certainly didn't seem that way to me at the time, the fight being an attritional, dour affair as the fighters' superlative skills cancelled one another other out. This was often the way when Herol fought boxers with enough resistance to withstand his punches. It's an overused word but Herol's style was simply *unique* and could never be found in any training manual. Moreover, his speed and awkwardness made him practically impossible to hit cleanly. What we also didn't know back then was just how good McCallum was. During the next decade he would win another two world titles in different weight classes and stretch the very best fighters of his generation to their absolute limits. In boxing, however, context is everything. And all we saw that night were two fighters not really putting on the show that punters had paid for.

The fight was also one of Herol's unluckiest, and would set the pattern for a further two world title challenges. In this case Herol's habit of physically barging his opponents with his shoulder would cause him to have a point deducted. That single point was enough to turn a close win into a close defeat and begin a run of broken dreams that would eventually leave him emotionally destitute.

PAIN

I do as instructed and go back the next day to sit with Herol and Karen in the hospital café. Herol again looks shaky but seems a little better. He's still not eating or drinking very much. Karen again does most of the talking. She tells me how the couple met at a boxing match in the 1980s, when Herol flicked a cigarette out of her hand and asked for her phone number. She recalls how she refused to give it to him, instead handing him a piece of paper with her home address on it. 'If he was serious about me, he would find me,' she says. The love in her eyes is palpable as she remembers that Herol duly appeared at her house the very next day.

The next bits are hazy. Somehow they split up after many years and Herol collects other women while losing money and property along the way. Cash is loaned out and never returned by friends whose names the ex-boxer cannot even remember; it's all standard fare for a prizefighter and yet the lessons remain perennially unheeded. It's also the reason why so few boxers abandon their gloves for a career in accountancy.

And then Karen talks about Herol's depression. Again it's all very well documented. About how he lost everything when he retired and was living in a shabby terraced house with no furniture. About how he drank a bottle of brandy and sharpened a knife and sliced through his wrists. It's easy to find out everything you need to know about this regrettable episode because, Herol, like so many damaged people, is willing to tell all and sundry every intimate detail of his life. Having bared every aspect of his physical self in its full unashamed nakedness within the ropes, he has simply moved on to exposing the contents of his soul.

But somewhere within Karen's words there lurks a secret. My radar is instantly aware of it. I can sense it nestling between the pauses and the silences which punctuate her story, in the knowing glances exchanged between the two.

'Was Herol abused?' I ask, so unexpected that it surprises both of them. 'Sexually, I mean?'

If I'd have done my research there would have been no need to ask this question. Because a couple of nights later, when I sit down to read Herol's ghosted autobiography it is all there in black and white. Herol was abused by a neighbour when he was just eight years old.

'That is where all his depression comes from,' says Karen, treating the episode as if it is a secret that only she and her partner know about. As if they are somehow unaware that the story is there in explicit detail for anyone who owns as Kindle and has a spare couple of quid. 'It's as if time stood still for Herol.'

And like a recovering alcoholic at a meeting, Herol's confession leads me to tell the pair about my own guilty secret, my own experience of abuse that I, too, kept to myself for too many years. Because this what the damaged do: eventually they tell other people, sooner or later they tell *everyone*. 'We have a lot in common,' I tell Herol. 'I'm just as fucked up as you are.'

* * * * *

Back at the hospital for the third consecutive day I take Herol for another slow, laborious stroll, this time to the cafe down on the first floor. He's a little perkier today but still unsteady on his feet. I get us drinks and we sit down at a side table. He wears a white hospital gown and nobody pays much attention to us. We talk about diet, a subject close to my heart, and Herol's voice becomes more agitated and excited. It is something that he's obviously passionate about, borne witness to by the fact that he is only seven pounds heavier now than his peak fighting weight over 20 years ago.

When many fighters retire they become bloated caricatures of their former selves. The termination of the strictest training regimen in sport often reveals the inner fat man lurking inside these beautiful thoroughbreds. Not so in Herol's case, as he looks almost exactly as he did during his dancing days. Like a teacher lecturing a naughty school kid, Herol tells me what I am doing wrong. It turns out that he is a firm advocate of the Montignac diet[59], something that I've dabbled with myself in the past.

Then the ex-fighter suddenly changes the subject. He tells me that the doctor informed him that morning that Herol's appendix had been so infected that he had been on the brink of death. 'I cried when he said that,' he admitted.

We chat for about half an hour until my daughter turns up to meet me. Only two days away from her 13th birthday and still in the early days of rehabilitation from her own hospital ordeal, she blushes when Herol speaks to her. Her presence is transformative. As if suddenly removing a dark veil, Herol springs into life: teasing the little girl, poking fun at her, pulling funny faces, affecting ridiculous high-pitched voices. It's obvious that the presence of an adolescent brings out the child in Herol Graham. At once, Herol is a young boy himself. The transformation in him is remarkable. It is a joy to witness.

The teasing and cajoling continues for several minutes and is only broken when Herol's friend Sedat arrives. Sofia and I head off to give the two men some privacy, pausing at the newsagent's to pick up a copy of the *Daily Mail* because, Herol tells me, he 'likes to read all the gossip'.

* * * * *

The next morning I have a long telephone conversation with Karen. The mood is celebratory: Herol is out of hospital and at home sleeping. I tell Karen what a privilege it has been to meet her, about how her triumph over cancer is an inspiration

59 The **Montignac** diet is a weight-loss diet that was popular in the 1990s.

to me. She tells me of her belief that the three of us met for a reason. She talks about the universe, about how nothing is accidental.

Normally I'd be racing to put the phone down but there is something in the way that Karen speaks that demands to be taken seriously. We plan to meet for dinner when Herol is back on his feet. I end the call feeling energised, my depression lifted.

* * * * *

Two days later, however, I receive a text from her. On Sunday evening Herol was rushed into hospital. Something has blocked his bowel and poisonous bile is building up in his system. He's in a very bad way. I tell her I'll be in to see him in the afternoon.

Green

HEROL Graham is slumped in a chair next to his bed, a doctor or it could be a nurse is leaning over him, fiddling about with something probably important. The ex-boxer seems not to notice the two of us when we arrive. It's immediately clear that there has been a dramatic decline in his condition. There is a tube protruding from Herol's nose that is attached to a triangular bag full of liquid. The bag is luminous green in colour. Radioactive green. The same colour as the piece of nuclear waste that Homer discards during the opening credits of *The Simpsons*. I had no idea that the body is capable of producing so toxic a substance. Surely it can't be possible?

Sofia notices this too and her pristine young face looks troubled. I wonder if I should discreetly steer her away from this vision of human misery; that she's too young to be witnessing another person in such obvious distress. But somehow Herol is aware that she's noticed. And although he can scarcely get the words out he breathlessly gasps, 'It's bile…You'll learn about it in biology.' And this simple sentence says so much about the ex-boxer. Even at this most terrible time in his life Herol is still striving to be considerate. Thoughtful. Polite. Not to do anything that will hurt or disillusion the confused child standing before him. It's a touching moment soon forgotten and probably noticed by nobody else but myself.

The doctor/nurse withdraws, leaving the three of us alone together. Sofia's face is painted in shock: she is incapable of hiding her emotions. There is an awkward silence which I attempt to fill by asking Herol routine, mundane questions. But Herol is in too much pain to respond and my daughter takes an empty seat by the window, shaking her head at me as if she's the parent and I'm the child. 'Don't ask him questions!' she commands. 'He doesn't want to speak. Just talk to him.'

For some reason the late Jonathan Rendall pops into my head. I tell Herol that I recently finished rereading Jonathan's book, that Herol was mentioned a great deal within its pages. 'Never heard of him,' grunts Herol, his voice barely audible.

I remind him that Jonathan even chose to close the book with a mention of Herol. I've even memorised the line, 'I sparred with him every day for years. And the thing is, I couldn't hit him, not once, for years and years.'[60] Surely he must remember him?

'I lot of people do that... Pretend they know me,' comes the muffled response.

So I try to I talk to Herol. I tell him stupid, inane stories about boxers I've met. I tell him about the time Muhammad Ali kissed my girlfriend at a book signing. About how he took her in his giant arms and passionately kissed her on the lips. Of how I was jealous: not because Ali was kissing my girlfriend, but because he had posed for a photograph with her and not me. In truth I would have killed to have been rewarded with a trophy like that. What made it worse was that my girlfriend had no idea who the person kissing her was.

In her eyes, just as in the eyes of the young nurse who attended to Herol the other day, Ali was just some anonymous middle-aged black man. And I quickly discover that I'm thoroughly useless at filling up the empty spaces. I realise this as the words splutter benignly from my lips. I understand this

....

60 *This Bloody Mary Is The Last Thing I Own*, Jonathan Rendall, 1997

as I continue to demand a response from the stricken ex-boxer and receive nothing in return.

'Stop asking questions!' repeats my exasperated daughter.

'Just keep talking,' groans Herol in a dead man's voice.

I ask Herol if he wants to lie down and he nods his head wearily. I carefully negotiate my way through the ganglia of plastic wires that entwine his body: the PICC line in his arm, the tube in his nose. Herol rises slowly to his feet like a 90-year-old, I put my hands under his armpits to support him, feeling heat and sweat on my fingers. It's like lifting a large rag doll stuffed with straw. The machine that he's hooked up to rings out an alarm, registering its displeasure at the clumsy way that I'm moving him. And finally, as my daughter looks on in increasing disapproval, I lower the ex-boxer safely on to the bed.

He begins to shiver. Not a normal kind of shiver but one that envelops his whole body. There is only a thin sheet on the bed which barely covers him. I look around and find a vacant bed and steal its sheet, which I lay on top of Herol and stretch to cover his feet.

It's seems ridiculous that he can be so cold and yet there is nobody from the hospital around to notice.

I take a seat next to him, the one that he had just been sitting in, and I feel his residual body heat warm me. My mind is empty now. I can think of nothing to say.

'Just keep talking,' urges Herol once more, lying stiff on the bed, his face screwed up in pain, his eyes staring glassily into the distance.

'Read to him,' suggests my daughter.

I look around in desperation for a magazine or a book but there is nothing suitable here. So I flick on my phone and locate a random e-book. But as I open my mouth to speak a woman and her child appear from behind the curtain.

The newcomer is tall and commanding. She calls to a nearby nurse who scurries over. 'I want to speak to a doctor now,' she demands. 'I want to know exactly what's happening and what you intend to do about it.'

She's sees me sitting down and I rise to shake her hand. She introduces herself as Natasha, Herol's daughter. The child is his granddaughter, Maya. The air pressure in the ward cranks up a bar or two as a young looking doctor scurries into view and nervously explains that Herol is back in hospital because his body has reacted to the appendix operation in an unexpected way.

Apparently scar tissue has built up around the site of the operation and has wrapped itself around Herol's bowel, blocking it. It can occasionally happen, the doctor explains, and usually clears on its own after a few days. It doesn't help, he says, that Herol told a white lie about having had a bowel movement on Friday. If the doctors had known this to be untrue they would never have allowed him to go home.

There is a calm authority about Herol's daughter that is instantly reassuring. Later, I will watch YouTube videos of a six-year-old Natasha being held aloft in her father's arms after his fight with Mark Kaylor[61] in 1986. It is impossible to reconcile the sweet, innocent child clearly bewildered by the hubbub that surrounds her in the ring with the tall, powerful, imposing and confident woman she has become. The doctor tells us that there is a very, *very* slight chance that the patient might have to have a further operation to remove the errant scar tissue. But that won't happen to Herol. He's pretty sure of that.

....
61 **Mark Kaylor** born 11 May 1961, London, England. Former British and commonwealth middleweight champion.

Lazarus

WHEN I arrive at the hospital next day Herol Graham is howling in pain. Howling. Really howling. It's a frightening sound that echoes around the ward and startles the other inhabitants. A sound I doubt that Herol ever made when he was inside the ropes, no matter how hard anybody struck him. If it's at all possible there are even more tubes attached to his body. He has them coming from his arms, from his nose and even from the tip of his penis. No medieval inquisitor ever devised such an elaborate torture apparatus. The tube in his penis is currently inducing an agonising burning sensation and Herol just can't control himself. He howls. And he howls. And then he howls some more.

It's difficult to know what to do when another person in your close vicinity is in such obvious discomfort. It's easier, of course, if it's a child. *Your child*. What you do then is simply pick them up in your arms and hug them for all you are worth. Such an act can sometimes make you feel better about yourself and there is a chance that the child might also gain some solace. In Herol's case I can't really do that. I should be able to but I somehow can't bring myself to hug another man. Instead I walk over to him and mumble words in his direction in the softest voice I can muster. And I take hold of his hand and clutch it in my own. I gently stroke the fist that was once an instrument of violence and I stare deep into his dark brown eyes.

Herol returns my gaze and for several long moments we say nothing at all. We remain holding hands, oblivious to the rest of the world. When I think about it later I am hard pressed to recall a time when I shared such an intimate moment with a member of the same sex. Herol, of course, may think differently; after all, is not the pre-fight 'stare-down' part and parcel of the boxing ritual? We regard each other for a very long time, until I begin to feel uncomfortable. Eventually to break the spell I declare in mock outrage, 'I'm going to have to stop holding your hand. It's getting a bit gay!'

There is the faintest trace of a smile on Herol's face and he weakly offers a Kenneth Williams ooh, matron-type retort. At his side, as ever, are Karen and Sedat. I kiss Karen on the cheek and embrace Sedat.

The doctor who previously spoke the other day to Herol's daughter Natasha and I had obviously been a little over-optimistic. Those scars he mentioned that afternoon did not go away of their own accord as he had suggested they might. In fact, even more scars have formed, creating the very real risk that the ex-fighter's bowel will have to be removed. Prior to arriving at the hospital I'd done the obligatory bit of Googling and discovered that those unwelcome scars have a name: they are called abdominal adhesions. I tell Karen everything I have learned about them and she confirms that this is what the doctors have been calling Herol's condition. In fact, there are eight of the deadly little blighters in total and they are effectively strangling his bowel. The next few hours, she has been told, are crucial. It is imperative that Herol undergoes a bowel movement. If he does not do so the bowel will effectively die and have to be removed. To spend the rest of your life without a bowel is a grim prospect.

The surgeon arrives with two or three doctors and tells us all that he suspects that Herol might be suffering from Crohn's disease[62]. Before he has a chance to explain the condition I find myself vociferously disagreeing with him. In his eyes it is plain to see that I am the worst kind of visitor – someone with a little knowledge aided and abetted by Google. I tell him I know all about auto-immune diseases and that Herol is definitely not suffering from Crohn's. The surgeon keeps his patience, although it's fairly obvious that he does not appreciate my unwelcome interjection.

When the group finally leave Herol turns to me and says, 'I could hear what they were saying about you when they were walking away. One of them said, "That guy is crazy!"'

We are advised it is imperative that Herol takes a walk at least once every couple of hours and with this in mind the three of us slowly attempt to haul him out of his bed. It's slow work: Herol is a dead weight now and the tangle of wires coming from him could easily be dislodged with the slightest mistake. I put my hands under one armpit and Sedat takes the other. Herol climbs shakily to his feet, his head a limp object hanging towards the floor, lacking the strength to straighten his neck.

The former boxer walks on the spot for about a minute but it's clear that even a limited activity such as this is far too much for him. I suggest that perhaps we should help Herol back into a chair but we struggle to do so. As Sedat and I gently lower him we become entangled in the wires that encircle his body. There is a very real danger that we might pull them out. When we finally have him back in his seat, Herol is sweating like he's just returned from a 10km run.

We try to encourage him to drink but he's not interested. Eventually, however, I manage to get him to take a few sips of a fruit drink that I've brought with me and it has an instant effect upon him. Herol tells us that he needs the toilet. I have to admit that this is the first time in my life that a grown

---

62   **Crohn's disease** is a type of inflammatory bowel disease (IBD) that can affect any part of the gastrointestinal tract.

man has indicated any desire to defecate in my presence. Ordinarily, such a request would naturally be greeted with less than enthusiasm but now the three of us, Karen, Sedat and I, look into each other's eyes with a mixture of joy and hope.

Once again we help Herol climb gingerly to his feet, me with one arm, Sedat with the other. It takes five or ten minutes to complete this difficult procedure. Curtains are drawn around his bed and a commode is wheeled into view. A young looking doctor pokes her head around the curtain and sees this happening before quickly beating a hasty retreat. Herol's surgical gown is loosened and he is lowered on to the commode. Even though he is desperately unwell, he is embarrassed by his predicament. He mumbles an apology, and then another. I tell him he has nothing whatsoever to apologise for.

The stench, of course, is appalling; although I'm having a slightly better time of it than the others on account of my diminished sense of smell, yet another symptom of hypothyroidism. I don't have time to reflect but later I will ponder upon the course that my decision to return to the world of boxing has taken me on. Would I have been quite so eager to revisit long forgotten memories had I known that the climax to such an undertaking would result in me sitting inches away from a one-time championship boxer while he had a poo? Probably not. It takes a certain type of person to harbour such an ambition.

Curiously though, this particular poo is greeted with celebration from all present. We hold our noses and make stupid jokes and laugh and, I think, instantly develop a closeness, a kinship, that can really only be understood by those who have shared such an experience. And this toilet session is no minor affair: It goes on for a very long time; Herol continues to mumble his embarrassed apologies and we continue to giggle.

We can hear other people in the ward complaining under their breath. Visitors are suddenly finding excuses to leave the building and inmates attempt to miraculously rise from their sickbeds. I very much doubt that Jesus ever considered using such a technique when he was busy resurrecting Lazarus. In the bed immediately next to Herol is a terminally ill patient who has been given five days to live (this news was whispered to me earlier on in the evening). If he has a god he must be wondering what on earth he's done to deserve this final indignity.

Press

THERE was a time when I used to attend press conferences two or three times a week. It was cheaper than getting tickets to the Christmas pantomime. The trick back then, if at all possible, was to try use them for your own purposes. When a promoter put together a press conference the obvious motivation for this lay in concocting a story for the newspapers that would help to sell tickets or to gain television coverage. We all knew that. For this reason it wasn't exactly unusual to be present to witness boxers theatrically bad-mouth one another in a manifestation of what gave every indication of being genuine antipathy. On occasion there might even be physical contact between boxers, such as when WBO heavyweight champion Michael Bentt[63] brawled with rival Herbie Hide[64] at a photo shoot outside a London hotel in 1994, or when British middleweight rivals Mark Kaylor and Errol Christie[65] rolled about on the floor outside a casino 11 years earlier.

....

63 **Michael Bentt** born 4 September 1964, London, England. Former WBO heavyweight champion of the world.
64 **Herbie Hide** born 27 August 1971, Amauzari, Nigeria. Former British heavyweight champion; WBO heavyweight champion of the world.
65 **Errol Christie** born 29 June 1963, Leicester, England.

In general, however, press conferences were a phenomenon that were just about tolerated by many of the people I knew back then. What was initially an opportunity to come face to face with your heroes soon became a tedious platform for rhetoric and hyperbole. More canny onlookers, however, might be able to gain valuable one-on-one time with a particular boxer and endeavour to satisfy sports editors by revealing a different angle on proceedings that rival newspapers did not have.

* * * * *

Naturally, angles are the furthest thing from my mind as I climb the steps of the Stonebridge Boxing Club in Harlesden with the intention of attending my first press conference in around 26 years. I've thought about this a lot recently: frankly I'm in dire need of a break from that hospital and it seems the next logical step for me. Since deciding to retrace my steps in boxing I've met a few fighters, a manager/promoter, an advisor or two, but now it's time to get back to the front line. It's no big deal really when you think about it. People do it all the time. But quite frankly I'm nervous as hell – exactly as I felt when I attended my first such event back in the days of four TV channels. But I needn't have worried. For as I look around the crowded gym there are already a couple of faces that I'm familiar with. Part of me feels pity that they are still here after 25 years; another part of me is envious.

Clicking away with a serious-looking digital Nikon is a photographer named Lawrence Lustig, who seems to have been taking pictures of boxers since Man Ray was still fiddling about with his pinhole camera. And just entering the building holding his six-year-old daughter's hand is Ed Robinson. Ed and I first met when he was Frank Maloney's fresh-faced recently graduated press agent. Subsequently he was employed in a similar role for Frank Warren before joining Sky Sports as presenter, a job he's been doing for almost two decades. Aside from Ed and Lawrence the rest of the people in the room are strangers who have come to see IBF super-middleweight world champion James DeGale undertake a live workout.

I'm handed a cup of coffee by a young attractive black girl. She introduces herself as DeGale's sister while displaying perfect teeth and complimenting me on the good manners that I never knew I possessed. She's charm personified, as is Ed Robinson when I go over to reintroduce myself to. I haven't seen Ed since 1996 but he's at pains to make me feel welcome. This, I realise, is what is easily forgotten about boxing: it's a sport where (almost) everyone makes you feel you're important.

As if to underline this point Ed offers to take me around and introduce me to everybody present. You couldn't buy this kind of attention. When I nervously decline he then proceeds to give me a precise description of what is happening here today: who is doing what to whom, what is doing which to when. He also gives me a comprehensive overview of all that's changed in boxing reporting since I decided to fall off the edge of the world. I can't help but be overwhelmed by his generosity and wonder whether I would bother to do the same if the roles were reversed.

Everything these days, Ed tells me, is about social media. The young men I see impatiently queuing to interview DeGale with their camera phones are in the unprecedented position of being able to evaluate customer feedback within hours of posting their videos to YouTube. These one-man bands are now important people and this is demonstrated by DeGale's willingness to accommodate them into his schedule. Sky are apparently anxious to emulate this phenomenon and there are clear similarities between the home brew approach of Ed and his social media rivals. Working for Sky Sports is apparently no Busby Berkeley production. Ed, with his daughter still clinging to his hand, has a solitary cameraman with him and tells me that when he gets back into the office it will be his job to edit the video.

Before I leave I bump into the ex-boxer Jim McDonnell[66]. I'm surprised to discover that he recognises me and even remembers my name. Jim is greyer and a little more careworn than I remember but he is yet another former professional who seems to be winning the battle against advancing years. Back in 1989 when Jim was preparing for his fight with Barry McGuigan[67]. I can recall spending several enjoyable afternoons at his house while his wife Kim attended to his young toddler. I ask him how that toddler is getting along. 'That toddler's standing next to you,' says Jim, pointing at the towering string bean of a man beside me.

Inevitably we talk about boxing and I remind him that I was there on the night that he beat McGuigan. Within moments it is impossible not to discern an anger and frustration in Jim's voice. A quarter of a century after he enjoyed an unexpected victory that night it obviously still appears to rankle that everybody made him the underdog prior to the fight. I quickly change the subject and tell him about Herol Graham and these things called abdominal adhesions that Herol has developed. About how I'm beginning to suspect they might be boxing-related, the cumulative result of thousands of punches taken to the belly. I tell Jim about Herol's second operation, and of how all we can do now is sit and hope that his body does not produce further scar tissue. And I let Jim know how disappointed Herol is that so few in boxing have been to visit him in hospital. Jim says he'll be be sure to drop in as soon as he can.

....

66 **Jim McDonnell** born 12 September 1960, London, England. Former EBU featherweight champion.

67 **Barry McGuigan** born 28 February 1961. County Monaghan, Northern Ireland. Former British and EBU featherweight champion; WBA featherweight champion of the world.

Frank

LYING next to my seriously-ill daughter on a collapsible hospital bed night after night will obviously not go down as one of the most fulfilling experiences of my life, although it certainly qualifies as being one of the most tedious. To fill the endless hours of boredom I begin blogging about my experiences. After a couple of days a comment from one of the doctors at the Whittington is posted on my blog. Later, another doctor tells me that all the medical staff have been reading it.

This leads to a conversation with the head of communications at the hospital who tells me that Sofia has been nominated to receive a bravery award. I ask her to make sure that Talya, the little girl with the injured foot in the next bed to my daughter, also receives one.

* * * * *

I take Sofia in to receive her award, which is a goodie bag full of sweets and pens and drawing books. She reluctantly poses for pictures in the petulant style of a moody 13-year-old and after a little prompting awkwardly hugs Tayla to her chest. A dozen or so doctors and nurses smile and cheer. It seems to me that this might just be the symbolic ending to Sofia's ordeal. At the back of my mind, however, is the feeling that something is once again not quite right with her. She looks pale and weaker than yesterday. When I ask her about it she tries to assure me that nothing is wrong.

With the ceremony is over we go to call in on Herol on the next ward and I'm pleased to say that people are finally coming to see him. Earlier that day Colin McMillan had paid a visit; nice, dependable, decent Colin. And now there is a middle-aged couple who I'm introduced to: Johnny Oliver, an ex-professional boxer who reveals himself to be the former trainer of the UK Olympic boxing team, as well as leading heavyweight contender Anthony Joshua[68]; his wife stands smiling at his side. The pair remind me of Hopper's portrait of himself and his spouse. Also present is a young muscular black man with a shaven head and thick beard. We shake hands and I'm told that this is Leon McKenzie[69].

I ask Leon if he can remember me at all, although once again there is absolutely zero chance that he will. The last time I saw him, I explain, was in the early hours of February 1990 when Leon was 12 years old. I remind him that I was sitting on the sofa in his father's house, another boxer named Clinton McKenzie[70], along with his uncle, yet another boxer named Duke McKenzie[71]. The three of us had fallen asleep while waiting for Mike Tyson to fight Buster Douglas[72]. A

68 **Anthony Joshua** born 15 October 1989, Hertfordshire, England. Current IBF world heavyweight champion.

69 **Leon McKenzie** born 17 May 1978, London, England. Former professional footballer.

70 **Clinton McKenzie** born 15 September 1955, Clarendon, Jamaica. Former British and EBU light-welterweight champion.

71 **Duke McKenzie** born 5 May 1963, London, England. Former British and EBU flyweight champion; IBF flyweight champion of the world; EBU bantamweight champion; WBO bantamweight champion of the world; WBO super-bantamweight champion of the world; British featherweight champion.

72 **James 'Buster' Douglas** born 7 April 1960, Ohio, USA. Former undisputed heavyweight champion of the world.

fresh-faced Leon had woken us up to watch what became one of the biggest upsets in boxing history.

If there is a pattern emerging from my decision to meet up with boxers after all this time it is this: every one of them seems to be damaged in some way – psychologically as well as physically – and every one of them is anxious to let you know that they are. Thus, within moments of meeting Leon I am given his story: of how he became a professional footballer and of how, upon his retirement he suffered greatly from depression which led to him taking up boxing.

Touchingly, Leon has brought Herol a gift. It is a poem philosophising the nature of life which he has had framed. With his head on the pillow, Herol reads it for a moment before quickly passing it on to me. As he does so I notice a frown flicker across Leon McKenzie's forehead. Like so many boxers he cannot disguise his feelings. He looks hurt.

Even for a prize fighter Leon's story is an unusual one. I tell him that not many people have turned pro at the advanced age of 34. I notice Leon tense up and immediately regret making the statement. It's obviously a sensitive subject for him. Johnny Oliver picks up on this, too, and softly proclaims, 'Age doesn't matter does it Leon? It's the number of fights that you have and how well you've looked after your body.'

I introduce my daughter to everyone there. She is greeted warmly and with gentle affection from these so-called hard men of the ring. But once again I can't help feeling that she's taken a step backwards in her recovery. She spends her time looking at Herol, who is still very weak and can hardly move, although all the attention seems to have cheered him up a lot.

Suddenly there is a commotion in the ward. The growl of a bear is followed by an apparition of Frank Bruno[73]. Although the weather is far from warm he's wearing long shorts and a

---

73 **Frank Bruno** born 16. November 1961, London, England. Former EBU heavyweight champion; WBA heavyweight champion of the world.

Hawaiian shirt. He looks slimmer and somehow smaller than in his glory days when his appearances on the BBC attracted millions of viewers and his unwitting catchphrase 'know wot I mean, 'Arry?' was the standard fodder of hundreds of stage impressionists.

His external appearance may or may not have diminished but that deep baritone of his could be used to warn ships away from clashing rocks. He shakes the hand of everyone present. He grasps my daughter's hand; she hasn't a clue who he is but cannot fail to notice the air of reverence which is bestowed upon him by all present. Bruno is yet another boxer with demons to battle. Like Herol he too has had to suffer the indignity of being sectioned. And like Herol his problems with depression have been liberally used as a vehicle to peddle newsprint.

In his heyday Bruno's imposing physical presence masked, I believe, an inherent shyness. And here today that shyness is readily apparent. When he takes my hand he refuses to look me in the eye. It's as if his thoughts are in a locked room. Still, he's taken the time out to visit Herol, which can only help to draw attention to the seriously-ill ex-fighter's plight.

For some reason Bruno's sudden appearance on the ward compels me to scamper away as quickly as I can. An article I wrote on Bruno back in 1988 was the first thing that I ever had in print and was in many ways responsible for my embarking upon the career that I did. But the element of completion, of circularity somehow fills me with discomfort. As he poses for pictures with Herol and Leon McKenzie I take my daughter's hand and gently lead her away from the ward.

* * * * *

Later that evening I contact Matt Christie, editor of the British trade paper *Boxing News*, someone I've barely spoken to before. I describe Herol's grim condition and he invites me to write a short piece on him for the paper as guest columnist. Thus, here is even more of an element of circularity for me: fully 28 years after last writing for *Boxing News* my name will appear within its pages once more. And as in the first time this occurred my byline is placed beneath a photograph of Frank Bruno.

Scream

STILL the hospital refuses to let us go.

At mid-morning the next day I receive a call from Sofia's school. It is only her fifth day back after a month-long absence and it's becoming more and more apparent to my wife and myself that there is every reason to believe we may have been a little unwise in hastening her return. Sofia is having difficulty breathing, I am told. I rush down to the school and pick her up. Then we immediately hurry back to the hospital. My second home.

The last few weeks spent finding ways of filling in time seems to have taught me nothing at all. Back in the queue for A&E and I'm already losing my temper.

And when the two of us arrive in a waiting room literally overflowing with hollering children and their world-weary parents I feel ready to scream. Time is slowed to a canter: trapped in a viscous paste that clogs up your joints and renders all movement impossible. High-pitched squeals stab at my brain. I stare with evil intent at anyone who meets my eye.

Progress is impossibly slow. After waiting for over an hour Sofia's name is finally called out and we are ushered into a small office where a youngish man in shirt and slacks asks the same questions that we have been asked a thousand times over the last few weeks. *How long has she been feeling ill? Has she been in contact with anyone? Has she been abroad recently? Is she allergic to any medicine?*

No! No! No! No! I reply. *Just look at your computer screen, won't you? It's all there in black and white. Stop asking stupid fucking questions and get on with making her well again!*

Of course, that's not what I say. Naturally it's not. I'm white and middle-class and – as I keep mentioning – I'm well brought-up. I don't say those words even though every fibre of my being cries out to. Instead I'm courteous, clipped court-eous. And serious. And attentive. And patient with my patient.

We're sent back into the waiting room, to the hordes of howling children. I try not to look but I'm struck by the ugliness of the room. I wonder – as I often do – at what point does a child stop being a child and become an adult: self-sufficient and capable of being despised for who they are as opposed to being cosseted for who they are not. Despite myself I train my eyes on the owners of the children, everyone single one of them on the wrong side of obese. Many of their offspring share that same physical characteristic. Some of them stuff their dribbling mouths with sweets and crisps. The children do the same.

And it's no small coincidence to me that they are all here. The mass of them. Cramming their bodies with poisonous fast-food. Cramming their children's bodies with the same to arrive at this, the inevitable conclusion: a hospital waiting room that leads to hell. Purgatory for the McDonald's age. I make a mental note to take more of a hold on Sofia's diet. I might even stick to it for a week or two.

More waiting. More interminable trickling seconds. What is it? An hour? Two hours? Three? A nearby child bellows into my ear without halt for a period of time that seems longer than I have lived. The discomfort is intense. It's as if someone is scooping out the soft pulp of my brain with a rusty potato peeler. I tell Sofia we're moving. There are a couple of chairs at the other side of the room that have recently been vacated.

She whispers something about not doing so because the child's parent will notice us move away and be offended. I tell her that she can stay here if she wants but I'm going. That's me obviously aiming for that Parent of the Year award again.

Finally Sofia's name is once more called and we are led into the A&E nerve centre: five or six women tapping away on keyboards, people in white coats randomly milling about, people in blue suits urgently scampering from room to room. I recognise many of the faces and they seem to recognise me. Perhaps they think I work here, or maybe I'm a mystery shopper come to evaluate their performance.

Sofia's blood pressure is taken. Her heart rate is measured. Those same questions are asked again. *Those same fucking questions!* She is instructed to raise her sweater. A cold stethoscope is traced across her flesh. Then it's off to the X-ray department, my third visit in as many weeks and again they seem to know who I am. I share a joke with the attractive radiologist about the difficulties of living with 13-year-olds (even in situations of severe stress such as this the male psyche still finds time to evaluate the sexual compatibility of any female it encounters).

This is when I take things into my own hands. When the X-ray is completed I barge in behind a technician and watch as an image of my daughter's lungs is cropped using a cut down version of Photoshop. There are three technicians in all standing in this little ante room with me and I can feel that they are uncomfortable with my presence. Nevertheless, I obstinately remain there, my eyes daring them to say a word against me, and take a long hard look at the X-ray.

What I see reassures me greatly. In the previous X-rays the hole in Sofia's lung was much more defined. Initially it could be seen as a large ugly black stain, and later as a smaller indistinct creamy smudge. Now I am relieved to see there is nothing there at all. I'm no expert, of course. I understand that clearly. But I'm *getting* to be an expert at looking for holes in my daughter's lungs. And to paraphrase Monty Python: this hole is no more; it has ceased to be; it is an ex-hole.

We go back to A&E while we await the doctor's official diagnosis. But he doesn't appear and one of those figures in blue instructs us to return to the screaming kids for some more punishment. He reveals that Sofia must now have an ultrasound scan, something which the doctor failed to mention. So we wait. And we wait. And we wait. *And we wait*.

We watch as newcomers arrive and are treated before us. And we wait some more as the room begins to empty. Running out of energy and patience I try to attract the attention of the one of the doctors lurking behind a locked door with a reinforced glass window. To all intents and purposes I have suddenly become invisible. I am wilfully ignored and/or I am genuinely not noticed. You decide. Finally I tell Sofia to pack her things away. 'We're leaving,' I say.

* * * * *

Later that evening I receive several phone calls from the hospital. One of the doctors wants to know why I left. When I tell him the reason there is silence on the line followed by a heavy sigh. Apparently we should never have been asked to return to the main waiting room. It was an administrative error. Whoever told us to do this mistook us for somebody else. The doctor apologises and then confirms my own diagnosis. It is indeed good news: Sofia's lung abscess has indeed reduced in size. He wants her to avoid overdoing things until it's completely healed. Other than that we have no cause for immediate alarm. Sofia stays off school for another three days and once again I'm on my way back to visit Herol.

Stars

THE next morning I take the article I've written for *Boxing News* about Herol Graham into the hospital. I'm keen for Herol and Karen to see it before it's published so that they have the opportunity to raise any objections. Herol lies on the bed, his condition unchanged from the last time I saw him, when the shadow of Frank Bruno was looming over him. I hand over my iPad to Karen and she puts her glasses on. She tries to look at it but appears to be having trouble. 'That's funny,' she frowns. 'I can't read it. I'm seeing spots.'

Karen returns the iPad to me and I read the article aloud. I have a captive audience, along with Herol and Karen the three other inmates of the ward and their visitors have no choice but to listen. When I'm finished Herol mumbles something about it being 'very poignant', although in truth I can't be sure if he even heard what I read. His mind seems to be elsewhere. Karen says I should go ahead and get it published.

The real reason I am here today is to give her a break: to let Karen have the opportunity to go home and shower and get some much needed sleep. With this in mind I sit myself down in a chair at Herol's bedside while his partner puts her coat on. We say our goodbyes and I suggest to Herol that we watch a film together. Before we get the chance to do this, however, there is an sudden disturbance at the other end of the ward. Someone is slumped in a chair by the door being attended to by a group of anxious looking people in civvies, not medical staff. It's Karen. I rush over to discover that she has just collapsed. You really couldn't make this up.

If you are going to collapse, the best place to do so is quite probably in a hospital; although that should obviously never be one's primary motivation for visiting. Within moments I've located a nurse, who scurries over to attend to Karen. Meanwhile, a doctor is hurriedly called. Karen's pulse is taken and her heart rate measured. She is then bundled into a wheelchair and I am instructed to accompany her downstairs to A&E. Apparently, this ludicrous piece of red tape is unavoidable. I'm guessing it's something to do with hospital insurance: the NHS can't have people dying on them when they're not actually registered to be on the premises.

A clearly disinterested hospital porter pushes Karen's wheelchair towards a lift. I'm caught in two minds: do I abandon Karen and stay with Herol? Or do I abandon Herol and stay with Karen? I decide upon the latter but before doing so I scurry back to him to let him know what is happening. He lies on his bed, strangely impassive. It's as if so much has happened to him over the past week or so that he has lost the ability to react to anything. His face is a blank canvas. I tell him to have his phone to hand and I will try to keep him updated.

We reach the A&E reception desk and I find myself queueing yet again. I really have lost count of the number of times that I've had to do this lately but it is no less a strain on what remains of my patience. Karen sits quietly in the wheelchair and watches. It is a good 15 minutes before we reach the front of the queue and then it's back to those questions again. *Those fucking questions.* I'm not going to repeat those questions to you.

We are finally ushered into the waiting room. Yet more people with bruises and cuts and cracked limbs and whatever else it is that brings them to a place like this. I get us both some water from a vending machine and while I do so some idiot approaches Karen and asks her if she is using the wheelchair that she is currently sitting in. It's a bizarre question that leaves us both temporarily dumbstruck. Then Karen's phone rings and she hands it to me, too shaky to answer. It's Colin McMillan calling to check if it's okay to post updates of Herol's condition on Facebook. Sweet, dependable Colin. I get him up to speed with what's been happening and tell him I'll be in touch if I have any news.

Karen is still seeing stars. She looks disorientated and delicate. Once again there is much to admire about this woman. While her partner hovers on the brink of disaster four floors above us, she talks about the universe and of the inevitable good that will come of all this. Of how this experience in this hospital is changing all of us for the better. And somehow I can't find it in myself to disagree with her. I think she's right.

* * * * *

It's quite some morning for all of us: long periods of boredom punctuated by tense drama. Karen is finally examined by a young doctor and it's eventually established that she has a urinary infection. Following her brush with the Big C, Herol's partner is something of an expert at monitoring her own condition. I listen as she discusses the effectiveness of different brands of antibiotics with the doctor. Finally, two or three hours after she initially collapsed, Karen is advised to go home and get some rest. I could have told her that at considerably less expense to the NHS.

* * * * *

When I return to Herol's bedside in the late afternoon he is sleeping. In fact, the whole ward is sleeping. There is a silence that has descended from nowhere and overwhelmed the place. All the nurses and doctors and porters and cleaners seem to have disappeared. Nothing moves. It is a stillness that is both comforting and eerie.

I sit down and draw solace from his gentle snoring. I idly flick through a book, scratch away at a crossword, play with my phone, before putting everything down and wallowing in the slow pulse beat of the silence, the unexpected bleakness. It's as though time has stood still and the world no longer exists outside this hospital ward.

And then, for no apparent reason, I find myself sobbing. The tears well up in my eyes and I staunch them with my fingers lest someone should witness my embarrassment. They dribble on to my cheeks and I shake my head and wonder who I'm crying for. Am I crying for my daughter, so very nearly lost to me just a short time ago? For Herol, twitching away beside me dreaming whatever dreams that must consume an ex-fighter? For Karen? For my father – the man whom I loved and hated in equal measures? Or for myself?

* * * * *

I nod off for a few moments but I am hauled out of my sleep by the sound of someone yelling a name. 'Herol Graham!' a voice calls out, followed by exaggerated giggling and laughter. 'Herol Graham!'

I open my eyes and without warning two infant-featured black men descend upon the ward. The atmosphere of tranquillity I had been enjoying is instantly obliterated. One of new arrivals pats Herol several times on the chest and when he gets no reaction roughly shakes him until he is dragged into consciousness. It turns out that the newcomers are both amateur boxers, protégés of the ex-champion. They speak in a patois that I can scarcely understand and jerk around the bed as if a strung out on amphetamines. Their appearance could be deemed threatening to some but somehow they fill the ward with joy.

I shake the hands of both men and find myself grinning as the taller of the two begins to dance around the ward, throwing punches at some invisible adversary. 'No,' gasps Herol, quickly getting into the swing of things. 'Not like that... Move your leg back a little... Put your weight on your front foot.' The punches fly and the laughter flows.

And suddenly everybody on the ward is smiling at this unscheduled training session. The man in the bed opposite is shaking his shoulders, probably happy for the first time in weeks. The terminally-ill patient to the right is grinning from ear to ear.

Session #5

'Y OU'VE not been here for a long time?' a Chinese accent says.

'I know... I'm sorry... It's not been... *Convenient.*'

'Convenient?'

'Yes. I should have told you really. I should have phoned. I'm sorry about that... I apologise.'

The usual herbal tea and notepad: It's as if she's been frozen in position here for all these weeks waiting for me to return. She might even be wearing the same clothing. In fact, everything is exactly the same: the walls, the clock, the desk, the chairs. Everything is as it was. Particularly the silence.

'It's a bit of a long story,' I say, before launching into a lengthy explanation for my absence. I tell her about Sofia, about the hole in her lung, the pneumonia. And she just sits there expressionless. Except for the very slight hint of a frown that creases her brow for a nanosecond there is no reaction whatsoever.

Then she says, 'I am sorry to hear this. Your daughter is better now?' Neither a statement nor a question.

'Yes... Well no... She's on the mend but it will be several months before she's completely well... She's only been out for a couple of weeks.'

'Couple of weeks?'

'Yes. Discharged. Let out of hospital.'

156

That familiar silence stifles the air. She stares into my eyes almost accusingly. The silence spans several long seconds and I find myself smiling back at her. 'Is there something wrong?' I ask.

Still silence. Then it suddenly dawns on me: she wants me to tell her why I haven't come to visit her since my daughter left hospital.

'Ahhh...' I say. 'I understand.'

More silence.

'I never really left the hospital,' I say. 'Literally the day after Sofia was let out I discovered that somebody I knew was in the next ward.'

'A friend?'

'Friend? Well, not really. I met him probably five or six times in the past... He's a boxer actually.'

'A boxer?'

'Well... In actual fact ex-boxer...Yes, it's a coincidence really because I've been doing what you suggested... You know, writing about boxing... I even had a piece published in a trade mag.'

Silence.

'But the boxer – Herol – has been very ill so I've had no choice but to give him some support.'

'Support?'

'Well not really support. I've just been visiting him as much as I can... Buying him a few magazines to read... Some food... That kind of thing.'

'But he is not your friend?'

'Sorry?'

Silence.

'Ahh... I get what you're driving at. Laura's been asking me why I've been visiting him so often, too. I told her that in initially going to see him I'd made a commitment to him. I couldn't really visit and say, "Thanks for the interview Herol. See you later – hope you don't die."'

'But he is not your friend?'

'Well I guess he is now. In actual fact I've gotten pretty close to him.' Images of Herol squatting on that commode flicker into my mind. 'Too close in fact.'

She takes a deep breath that might almost be a sigh. She stares at her notebook. 'You spoke about another friend in hospital,' she says.

I think for a moment. 'You're probably talking about Michael... Michael Watson.'

'You didn't stay with him in hospital?'

'No. I told you I didn't. I told you why.'

'But he was your friend?'

'Yes.'

'And Herol is not your friend?' She pronounces the name 'Heror'.

'Well not initially,' I say.

'But you did stay with Herol?'

'Yes.'

The traditional period of silence that ensues allows her questions to swill around inside me. Michael was my friend and I essentially abandoned him all those years ago when he was seriously ill in hospital. Herol was not my friend but I seem to have made it my mission to stay with him.

'I guess what you're implying is that I have a guilty conscience,' I say.

Gone

AND maybe it is a guilty conscience. It seems an incredibly simplistic conclusion to be reaching but how else can you explain my transformation from Victor Meldrew to Mother Theresa? However, the time I spend with Herol Graham is not entirely altruistic. I understand that.

On one occasion Herol tells me about a dream he has had. About how he found himself my waiting in a queue for heaven and hell, purgatory no less. He has tears in his eyes when he is finally told that he doesn't belong there. 'They told me to piss off...' he recalls, '...nicely.'

* * * * *

And so I continue to fit my hours around my daughter and around Herol. I try to visit as often as possible and each time I see him I am aware that I am needed less. Boxing finally rallies around one of its own. Every day a broken nose... A thickened brow... A young fighter come to pay homage to a page from history... A careworn trainer's unflinching gaze... Boxing hasn't forgotten Herol after all, it's just dragged its feet remembering him.

I drop off flowers for Karen and an Easter egg for Herol and we take Sofia away for a much needed weekend break. It rains, naturally it does. And we spend most of the time closeted together in the hotel room. When I return to the hospital I'm surprised to see that Herol is sitting upright on the chair by his bed. There is colour in his cheeks and laughter in his eyes. Surrounding him is a pile of old boxing magazines, most of which have his face on the cover. He finally has energy. He no longer moves like an old man. It would appear that the second operation has been successful.

Sofia joins us and has her picture taken with him. She's looking a lot healthier, too, and out of nowhere I'm suddenly beginning to see an end to my period of exile in this hospital. Herol smiles into the camera and rearranges my daughter's fingers so that her fist is pointing towards the lens in that all-too familiar pose.

* * * * *

My face has become so well known in the hospital that a few days later I'm asked to speak at a conference of doctors and consultants. How very grown up for this 53-year-old juvenile delinquent. My task is to detail my experiences in the hospital from the perspective of a parent with a sick child. So I tell my story: of Sofia and Herol and boxing. And in doing so I'm aware of the positive effects that this experience have had on me. By the time I finish speaking somebody at the back of the auditorium is crying and for a moment I wonder if it might be Herol or Karen, whom I had invited along.

But when I look they are not here. And when I go back upstairs to Mercer's ward Herol's bed is empty and some other unfortunate is already being wheeled into it. Death goes on.

Loss

BOXERS are adept at deception. It's something they do better than an awful lot of politicians. And one of their myriad acts of subterfuge is that they would have us believe they are normal creatures, that they do normal deeds and behave in ordinary ways. When you meet them face to face their physical appearance may strike you as unremarkable. But that's just another deception. Because it doesn't take me long to realise that there is nothing normal about the person sitting at my kitchen table right now.

It isn't anything to do with the conspicuous lack of extra poundage on his long, too lean frame. Nor is it the glowing skin: firm and freshly scrubbed and ridiculously absent of wrinkles of any description. And it's not the way he talks or moves or smiles or frowns or grimaces or coughs. It's nothing at all that you can put your finger on. This courteous, quietly spoken man-boy is just *different*. There's no other way of describing it. *Different*.

Sofia has now been out of that hospital for more than three weeks. As soon as she spots the back of boxer Frank Buglioni's head she scampers off to hide in her bedroom. Frank, you may remember, was at the gym a lifetime ago when I met with Steve Collins. Since then we've exchanged a few messages and the young fighter has very kindly sent words of support for Sofia. She doesn't know that, of course. She's just a 13-year-old girl and as far as she's concerned a very good looking stranger has just walked into our house; he mustn't be allowed to see her blushes.

A little while ago Frank asked a favour of me. He told me he was having his website redesigned and asked if I would mind writing a piece about his last fight: his WBA world championship loss to a Russian named Fedor Chudinov[74] in September 2015. I told Frank it would be an honour. However, if we were going to do this it had to be different to the standard 'So-and-so threw a left hook… Whatsisname threw a jab' sort of fight report.

For this reason our plan is to watch the Chudinov fight together and talk about what might have been in possibly excruciating detail. I've never done this with a boxer before and I can't say I've heard of anybody else doing it. I believe it's a particularly brave thing for Frank to agree to. After all, not many would want to rake over the coals of what must be one of the undoubted low points of their life.

It would be the equivalent of you or I being forced to relive the minutiae of a particularly cringeworthy date in which you loudly belched as you reached over for that first tender kiss. Or an embarrassing job interview that you undertook not knowing that you had a piece of cabbage wedged between your incisors. I understand, of course, that such comparisons are a trifle egregious – for since when was a boxer ever anything other than brave?

* * * * *

Thankfully the Frank Buglioni who takes a seat next to me today is nothing like the figure of the latter rounds of the Chudinov fight that will remain eternally searchable on YouTube. Remorseless pressure and relentless punching from

74 **Fedor Chudinov** born 15 September 1987 Bratsk, Russia. Former WBA super-middleweight champion of the world.

the Russian WBA belt holder had reduced *that* Frank Buglioni to an exhausted caricature of himself. The person sitting beside me is, however, unmarked by his ordeal. A sickeningly fresh-faced picture of youthful vitality that makes me feel like punching him myself right now.

A little small talk: Frank tells me more details about his split with promoter Frank Warren. As before I find it difficult to hide my concern. Then Frank drops the bombshell that he has also parted company with Steve Collins and my worries are instantly amplified tenfold. Being a boxer in the digital era is rather like being a contestant on *The X Factor*: unless you get that number one hit in double-quick time you're pretty soon humped and dumped. Only five months earlier Frank had been fighting for the WBA world super-middleweight title – the very pinnacle of a prizefighter's ambitions – and now his future, to put it mildly, seems uncertain. Or at least this is my initial impression.

But I'm wrong. Frank's disarming honesty and common-sense approach convinces me so. With a nonchalance that belies his tender years Frank explains that these decisions were his, and that he made them purely in the name of good business practice. 'I was prepared to work with Frank Warren again,' Frank tells me. 'But I thought let's see what else is out there. I don't want to do anything behind anybody's back. I want to do things properly.'

I've heard boxers attempt to deal with disappointment before. And I've been present when blatant untruths have been issued with an audacity that would put to shame any government dossier ever compiled on WMD. But Frank is earnestly and eminently believable: he's had to stop working with Steve Collins purely for financial reasons and he's keen to manage himself, which is a very bold step that few boxers ever take.

This means that he will have to personally barter with promoters for the best price he can get whenever he boxes.

He's going to have to learn to fight outside the ring as well as in it.

* * * * *

I click the YouTube 'play' button and tell Frank to prepare himself for some fairly dopey questions. The blocky image on my iPad reveals his Russian opponent Chudinov climbing through the ropes. Small. Clean limbed. Ape-like. Hairless torso. Muscled. A good head shorter than Frank. Watching the Russian immediately brings to mind an issue that is perennially debated on social media.

I halt the playback and ask Frank whether he genuinely considers the title he fought for to be a true 'world' title.[75] It's an awkward question and his answer is not entirely unexpected, 'It's 100 per cent a world title,' he says firmly, as if used to and bored of answering this question. 'The WBA, the IBF, the WBC, WBO – if you're a world champion of any of them you're a world champion. People on social media don't know how hard it is being a professional boxer and getting to that world title level.'

We restart the video and watch the figures onscreen warm-up in their respective corners. 'What were you thinking about at that moment?' I ask. 'Were you thinking about your dad... About when you were a kid dreaming of being a world champion?'

'The fight was the only thing on my mind,' he says. 'I was just visualising myself lifting the belt. It was something that I'd been preparing for the last year, and then very intensely for the last ten weeks.'

'Did you have any doubts in your mind at all as to the result?'

....

75 In boxing the proliferation of governing bodies often results in there being multiple world champions, making it usually impossible to ascertain who is the 'real' champion of the world.

'No. None at all. Prior to the fight I was actually full of confidence. The way that I fought in the gym was better than ever before. I pushed it that extra level.'

Had he spoken to his opponent in press conferences leading up to the fight?

'Not really,' says Frank. 'His English wasn't great but we'd shaken hands when we first met. Obviously I didn't shake his hand at the weigh-in because I was in the zone. People saw that as disrespectful and some had things to say about it but I'd like to challenge them to be in my situation. To prepare their mind and body the way I did and then shake someone's hand you're about to fight to the death.'

We stop talking for a moment and watch the introductions to the fight unfurl. The on-screen Frank looks pensive as he prowls the ring, the Russian unperturbed, all business.

ROUND ONE

'I presume you had a fight plan?' I ask as the action kicks off.

'Yes, it was to box, move, draw him on to the shots, make him use his legs because in his last fight every time he used his legs he needed to take a breather. Obviously it didn't work the way we thought it would do.'

'It must be so hard when you're doing everything you can but the other person is still beating you,' I say. 'Surely no amount of money can compensate you for this sort of punishment.'

'You wouldn't be fighting for a world championship unless you didn't love boxing,' replies Frank. And I think it's hard to love a business the same way as you love a sport.'

As the sentence leaves his lips there is a cheer from the YouTube crowd. Frank has just enjoyed his first success of the fight: he connects with a couple of right hands but they scarcely make a dent in the perpetually advancing Chudinov. The Russian moves forward like an automaton, throwing punch after punch at the retreating Buglioni.

'He had a great jab,' says Frank. 'And he's thickset and strong. I wasn't expecting the jab to be as good as it was. In fact, I've never come across anyone with a jab as good as his.'

'How did that affect you?' I ask. 'If I'm hit by one punch it's more than I can take. But he was throwing dozens and many of them were connecting.'

'I would say after the seventh round I started to feel the pace,' admits Frank. 'It was getting tougher and tougher and he wasn't tiring.'

So tough in fact that with no more than two minutes on the clock Frank is already running out of places in which to retreat. He rests his back on the ropes and attempts to use them to leverage his own punches.

'Did you plan to do that?' I ask, already knowing the answer.

'Once my back was on the ropes the plan was to try to move away,' says Frank. 'But he was very good at cutting off the ring and reserving energy.'

I find myself wincing as Frank tries to fend off the first-round barrage. I tell him I don't like to watch him fight. He ignores the comment.

'Did you work on your jab?' I say.

'Yes. I've been using the jab.'

'So why weren't you using it here?'

'I was trying to keep him at range and when he comes in, throw the flurry and move away again. But I shouldn't have been away so quickly. I should have thrown a second phase of punches.'

I tell Frank that perhaps he should have stood his ground more. Although I'm all too aware that it's easy for me to say.

'If I fought him again I *would* hold my ground and go to war with him,' he replies. 'He's so good coming forward I'd like to put him on the back foot and see what happens.'

As the round comes to a close Frank reveals to me that prior to the fight he had perforated an ear drum.

'Jesus!' I exclaim.

'The other thing is that making super-middleweight was just taking a little too much out of me,' he adds.

'You really shouldn't have been fighting at all,' I say.

'Yeah but world titles don't come along too often. My dad wanted to pull me out but I said, "I don't care if I've got two broken hands!" It was the biggest opportunity of my life.'

'I suppose that in reality it's rare for a boxer to ever be 100 per cent fit.'

'Yeah… If you push yourself to the limit you're inevitably going to have an injury or illness. It's as simple as that.'

ROUND TWO

We watch as the second round carries on from where the previous left off: Chudinov stalking, Buglioni retreating. Chudinov metronomically launching punch after punch, Buglioni trying in vain to pick off his opponent. It's painful viewing.

'But this was the best I could have performed,' insists Frank. 'The actual best. That's why I'm not disappointed by the result. He was the better man on the night.'

I ask the boxer about his opponent's power. What did it feel like being continually hit by the champion's punches?

'They weren't concussive but every one was solid,' says Frank. 'And he had very fast hands. But I've been working on crossing my arms on the inside so I didn't take too many uppercuts. I was rolling with a lot of the punches. Even though he was winning most rounds I was having flashes of success. So I was still positive.'

'But I just want you to stop and use your jab,' I say. 'I think it could be a phenomenal weapon.'

'Yes, my jab's good when it lands,' agrees Frank. 'It's very solid.'

ROUND THREE

As we look on it suddenly becomes apparent that Chudinov appears to be slowing down for the first time.

'He's taking a breather,' observes Frank, as he finally begins to force his way into the fight.

'See… that's nice,' I say, pointing out a body shot that Frank sweetly delivers.

'Yes I was having a little bit of success working to the body. I think he felt a few of my shots.'

'How quickly does time go when you're in the ring?' I ask.

'The minute break in the corner was going very quick,' says Frank. 'But the three minutes were *definitely* three minutes long.'

'When you're exhausted I expect it seems like six minutes?'

'Yes, of course. When he catches you with a good body shot or in your face it seems longer.'

'Now all of a sudden you're planting your feet and throwing punches,' I say.

'Yes I'm going back to my instincts.'

'And your instinct is to fight him, not to back away?'

'Yeah.'

ROUND FOUR

Round four begins and Frank makes another confession. 'I think it was about then that the other eardrum went,' he reveals.

'Oh no! What did that feel like?'

'It's like a ringing in your ear, a very, very bad headache. It didn't really affect my balance.'

'I take it you didn't mention it in the post-fight interviews?'

'No. You can't do that. But I had a lot of injuries in that fight. When I took the drug test afterwards my body wasn't absorbing any water and I was vomiting from exhaustion. And the urine I passed was just blood.'

'Do you ever wonder why you do it?'

'The next day I was pretty sore when the adrenalin had worn off. But I thought it was a great night and a great experience. I loved every minute.'

ROUND FIVE

'Are you starting to feel the pace now?'

'Yes but I was having a little success and occasionally hurting him so it gave me the incentive to carry on.'

'Had he hurt you yet?'

'Only with the shot that burst the ear drum.'

I wince and try to talk about something else, 'What does your mother think of you fighting?'

'She was actually there that night. She didn't want to miss my world title shot. I think she took the defeat quite hard.'

'It must be difficult to watch somebody hitting your child.'

'I suppose so. The only thing that was going through my mind was, "I need to beat this man and I can do it!" I know that when I hit someone I can hurt them. And I tend to be quite a good finisher.'

'His punches don't look particularly hurtful, I say. 'Although I'm obviously not the one taking them.'

'Yes but it's the cumulative effect. The gloves are important here. He wears Rival gloves and they're very compact. And I usually wear Grant gloves which are a puncher's glove and slightly bigger so that you can get more wrapping around your hands. Sometimes when a glove is too tight it can make your hand go numb.'

ROUND SIX

We watch as Chudinov continues to up the tempo. Frank is visibly tiring now. His face is marking up and more of his opponent's punches are getting through Frank's guard.

'That's looks painful,' I say.

'Not really. You take a shot and you deal with it. You try to have your chin down so you take them all on the forehead.

If you take an uppercut to the nose you can feel that a little bit more. Body shots can hurt and sometimes you get a thumb in the eye.'

'But he wasn't dirty?'

'No, not at all. Just businesslike. I'm kind of the same really. I just get on with the job. I don't really enjoy gamesmanship.'

'It seems like you're suddenly getting a second wind.'

We look on as Frank finally gets his turn to land a few punches. Then, as the bell to end the round sounds, Frank suddenly connects with a booming right hand and the Russian hits the canvas hard. The crowd are screaming as the referee steps in to separate the fighters.

A moment or two later he indicates to the ringside judges that two points are to be deducted from Frank's score[76]. The referee clearly believes that Frank landed his punch after the bell.

I rewind the YouTube video. Frank and I review the action meticulously. It's arguable but fairly clear to me that Frank's knockout punch landed exactly *on* the bell. The sound of bell can still be heard as the punch connected. Deducting two points from his score was extremely harsh, bordering on unfair.

'Towards the end of this I landed a few shots and it spurred me on,' says Frank. 'It would have been nice if I'd landed that punch 20 or 30 seconds before the bell. We might be sitting down having a different conversation right now.'

'His recovery was superhuman,' I say, as Chudinov instantaneously springs to his feet, apparently fresh as a daisy.

....

76 In boxing the winner of a round is usually awarded 10 points and the loser 9. If a boxer has enjoyed a particularly large advantage during a round, or has knocked his opponent down he will be awarded 10 points and his opponent 8. For infractions such as illegal or late punches, incessant holding or other unlawful activities a boxer may have one or more points deducted from his end of round score, as in this case.

'He bounced back didn't he?' says Frank. 'And I thought it was a bit unfair taking two points off me because it was on the bell. And it was only because I dropped him. It shouldn't make a difference.'

'I agree – it's very, very harsh.'

'So you know with two points gone it's Goodnight Vienna,' says Frank. 'If the referee hadn't have done that it would have been a 10-8 round to me. Instead it's a 10-7 round to him – that's a five-point swing.'

ROUND SEVEN

Now it's Frank's turn to attack. With Chudinov still shaky on his feet Frank throws punch after punch at his opponent in an effort to end the fight.

'You're obviously tiring,' I say. 'But the adrenaline is keeping you going.'

'Yeah. I'm thinking if I'm going to win it I better go out and do it now.'

'And you've maybe only got about half a minute before the exhaustion takes over?'

'Yeah. I was kind of winging the hooks in.'

'It's a terrible thing that this half a minute is so crucial to your entire career.'

'Massively, yes.'

And even as we speak Frank's punches are becoming slower. His arms suddenly look as if they have lead weights tied to them. Conversely, Chudinov seems to finding a new lease of life. The pendulum has swung.

'I put so much into that first 30 seconds to try and hurt him and tired myself out,' explains Frank. 'That's when his shots start to really tell.'

'At this point in the fight was there any strategy left at all?'

'Yes, I was trying to fight in bursts but they weren't frequent enough or long enough to have any telling effect. And Chudinov tended to win the rounds because he was consistently on me all the time. In order to win I had to put my level above his and I couldn't do that.'

ROUND EIGHT

As the bell for round eight sounds I leave the room for a few moments and Sofia conveniently appears from nowhere.

'Hi, you okay? Recovered now?' I hear Frank ask. 'What a terrible incident!'

I return and put my arms around her shoulders before introducing the pair.

'She's tall now,' I say. 'She going to be a big one.'

'That's probably what caused the illness,' says Frank. 'When you've had a growth spurt your immune system is weak. All your energy goes into growing.'

'I didn't think about that,' I say.

'A lot of young athletes get injuries and illnesses because they're training all the time and it's too much stress.'

'That's an interesting theory.'

'When I was about 12 or 13 I had bouts of glandular fever every time I got taller. The specialist said that it was because I was weak. But there's a few things you can do to boost it: Carrot and ginger juices… Manuka honey… Echinacea… Garlic.'

I point Sofia's head towards the iPad screen. 'We're watching Frank fight,' I softly say. 'Wanna see?'

'Getting banged up,' says Frank grimly.

'Frank is fighting for the world title – can you believe that?' I tell Sofia. 'I don't know if you like boxing, do you?'

'I don't know,' Sofia replies dryly.

ROUND NINE

It's more of the same for Frank now. Monotonously more of the same. The Russian's piston-like punches never stopping. Frank retreating, attempting to connect but never quite managing it with any real authority.

I feel guilty for putting Frank through this.

'I remember at the end of the ninth coming back to the corner and Steve saying, "Only three more rounds!" recalls Frank. 'And I was thinking, "Three more rounds? It seems like a lifetime!"'

'He can't win it on the cards now,' says the commentator. 'He's got to knock him out!'

ROUND TEN

Round ten begins and the pattern of the preceding rounds continues. It's barely worth mentioning what's happening on screen right now so we talk about Frank's training methods instead and proceeds to give me a detailed explanation of the training model that he adheres to. In this model the brain is made up of three parts: the first governs automatic functions; the second controls ego and emotions; and the third concerns the logical functions of the brain.

'When you're training obviously you do things over and over again,' says Frank. 'These are automatic thoughts and functions. When you go into a fight you want to run off your instinct, because it's so much quicker. It's something like ten, 20 times faster than human thought.

'If someone throws a jab and you think to yourself, "Okay, jab coming, catch it, block it, throw a counter!" then you've already been hit three or four times. But if you don't even think about it and just react instinctively – that's your instinct at work.'

'That's very interesting,' I say. 'Do you think all boxers do this?'

'Yes. To get to the top level of any sport you need to rely more and more on your instinct. And to have a good funct-ioning instinct you need to do the practise.'

'But are other fighters consciously aware of this? Do they think about this like you do?'

'Maybe not. They probably just do it automatically. When

your emotions kicks in you'll be thinking, "I'm under pressure here! It's getting too hard! Let's quit! Let's quit!" So it's down to your logical functions to override it, to say "No, I've trained too hard for this!" And then your reason and logic will kick in.'

Frank tells me about how he visited a psychologist prior to the fight, about how he uses hypnosis and visualisation techniques.

'Because of this I went into the trenches a hundred times before I fought Chudinov,' he says. 'In my head I'd already beaten him so many times. When I was in the ring this is what drove me on.'

'Unfortunately I guess all of this must cost you money,' I say.

'Of course – it cost a small fortune,' says Frank. 'But what I learned leading up to this fight is an education for life. Everything I've learned about how to fight and deal with copious amounts of stress and pressure. After a fight like this everything else is a walk in their park.'

ROUND ELEVEN

'We're having a trade-off,' says Frank to Sofia as the three of us grimly watch him continue to lose the fight. 'And he seems to be getting the better of it.'

'You're really tired, aren't you,' I say.

'Yes, I am but I'm still thinking about trying to land and hurt him.'

'Did you think by this stage that you'd lost the fight?'

'No. I still thought there was a chance.'

'How do you feel about seeing yourself looking so tired on-screen?' I ask.

'It's not a shock really. I *was* exhausted.'

We watch as Chudinov connects with a hard looking uppercut.

'That looked like it might have hurt,' I groan.

'Yeah,' smiles Frank.

'It's good that you're laughing about these things.'

ROUND 12

The bell rings for the final round and it's no use pretending that the fight was even close. Even Sofia standing quietly beside us can see that.

'At this stage you must have known that you'd lost,' I say.

'Yes. I was a little bit spaced out. That's a good description,' says Frank. 'It was an exhausting fight and you don't always think clearly afterwards. There was a lot of things jumping around my head: I was disappointed with the two-point deduction, although it wouldn't have made any difference to the result of the fight.'

'You don't seem to be angry about that decision,' I say. 'A lot of people would be very bitter about it.'

'No. Anger doesn't really come into it. It's not in my emotions,' says Frank. 'It was an honour to be fighting for the world title. A great experience. A great achievement. I just want to move on to better things.'

'What do you think was the main difference between you and Chudinov?' I ask.

'Well he just didn't expend any unnecessary energy,' says Frank. 'He'd obviously trained so long on the bags that his muscle memory could punch all day. He just let them flow naturally.

'I've learned a lot from him. Rather than fighting in bursts that use 100 per cent of your energy I'm going to drop it right down to about 87 per cent, which is still going to do a lot of damage, but is more sustainable.'

Frank talks about his plan to fight at a heavier weight and how it's going to help him. 'Give me another four years,' he says.

I offer him an unprovoked suggestion, 'My feeling is that what needs to happen…'

'…Is that somebody gives me an iron bar?'

'…Is that a big name is fighting and his opponent pulls out

and they bring you in at the last minute.'

'Yes. Course.'

'You need a big name,' I tell him. 'You need a big win. You must have thought that yourself?'

'Yes. But I'm happy to take my time. Rebuild. Go and do some very high quality sparring.'

* * * * *

I thank Frank for his generosity. I tell him that hopefully there will come a time when he can return to my kitchen and together we can watch him win that elusive world title.

'That's why I'm here and why I speak to you so often because I respect what you do,' says Frank. 'And I've got a lot of trust in you.'

'Well that's very nice of you.'

'If not I'll have to send someone round.'

'Do you see that Sofia?' I say. 'Somebody who finally respects what I do... We should have him stuffed.'

Supertent

SINCE my reunion with Michael Watson late last year at that pub tribute in Ware I've been harbouring another guilty conscience. I can feel myself blushing every time I think about my drunken behaviour that night. It was not what you would call one of my finest hours. It didn't exactly help matters that I texted Michael's friend and carer, Lennie Ballack, the morning after my stellar performance, with throbbing head, only to receive no response. A further text that I sent to Lennie on New Year's Day also met with a similar reaction. Finally, a third message sent two weeks later was greeted with yet more unremitting silence. I could only conclude that my whopping size 11s had definitely stomped on the wrong feet that night. It had taken me more than two decades to get back in touch with a man who had once meant so much to me and I'd managed to alienate him in just a couple of hours.

But I try once again. For some reason I try. More than five months after my emotional meeting with Michael I call Lennie once more. This time, however, I get through straight away and I'm relieved to hear the pleasure in Lennie's voice when I let him know who he's speaking to. He explains how he lost his phone soon after meeting me and has been waiting for me to call. He tells me that Michael keeps asking about me. And he's lavish with his compliments: he calls me a 'great writer', 'the man', a 'legend'. It's a little over the top – a lot over the top actually. And my spider-sense is immediately tingling. But at least it looks like I'm off the hook.

I don't need to tell you that I'm taken aback by Lennie's extravagant praise. I'm none of these things. Obviously I'm not. To paraphrase the great boxing writer Bert Randolph Sugar: I'm not even a household name in my own household. I'm perplexed. Surely Lennie must be confusing me with someone else? Either that or he's trying to make me feel good about myself and has simply misjudged the quantity of his flattery.

* * * * *

The three of us arrange to meet for lunch in a restaurant in London's Stoke Newington and for once I'm actually late. Ordinarily, as I'm sure you're gratingly aware of by now, this would bring me out in hives but on this occasion I'm strangely relaxed. This could be because I'm nowhere near as late as Michael. When I finally catch sight of him coming through the door, however, it's easy to understand why he might have trouble adhering to anything so straightforward as a schedule.

As he was last time that I saw him, Michael is walking unsteadily behind his friend Lennie, one hand on the other man's shoulder. Michael's footsteps are slow and measured, always, it seems to me, on the brink of disaster. His glasses hide whatever expression might be on his face but straight away I'm left wondering what it must be like to have to endure such indignity for someone whose physicality was once such an essential part of his being. It's hard to imagine what he is thinking: after almost 25 years of this has he grown used to having to rely on another for such a simple, everyday task as walking? Or is it still an endless cause of heartache, a daily reminder of all that boxing has taken from him?

I climb to my own feet and move towards the door. We embrace. Michael wraps his arms around me and I wrap mine around him. Like Cathy and Heathcliff. I can feel his body heat. I can smell his aftershave. We stay locked in this position for a long time, for too long. For so long that the handful of people in the restaurant stop eating and stare towards us in puzzlement. I feel my hug become desperate, as if I'm trying to squeeze away a quarter of a century of mistakes. Because mistake is the word that I cannot exorcise from my mind. Mistake. Error. Mistake. There's is nothing I can think of that is more appropriate to what I'm feeling.

I finally let Michael go and place an arm around his shoulders so that I can help him to the table. On shaky legs he finds a seat; nothing at all seems to be easy for Michael. Lennie goes to find a parking space, leaving me alone with his best friend. We gaze into each other's eyes in a manner that we never used to all those years ago when everything seemed to be moving too fast to take a breath. Michael holds my hand in his big, meaty fingers. He is generous and unreserved with his emotions, almost as if his injury has set something inside him free. He tells me he loves me and, even though I've a hunch that this might be a phrase that leaves his lips at least once or twice a day to a wide range of recipients it is enough to make the tears flow.

I lower my head and dab at the corners of my eyes with the tips of my fingers. 'I'm sorry,' I stutter. 'I get very emotional these days. It's since I had a kid... Since she was born everything seems to make me cry.'

But that's a stock phrase I often use and it's only partially true, particularly right now. Because sitting here in this anonymous café with an ex-boxer named Michael Watson is already too much for me to deal with. I look at his face and see it super-imposed over the face of the beautiful, streamlined boxer that I used to know. I see the hunched, rounded shoulders across from me and imagine somewhere inside him the athlete's body of long ago, not an inch of fat covering his superbly defined abdominal muscles. I remember I once touched those muscles, it must have been not long before his fight with Nigel Benn in 1989. They felt as if they were carved from alabaster.

Here is the living, breathing embodiment of everything I have ever done wrong in my life. This is what I'm thinking as Michael's soft features re-arrange themselves into a smile. His affection is unrestrained but I'm conscious that I have no right for him to be smiling at me. I simply do not deserve it. There is nothing I will ever to be able to do to make things better. In the quiet of the afternoon, amid the gentle chimes of knives and forks, I yet again attempt to explain my absence from his life this past quarter of a century.

I tell him once more about visiting him in hospital the night after his injury, as if repeating this anecdote will somehow erase my mistakes. But he stops me, 'It's not an injury,' he says. 'It's an accident.'

I remind him again about how I was warned off that night by one of his friends, implying that but for this I would surely have been there for him. And then I look down at the table and apologise for not being there. Just like the one I recently made to Derek Williams, it's a long overdue apology that I am ashamed to be making.

'Don't worry about it,' says Michael, matter of factly. 'I just thought you were a busy man.'

The combination of my defective hearing – yet another symptom of my malfunctioning thyroid – and Michael's difficulty in speaking makes for a troublesome couple of hours. When Lennie joins us at the table I notice how he will automatically sense when Michael's words are in need of clarification and subtly step in to help his friend. Also apparent is Lennie's habit of assuming control whenever relatively complex sentences are called for. He does this instinctively – he's had 24 years of practise.

Later, while Lennie is ordering at the bar, I tell Michael of my admiration for his friend. I tell him that Lennie deserves some form of recognition. That in an ideal world he should get an MBE or a CBE or whatever it is they give to saints, pop singers and crooked bankers these days. Michael grows visibly excited at these words, 'Tell him what you just said to me,' he announces eagerly when Lennie returns to the table.

We talk about old times. Naturally we do. And Michael's disappointment about the way things have turned out becomes apparent. Although there genuinely appears to be not a trace of bitterness about his condition, Michael feels increasingly let down by the people who surrounded him. He reels off a long litany of names, including former managers, promoters and other random associates. It's the sort of list that could easily bankrupt the publisher of this book and is marked not by frustration but by anger at what could have been.

Although Michael holds no animosity towards Chris Eubank, the man who delivered the blow that had such a devastating impact upon his life, he remains adamant that he won their first encounter in June of 1991, three months prior to the accident. Indeed, in domestic boxing that disputed points loss remains to this day one of the most hotly debated talking points of the past few decades. 'If I hadn't lost that fight,' says Michael, 'there would have been no need for a rematch… And no need for this.' He points a finger towards his head.

I tell him about how I've returned to writing about boxing, and about my decision to try to meet up with people from my past after all these years. The pair listen to my words respectfully and when I finish speaking they thank me for my openness. I tell them they have nothing whatsoever to thank me for.

Then Lennie moves on to what might be the real reason for wanting to meet me today. He explains that somebody recently contacted Michael wishing to make a movie about his life. Although this didn't end up happening, they think that I might be able to help. They also want to sell Michael's story to a newspaper for a 'lot of money' and think that I might be the man to get this done.

I'm confused again. 'Things must be bad if you're pinning your hopes on me,' I joke. Except I'm not really joking. The earnest look on both of their faces, however, forces me to take their words seriously.

I tell the two men that they are in a chicken and egg situation: that in order to have a movie made about him Michael would need to radically increase his public profile; and that in order to get a lot of money for a story in a national newspaper he would have something very controversial to say for himself, or at least have something in the pipeline, such as a movie, for example. My words are greeted with ill-concealed disappointment but Michael grasps my hands tightly again and tells me that I'm now a member of 'Team Michael'. He says that he wants to produce a second autobiography[77] and that I should write it.

And then the pair move on to their idea for buying an empty building in Stoke Newington and converting it into a gym for underprivileged youngsters. I tell them that this is altogether more achievable, and ask if they have looked into the idea of applying for a lottery grant. This seems to turn a light on in their eyes and the conversation accordingly brightens.

Lennie leaves the table and for the second time I'm left alone with Michael. I pull out my iPhone and show him a picture I took a few days earlier of the 12in scar on Herol Graham's stomach. Michael looks shocked at the image and stares at it for a few moments open-mouthed. 'I love Herol,' he says. 'And I love you too.'

Apparently word has gotten around the notoriously incestuous boxing community of my multiple visits to the stricken fighter. Michael stares into my eyes and, just as he did when I was first reunited with him months earlier, he tells me that I have 'the spirit' in me. Once more I tell him that I'm

77 **Steve Bunce** born 3 December 1962, London, England. Journalist and broadcaster.

not religious and again he responds by assuring me that he, too, is not. 'I don't believe in organised religion,' he says. 'Just Jesus Christ.'

I change the subject and tell Michael about how many damaged boxers I've met in the past few months. About how scarcely any of them seem to have escaped their past without suffering some form of depression. Michael's eyes widen when I tell him about Herol's attempted suicide.

'He's a damaged person,' I say.

'He was abused as a child,' says Michael.

'Yes, I know.'

'I always thought that you were damaged,' he continues.

'Really?' I say, genuinely surprised. Not by the fact that he might have sensed this, but that he remembers sensing it.

And then it's Michael's turn to change the subject, 'You know I had a seizure before Christmas?' he says without warning.

'Yes, I heard,' I nod.

'I went to the gym for the first time in years and I overdid it,' Michael continues. 'I started sweating and I should have stopped.'

'I saw it on YouTube,' I say. 'Everything anybody does that's related to boxing is on YouTube these days.'

Then we talk about Glyn Leach, the editor of *Boxing Monthly*, my one-time colleague who suffered a seizure in 2013 and then tragically died several months later. He was only 54. 'You have to be careful with seizures,' I advise him, somewhat blithely.

'Yes, I know.'

Finally, I ask Michael Watson the question that I have been avoiding all afternoon. 'Have you heard from Eric?' I ask.

No surname is needed. We both immediately know that I'm referring to Michael's former trainer Eric Seccombe, the part-time taxi driver who was at once father, trainer and life mentor to Watson when I first met the boxer in Islington in the mid-1980s. When I had mentioned Seccombe's name at the Nigel Benn tribute dinner last October I had been discouraged by Michael's reaction. On that occasion it was as if a switch had been turned off inside the boxer, leading me to believe that something must have happened between the two that had irreparably damaged their relationship. Nothing unusual in boxing.

'You know that he was at ringside for the second Eubank fight?' I say.

'Was he?' says Michael, surprised.

'He was crying when you got carried out of the ring.'

'Was he?' Michael repeats, before staring wistfully into the distance as if overcome by emotion.

'I'm amazed that you don't know that,' I add.

'No I didn't,' says Michael sadly shaking his head, the first time I've seen a hint of sadness in his eyes all afternoon. 'I'd love to see Eric.' He stares into the distance sadly.

Back at the end of the1980s, Eric was in his mid-to-late-50s. He was a small, stout figure, not much more than five feet in height, I'd guess. Everybody who met the quietly spoken trainer liked him immediately. In the often cruel world of boxing he was a beacon of kindness. 'He'll be in his 80s by now,' I say.

'Will he?' say Michael and Lennie – now back at the table – in unison, both hoodwinked by the passage of time.

* * * * *

I leave Michael and Lennie and head off to my daughter's parents' evening. Lennie escorts me to a nearby taxi firm and as we walk I tell him that I'll try and see if I can track Eric down. While I wait for the cab to arrive I watch from afar as Lennie leads Michael to his car. Once again progress is painful: Michael unsteadily holding on to his friend's shoulder as if his life depended on it. But then something remarkable happens, something magical. The sound of laughter suddenly fills the air as without warning Michael climbs on to his toes and starts to aim jabs at his friend. Lennie drops into a crouch and throws his own mock punches in response. The two men giggle, unaware that they are being watched. And then Michael raises his arms to his face and ducks forward in a crab-like stance.

For a few brief moments I'm watching Michael Watson fight Nigel Benn. I'm in a supertent in Finsbury Park and thousands of people are cheering. Michael's bearing, his body language, exactly recalls that night. It's eerie and sad and uplifting. I could easily be dreaming this but I'm not. This is really happening. I want to go back to that night. I want to be who I was then. I want Michael to be who he was.

* * * * *

When I get home I put out an APB: on Facebook Ben Doughty asks if any of 'the brethren' knows Eric's whereabouts. After several days of silence Ben gets back to me. His friend, media personality and sometime boxing promoter Spencer Fearon, has a lead. Spencer puts me in touch with another ex-boxer named Jason Matthews, who claims to have Eric's number but the trail runs dry. Eric seems to have disappeared off the face of the earth.

Then I have a thought. Eric, I recall, had at least a couple of children. I can remember seeing grandchildren when I used to visit Eric's small council flat in Islington. I contact Lennie and get their names. One of them is called Terry, which is quite unusual because this person happens to be female. After only a cursory search on Facebook I find her. When I scan through her posts there is a picture of her standing beside her older but still very much alive father. I message Terry and wait for a response.

Stare

I WISH *people would leave Jesus alone.* This is the thought that strikes me as I wait in line to steal a few moments from the busy life of a former professional boxer whose nickname used to be 'The Dark Destroyer'. *I'm sure Jesus has got plenty of other things to worry about.*

I'm standing in the ornate surroundings of Trinity House near Tower Bridge in London. Paintings of Prince Philip, of Earl Mountbatten, of Charles I hang from the walls overlooking a rather gaudy and grandiose screen that has been erected in the centre of the room proclaiming 'Conor Benn' in big white letters in a font that is designed to mimic, one assumes, street graffiti. Conor Benn: given name of the son of the man who is currently telling a small digital camera that he has recently discovered Jesus. Conor Benn: 19-year-old offspring of Nigel Benn, of whom there are great expectations.

For me it's the climax of an impossibly uncomfortable morning. Standing here awaiting my turn gives me plenty of time to think about the events that led me to be here. The morning, of course, begins with my customary struggle to find the venue. It's embarrassing to keep admitting this but, yes, I am once again half an hour early even after being dragged hither and thither by my misfiring sat nav. My discomfort at standing outside the venue aiming inane small talk at the shaven heads and muscles guarding the entrance is exacerbated by the appearance of Johnny Nelson[78], who does rather a good job of blanking me. 'I thought you were going to nick my sandwich,' he says in his northern accent, eyes stubbornly pointed towards the pavement, before racing away at a pace far greater than any he ever used to achieve inside the ropes when he was the WBO cruiserweight champion of the world for a record-breaking 14 fights.

I could be imagining things but he refuses to meet my eye. It could be that he really does not remember who I am. That's entirely possible. After all, I did not see him for more than two decades until I bumped into him back in 2014 and shared lengthy reminiscences at the funeral of *Boxing Monthly* editor Glyn Leach. It could also be that he doesn't much care for me – it wouldn't be the first time. But I don't think that's the case.

When Herol Graham recently fell seriously ill we exchanged a number of Twitter DMs. He knew who I was then. He asked for and I gave him the address of the hospital. For whatever reason he never arrived and this is why, the most cynical part of me is thinking, that Johnny is so unwilling to engage me in conversation. I could be wrong. I hope I'm wrong. And if I am I'll go down on my knees and beg his forgiveness; I'll present *Match of the Day* in my vest and underpants.

Inside the venue are rows of elegant chairs set before a table festooned with mikes and the obligatory drinking water. Possibly increasing Nelson's discomfort, I take a seat directly behind him. Again, I might be imagining things, but he scrupulously manages to avoid turning in my direction for the full hour or so of what transpires.

Another press conference. That is the reason I am here. I'm at my second press conference in a week and already

78 **Johnny Nelson** born 4 January 1967, Sheffield, England. Former British and EBU cruiserweight champion; WBO cruiserweight champion of the world.

there are a few familiar faces leaping out at me. I watch as a journalist from, I think, the *Daily Mail*, swans into the room stonily shaking a few hands as if it's something he's expected to do. I see the photographer Lawrence Lustig circling the room. Years ago when I regularly attended press conferences I never actually managed to speak to this diminutive photographer, and I guess I never will. I see a few other old faces. I don't remember their names and I'm keeping so far out of sight that they won't get the chance to remember mine. Then Nigel Benn walks in.

What is it about Benn that makes me dislike him so much? My eyes follow his progress through the room. He is wearing a cream suit that isn't quite a suit. The trousers are a semitone lighter than the jacket. On his feet are gold shoes that surely only someone with a certain opinion of themselves would be comfortable wearing. He sports a cream waistcoat. There's nothing in the manner in which he dresses that should elicit my dislike, but it's there, lurking away. I watch as he shakes the hand of the aforementioned Lustig and shares, presumably, some well-worn yarn from eons gone by.

Then I see the photographer take something out of the bag he is carrying. An item of clothing. A jacket. He unfurls it and begins to force his arms through the sleeves. I've seen such a thing before. It is the team jacket of the grandly named World Sports Corporation, a promotional outfit headed by Ambrose Mendy back in the late 1980s when he was still on friendly terms with Benn, along with business partner Frank Maloney when he was still on friendly terms with his masculinity.

The jacket is shabby and crinkled. It's interesting to see such a curio but it brings a tear to the eye of nobody present here. It is a spandex reminder of equally shabby and crinkled bygone days. Best put back in Lustig's bag.

I watch as Benn makes his way slowly to where I am seated. A handshake for someone. A kiss for somebody else. A man hug and a joke for Johnny Nelson. And then he spies me and

I'm surprised to be holding his hand in mine for the first time in 29 years. On the last occasion – ringside at some long-forgotten fight – Benn had greeted my handshake with the words, ''Ere – ain't you got small hands!' And even though I'm sure my hands are pretty much the same size as they always were I only get an 'all right?' for my troubles this time. 'Fine thanks,' I reply, lowering my voice in, one assumes, an attempt to sound tougher. 'How are you?' Benn walks on by. He hasn't got a clue who I am. Understandably so. Neither have I for that matter.

Benn-the-Elder continues to circumnavigate the room. A high-five for Alan Minter and his son Ross, both appearing from nowhere in the manner of pilot fish. Another handshake and a very long conversation with *Sun* doyen Colin Hart, surely a fine example of a boxing oxymoron if ever there was one. And then Benn Jr arrives. Although he shares some of the facial characteristics of his father, Conor Benn's features and general demeanour appear on first impressions to be unsuitable to the career on which he is about to embark. When you met Nigel at around the same age there was never any doubt that his face fitted his profession as surely as his giant fists fitted his gloves. Here I find myself wondering. Conor's skin is tanned rather than 'Dark'. His face is thin and sensitive, not so much 'Destroyer' as debater. When he speaks he is polite and articulate and gentle. The nickname 'Tanned Debater' is, however, unlikely to be such a ticket seller as the one adopted by his father. I instantly warm to Conor in a way that I never did with his father. Possibly not a good omen for his ring career methinks.

The room begins to fill up. Among the one or two faces from my past there are several dozen that I have never seen before. Black faces outnumber white by a possible ratio of three to one. Digital phones with audio recording apps outnumber pencil and notebook by a probable ratio of 100 to one. I have such a device myself. I switch it on.

Conor and Nigel sit at the main table occasionally blinking at the clicks and twinkling flashes of the photographers. Sandwiched between them is Eddie Hearn, son of promoter Barry Hearn. It is the first time I have been in his presence, although I have been forewarned as to what to expect. 'Tall, handsome and charming' is how my wife described him to me when he recently visited the offices of the company she works for, who, by coincidence happened to sponsor Eddie and his father's company Matchroom Sport. I could not have put it better myself.

Hearn confidently mouths the introductions. He is slick and cocksure; he reminds me of a prime TV chat show host. His Colgate smile could not be whiter. His haircut could not be more just so. His charm could not be easier. If it wasn't for the Essex brogue we could easily be looking at a future candidate for the American presidency. Then he gestures towards Nigel Benn. Somehow he manages to gesture perfectly too.

There is a sense of expectation in the room as Benn Sr theatrically clears his throat. Then a long uncomfortable silence. People start to turn and look at each other, wondering what is about to happen next. Finally it dawns on the room that he is about to cry. And cry he does. Nigel Benn is having a good old cry. He's worse than me. At last a reason for my dislike of the former knockout specialist. For despite the obvious emotive qualities of the occasion – a 'legendary warrior' passing the torch to his chip off the old block no less – there is nothing that will ever convince me that Benn's tears are anything other than of the crocodile variety. To my mind he's hamming it up. But give him his due: he serves up top quality ham. Nothing tinned here. He knows how to pluck away at those ol' heart strings. He's a Grade 8 plucker. In tomorrow's red tops more than one journo will lead with those tears.

What follows is a lengthy, meandering monologue from Benn. He tells the story of how he sparred with his son three years ago and 'broke his nose' and 'chipped a tooth' (has Australia never heard of the CSA?), and of how his son later returned in time-honoured Rocky Balboa fashion to exact his revenge by giving his old man what for. He remembers the occasion when he learned that Conor had been bullied and of how he proceeded to trawl the streets searching for the perpetrator only to discover that his son had actually been fibbing, that Benn Jr himself had initiated the violence. Cute. 'Yeah but did you beat him up?' Benn recalls asking, before colourfully demonstrating his relief and/or pride at his son's response with a loud yelp of triumph.

Yet despite myself I can't help but smile at these little fairy tales. Somehow they are sweet. Physically assaulting your son in any other walk of life would surely be evidence of criminal psychosis, as would encouraging your child to assault other children. But this is boxing. Of course it's boxing. And boxing has its own set of rules that set it apart from society. And although Benn's anecdotes may or may not be true this is beside the point. This is boxing: a pastime built upon deception from the foundations up. When even the boxing ring itself is actually square it is wise to take everything you are henceforth told about the sport with a pinch of smelling salts.

Occasionally, Conor will have the temerity to attempt to make his own contribution to the proceedings but his efforts are good-naturedly and methodically swept aside by his father. 'This is about you, not me,' says Benn Sr on more than one occasion. But it's clear to all that it's not. Benn Sr's good at this. An expert. He has the haggle of journalists and social mediatricians in the palm of his fist. He whoops and cries and sobs and shrugs and smiles and winks likes Olivier in *Richard III*. Like Robin Williams voicing Aladdin. 'Don't worry,' he reassures his son, not even pretending to conceal his accomplished array of PR talents. 'You'll get used to these. It'll be like water off a duck's back.'

The press conference judders to a halt. In four days' time Conor is making his professional boxing debut on the undercard of the Anthony Joshua-Charles Martin IBF heavyweight title fight at the O2 in Greenwich. He will be fighting someone from Bulgaria known as Ivailo Boyanov; it's safe to say that if I was a betting man I'd put a couple of quid on my mother-in-law giving Boyanov a decent argument should they ever meet in the ring. But the real battle, however, is about to begin right here. To a man the press observers leap to their feet and scurry towards their quarry. First to reach Benn senior is a television crew. A disorderly scrum forms around a seated Conor.

I find myself standing next to the journalist from, I believe, the *Daily Mail* whom I noticed earlier on. I can't for the life of me remember his name so I sneakily Google it on my phone. 'How are you Jeff?' I say eventually.

The man turns toward me, a look of utter disdain on his face. 'Don't call me Jeff!' he spits. 'I hate Jeff!'

He turns away in disgust and I offer an apology. 'We met at Glyn Leach's funeral,' is my flustered explanation, letting him know my name.

He looks at me again and his face softens. 'It's Gareth not Jeff,' he says, and then, 'Yes, I remember. You've written a few great books.'

I apologise again for getting his name wrong and mumble a grateful thank-you for the unexpected compliment.

'It's just that I hate Jeff,' he continues. 'Jeff is a liar!'

* * * * *

Things move at a pace that would frustrate a paraplegic snail. People are taking far too long to interview the Benn clan. Journalists petulantly snap at each other and stamp on one another's toes. It's as if someone has fed the kids coffee in the queue for Santa's Christmas Grotto. I decide to give up on Benn Jr. In truth, other than to wish him well, I have no real reason to speak to him. So I nervously shuffle towards his father and stake my tentative claim.

A tall black man with a video camera is questioning Nigel Benn. I listen as he talks about finding Jesus, about how he smoked throughout his career – Benn not Jesus – about how he is a better and fitter fighter nowadays than he was back then – Jesus not Benn. That such an array of statements stretches the bounds of plausibility to breaking point is largely irrelevant to both perpetrator and victim of these colourful pronouncements. Everybody present here today is aware of this. But the pressure to provide precious content for the butter mountain of media outlets that need to attract mouse clicks or finger-pokes is clearly etched upon everybody's faces.

It seems that everyone here has their own radio show, or their own YouTube channel, or their own TV show on some faceless digital channel. Further evidence, if any were needed, that the proliferation of digital data currently available to anybody who possesses a touch screen only succeeds in undermining anything of any relative substance. Content and information are so readily available that they no longer have any value. Stories are like salmon swimming upstream: pluck one out and it looks very much like the one before it; and the one after.

It's noticeable that the only people not queueing to get a tiny little piece of a Benn of some description are the handful of old timers; fingers still smelling of newsprint. They stand talking amongst themselves on the peripheries, toothless old lions waiting for any scraps that might be left on the carcass once the feeding frenzy is over.

For some reason I move over to Colin Hart. He looks older and, if he could remember who I am, I'm sure he would think that I look older too. I tell him he hasn't changed a bit, as I'm learning one is expected to do. I remind him that the very first story I ever had published in a Sunday newspaper went out under his byline. 'In those days they'd put my name to any old crap,' he says, oozing charm. Nice to see you again too.

I decide to use a little muscle. If you can't beat them, beat them. I discreetly shoulder my way to the front of a throng of jostling journos. I get angry glares from a few of them but I puff out my chest and pretend not to notice. I wait for five... ten... 15 minutes while Nigel Benn grunts and heaves his way through his 20th or 30th monologue of the last half-hour. *Yes... I've heard that you've discovered Jesus... Yes ... I know that you used to take drugs... Yes... I'm aware that you once attempted suicide... Hang on a minute... I actually didn't know that...* Apparently, announces Benn, he once locked himself inside a car and tried to finish himself off with a combination of carbon monoxide poisoning and pills. That's what you call a belt and braces approach.

It's not funny, I know that, and I don't doubt the sincerity of Benn's words, but is there an ex-boxer around who has *not* tried to end it all with an overdose? This is what I'm becoming increasingly aware of. I'm surprised that the sport isn't sponsored by Nurofen.

Forgive me that one, won't you? Because I'm getting weary standing in this line and my frustration is in overdrive and this is not how I remember press conferences and I'm relieved that but for this brief sojourn I'm no longer a part of it.

Somebody nearby is complaining about the duration of Benn's current interview. A baby-faced press officer in a grey jacket shrugs his shoulders and advises him to button it – his mouth, not the jacket. Standing shoulder to shoulder with me, another tall black man is chewing his lip. I ask him who he works for and he mumbles something about William Hill. He doesn't want to talk to me and I don't really want to talk to him. But when you are close enough to taste the Polo mint the other person is sucking it is difficult to avoid at least a cursory attempt at verbal communication. Then – at last – it is my turn.

STARE

I hoist myself in front of Benn and he slowly runs a pair
of unblinking eyes over me, not in an unfriendly way as it
happens. But I'm suddenly overcome with a rush of nervous
energy and when my voice finally surfaces it is weak and
shaky. I find myself experiencing feelings of inadequacy which
I can find no real reason for. In the past I've shared time with
boxers of a similar stature to the erstwhile Dark Destroyer –
even Muhammad Ali if you will allow me to name drop – and
usually had very little problem being myself.

But Benn does something strange to me. We have weird
chemistry. He sets my teeth on edge. Damp patches form
around my armpits. The top of my head begins to sweat. I
have an over-powering urge to break wind. I'm frightened
of him. That's it. Frightened. He scares me. There's no
rational reason why this is happening but happen it does, in
a primeval kind of way that I can no more control than I can
prevent the hairs on my arms standing on end when I listen to
a particularly moving piece of music or stop the goosebumps
from puckering when I see an old family photograph that
evokes aching nostalgia. And although I'm perfectly aware
that there is zero chance that Benn will suddenly tear off
his cream not-quite-a-suit to reveal black Dark Destroyer
shorts and slashing fists, there is something about him that
makes me struggle in a way that is beyond my control or
comprehension.

I offer a brief introduction, feeble in its execution: I
remind him about the ring entrance music that he used before
his 1989 fight with Michael Watson, an obscure reggae track
by Conroy Smith entitled 'Dangerous'. I tell him how to this
day the memory still chills me to the bone. This seems to spark
some interest in the ex-fighter's eyes. I then tell him that he
won't remember me but we crossed paths a long time ago
and that... He interrupts me, 'You just do what you have to
do, mate,' he says. In other words: *Get the fuck on with it – I'm
a busy man.*

I tell him that I'm going to ask a really stupid question. That we both know what the answer to that question is, but that I want to hear him answer it in his own words.

'Yeah?' he grunts.

'How dangerous do you think boxing is?' I ask.

Time seems to stand still. Benn ceases all movement and locks his eyes on to mine. He stares into me. And he stares… And he stares… His eyes scrutinise the deepest recesses of my soul. It's as if I've just asked him the worse possible question that anybody can ask another human being. He stares… Two seconds go by… Three seconds… Four seconds… Insubstantial time intervals on paper but an indescribably uncomfortable eternity when you have the shaven skull of Nigel Benn poised inches away from your face. He stares… Five seconds go by… Ten seconds go by and still he doesn't answer. Finally, fully 12 seconds after I initially asked the question the former prizefighter at last responds.

'It's dangerous like any sport,' he growls. 'But you get more injuries in football, in car racing than you do in boxing.' Did it really take him that long to come up with this stock response?

But then I get an insight into the reason for the long gap before answering.

'I'm not going to say something and you take it out of context,' he warily announces. 'Boxing's a sport. A contact sport… Martial arts… Rugby… You get more injuries in American football than boxing. All of them sports are dangerous. I'm not going to separate boxing from any other sport.'

Just as I did Steve Collins a few months earlier, I tell Nigel Benn that rugby is more dangerous than boxing in my opinion.

'Absolutely,' he agrees. 'Look at all them cauliflower ears.'

* * * * *

I leave the building feeling depressed and shaken, ashamed of myself, ashamed of the fear that Benn evoked in me, aware that I shouldn't be feeling this way. I was never a great fan of press conferences when it was my job to attend them over a quarter of a century ago. I'm even less so now.

Bone

THREE days after the singer Prince dies I make the short trip to North Finchley to meet a Prince of a different kind. I have ambiguous feelings about what is about to happen: I'm looking forward to meeting Mark Prince because everything I've read him about suggests an inspirational person; and I'm dreading meeting Mark because I sense that I am about to bear witness to a measure of pain that is incomprehensible to most people.

Mark – or Prince, as he prefers to be called – was there at the very start of this journey that I find myself on. Fate had conspired to have us sitting at the same table on the evening that I came face to face with Michael Watson for the first time in close to a quarter of a century. On that night, you might recall, Prince expressed surprise that I didn't know who he was. On face value he appeared to be one of any number of ex-boxers sitting there in that sweaty banqueting hall but now that I've found out more about him I can understand that his incredulity had nothing to do with hubris or conceit. And it is for this reason that I'm secretly pleased that there is no answer when I ring the bell to his office.

Even so, I go through the motions of expressing frustration at our broken meeting: I call his office landline and leave a message. I even ring his mobile. But just as I'm about to hang up Prince answers and in a fractured baritone that is a mixture

198

of broken pause and 'yeh bros!' I'm given some garbled excuse about his dog having a lump on its leg, and his son's trainer dying. And as I listen I find myself relieved that I've managed to avoid coming face to face with Prince. He tells that he'll call me back to arrange another meeting but we both know that he won't.

* * * * *

I've somehow managed to flip on 'do not disturb' mode on my phone, so when Prince calls me back the following afternoon I don't hear it. And several hours have already transpired by the time I finally notice I have a missed call and pick up his voicemail. More out of guilt than anything else I call him back and he tells me that he'll be in his office within the hour if I still want to meet him. I don't really want to do it but I'm nevertheless quickly on the move.

* * * * *

On the doorbell to his office the words 'Kiyan Prince Foundation' are scrawled in biro. And this, more than anything that happens in the next three or four hours, brings home to me the desperate sadness that will always envelop Mark Prince. In the 1990s Prince was a boxer campaigning in the light-heavyweight division. And a good one, too. Good enough to win a trinket called the WBO intercontinental light-heavyweight title in only his 14th fight; talented enough to unsuccessfully attempt to claim a version of the world title in 1998 in only his nineteenth.

For most people exploits such as these would be a story in themselves but in Prince's case they are simply footnotes. For Prince's life took on an indescribably tragic complexion in 2006 when his son Kiyan was fatally stabbed outside the school gates by another schoolboy.

Like many people I can remember the news reports concerning this horrific incident. But there was nothing to correlate the death of Kiyan with the man who shared a dinner table with me back in October. All I remember of the Mark Prince I met that night was a certain intensity, a discernible rage that I assumed was related to the fact that Prince was in the midst of a ring comeback at the age of 44 that had been routinely rejected by the British Boxing Board Of Control. What I didn't know was that Prince was making that comeback as a means of drawing attention to the Kiyan Prince Foundation, a charitable body that the ex-boxer set up in the months that followed his son's murder.

Other than a number of messages that we've exchanged via Facebook, Prince and I have not met since that night. I have, however, been intrigued to watch the videos that he regularly posts which show him talking to groups of mesmerised children in school assembly halls around the country. Prince is very clearly on a mission and a good portion of that intensity I recognised before is still present as we shake hands and climb the stairs to his office. He is a tall, handsome black man whose eyes are alive with energy.

The office of the Kiyan Prince Foundation is small. There is just enough room to fit a couple of desks and three chairs. Every inch of wall space is covered in photographs, mainly snaps of boxers or of Prince posing with various celebrities. On the wall opposite Prince's desk is an image that he must stare at every time he lifts his eyes from his computer screen. A large poster depicts his lost son Kiyan decked out in QPR colours, a football at his feet. Kiyan was a prodigiously talented footballer who was due to sign professional forms with the club. In the picture he looks uncannily like his father. The sadness in the room is palpable. You can breathe it. Taste it. Smell it.

Prince invites me to take a seat opposite him but I move to the one alongside him instead. He asks me why I want to see him. In the almost ten years since Kiyan died Prince must surely have met his fair share of sharks and charlatans. He looks at me with undisguised suspicion as I choose my words very, very carefully. I remind him how we met. I describe my reasons for abandoning boxing and why I've decided to write about it once more. I talk about my father, my depression and my therapist. I'm well practised at doing this now but I'm also ever vigilant that I should tread carefully. Prince is a boxer. He has a boxer's build. His biceps are prominently on display. He is not a man you'd like to pick a fight with. But there is a wholly understandable fragility about him. I have no desire at all to risk adding to his torment.

But it doesn't take long for a light to flicker on in his eyes. The frankness of my words, I think, make him relax. The fact that it transpires that we have a number of mutual acquaintances also brings down his guard a little and he starts to do what all boxers tend to do: he talks about boxing. Initially it's minutiae. Prince describes the early days of sparring with Michael Watson and how Frank Maloney attempted to sign him but when Prince 'didn't get any positive vibes from him' he chose not to go with the diminutive manager.

He talks about how Ambrose Mendy also tried to tempt him. There's a note of resignation in his voice when he tells me he thinks that all promoters are thieves. I quickly counter that it's the promoter's job to make as much money as possible. 'Yes, but I think it would be awesome for a promoter to try and do the opposite,' he responds. 'Because it's not going to change your life – you're still going to make money. If you've got a good fighter he will always make you money.'

We talk about the fact that boxing is run by an essentially self-appointed, self-regulating governing body and that the money which emanates from the sport is always going to attract the shadier aspects of society. 'It's a money-making, scam artist business,' agrees Prince.

'And yet,' say I. 'You can't keep away, can you?'

Prince smiles at me guilty, as if I've caught him out. 'Yeah,' he says. 'Because fighters love to fight. It's like a drug in itself. I don't know what it is about boxing, I really don't. But you just love it so badly.'

* * * * *

The origin of Prince's bad love is an all too familiar story in boxing: Troubled childhood. Drugs. Violence. Crime. And then corporeal redemption through the giving and receiving of punches.

'I was a very aggressive, want to tear your heart out kind of fighter. I loved to hurt people,' he tells me as my eyes crawl across the tattoo of his son's name stretched across his neck.

Twenty fights. A minor title that he is understandably proud to have won but which many people will question the value of. A shot at a fragment of the world title. And then a mysterious knee injury, the mention of which makes Prince shuffle in his chair awkwardly when I query him about it. And obviously no money. Obviously.

'I was just surviving when I fought,' says Prince. 'The Board[79] was right when they told me at the start that everybody thinks they're going to be a Nigel Benn but only five per cent are. Well I said, "I'll be that five per cent."'

'And were you?'

'No.'

There is a thickness in the air as Prince continues with his story. In other circumstances one could almost be forgiven for stifling a yawn: the tale of the boxer who retires to plot a comeback that is doomed to inevitable failure is, after all, nothing new. In Prince case's, however, that story takes on an entirely different complexion when you realise that he waited 14 years before choosing to step back into the ring. Very few boxers have returned after so long a gap; and even fewer have done so and experienced a happy ending.

'I didn't ever think I'd be back in the ring.' he says. 'I was 44 when I started back. When you can't fight any more hearing that news breaks your heart. You've got all the time to sit thinking about those words. It's lonely. It's depressing. And you don't know what future you've got. And that's even before you think about your kids and how you're going to keep a roof above your head. When I retired I didn't announce it because I just couldn't handle saying it.

'Then after 13 years out of the ring I thought, wait a minute, I'm training. Why am I not boxing? I'm squatting my arse off. Jumping around.'

It's standard fare. It's the sort of conversation that I've had with a boxer on many an occasion in the past. It's a flavour of dialogue that Prince is also undoubtedly tediously familiar with. Because there's a sense here in the quiet of this haunted room that we both know what we should really be talking about.

I broach the subject. Awkwardly. Nervously. Meticulously. 'I'm worried about asking you questions, to be honest,' I stutter.

Prince instantly knows what I'm talking about. 'Please don't be,' he says with a dignity and humility that is heart-crushing.

So I tell him about Sofia. About how she almost died a short while ago. I tell him about the thoughts that went through my head. About how I'd always told my wife that I'd kill myself if we were to lose our daughter. 'Because it's only when you have a child,' I explain. 'That you realise what an amazing, incredible thing it is.'

'That's right.'

'We're genetically programmed to instantly fall in love with them. And we'd will kill to protect them.'

'And you'd give your life for them.'

I find myself focusing in on Prince's eyes. 'I just don't know how you do it' I say, turning my head to look at the photographs that cover the walls of the office. 'For a start you're constantly reminded of Kiyan.'

'Yeah,' he says softly.

'I don't know whether I'd want to be reminded. I don't know whether I wouldn't want to be reminded. I don't know. I guess you have days when it's both for you?'

'Look at the work I do,' says Prince, resting his eyes on that giant poster of his beautiful son kicking a football. 'That constantly looks at me. I talk about Kiyan. Kids ask me questions. He was a strong lovely, lovely boy. A character.'

I tell Prince that I remember seeing it on the news at the time. That it was the QPR connection that I found most upsetting, the fact that Kiyan was on the cusp of a career in football, that he was being lauded as one of the most talented young players in the country. 'I really hate to talk about it with you,' I confess.

'I've got to live with it every day,' Prince shrugs. 'I've got to use it. I've got to teach with it. Inspire with it. Motivate with it. And it's opened up my own life now. So I have to use my own life, everything I've done... Running away from home... Being into drugs... Being a criminal... I have to use it all because now it's all become useful as a teaching tool for the kids.

'So I had a choice to put down this crap. Put down cocaine, put down drugs, put down Es, acid tabs, drink, and focus on something; to become someone because that was always my dream when I was younger.'

There's a silence in the room as the words fall away. There are many such silences as the light begins to fade. As happens too often these days I once more find myself on the verge of tears. It something about the desolation in this place, the memories and the aching stillness. The sense that this man, so used to fighting alone inside the ropes, has surely never encountered such loneliness as he struggles to come to terms with what has happened to his world.

Prince tells me about the days after his son's murder and his decision to create a charity in memory of Kiyan. Even though he had split with his partner Tracy Cumberpatch, the couple found solace in each other's despair.

'I was hugging his mother Tracy, crying. You don't turn on each other in grief. You turn to each other because you're the only person who can understand it. You're both going through this terrible pain.

'I said to Tracy that I don't believe that Kiyan has died for no reason. I believe that God has a plan in all of this, as horrible and as painful as it is. And I think there's a part that I've got to play. Let's start a charity and then see.

'So I just took it down to basics. I said, "I'm a dad to my son. How Kiyan turned out proves how good I am at bringing up my boy. He listened to what me and Tracy said. He took our advice.

'He was well-schooled and brought up and he was the product. He wasn't just doing well in football, he was doing well in his life as an individual. That's a testament. His character... His goodness... His kindness... Having the head teacher speak about him at awards ceremonies, saying how he's a role model... I've got that as a template so why don't I use it and show the kids?" This is what proves that life is not about money. Life is about character. The quality of who you are as an individual.'

So based on this philosophy Prince did a remarkable thing. In a single-minded mission to try to prevent any repetition of the terrible thing that happened to his son he began touring schools and telling his harrowing story to school kids.

'That's why I've been given this position,' he says. 'This is what I do. To me his death didn't end there. The journey continues. Because of Kiyan's murder there have been many kids that have been awakened to their true potential.

'I think this guy that's killed Kiyan, he done more than just take a life. He's stopped many other people's lives from being impacted by that young man.'

To illustrate his point, Prince singles out another picture on the wall, 'There's all my kids. We all miss Kiyan.' He recites the names of his surviving children with a tenderness that would melt the coldest heart.

And even when Prince decides to bring God into the room it's impossible for me to hold it against him. When Prince speaks about God it is with the fervour of a Deep South evangelistic preacher. He talks for a long time. He talks about love and peace with an intensity that can only have been borne of pain.

Only when his voice finally beings to trail off do I interrupt and, just as I did with Michael Watson, tell Prince that I am an unbeliever. 'It would be easy to think that there's a higher power,' I explain, 'But I'm not going to.'

And it suddenly strikes me how often over the last few months I've found myself awkwardly listening to a boxer wax lyrical about God. The more that I consider it the harder it is to think of any boxer who is not at pains to talk about some kind of divine being.

From Michael Watson telling me that he doesn't believe in organised religion, to Herol Graham telling me of his vision of heaven and hell. There is a connection somewhere. A connection between boxing and the need for some form of faith. Obviously there is.

Although I don't believe in God, I tell Prince, conversely I've felt a lot of love in boxing over the past few month.

'I hear you,' he agrees.

'It's perverse because it's boxing we're talking about,' I say. 'People hit each other. They knock each other out. They hurt one another. But on the other hand there's an awful lot of love. I don't think you get that in football, for example. It's not surprising that a lot of boxers end up finding God.'

'Of course, man. Look man, God is love, man. And that's all I have pouring out of me.'

'But I can also see you've got a lot of aggression in you, that's clear to me,' I say. 'You're obviously formed by your pain. They say there's nothing worse than a child dying before you.'

'Yeah and you only know when you know. And I don't want no one to know. I don't want no one to join this club.'

Prince describes his experience of attending a support group for parents who have lost children in the months after the tragedy.

'I didn't even like being there. I don't see myself as a victim. I don't like the whole thing of looking at everyone together and seeing the look in people's eyes. I still see pictures of myself with that same look.'

'Is it on your mind all the time?' I ask.

'No it's *inside* me all the time… I could be talking about it just fine and the next moment it just pops out and you're breaking down. Sometimes you make just a noise… A noise.'

We're looking deep into each other's eyes now. Prince's might be filling with water but it's difficult to say. And I feel myself start to crumble. I find myself relieved that Prince is doing most of the talking because I'm finding it hard to get any words out. And I understand exactly what he means about it being inside you all the time. When he talks about that and he talks about making that noise, Prince is describing exactly how I've felt and still feel since my father died. As I sit here with this remarkable man it dawns on me that sometimes it takes another person to articulate your own feelings before you can begin to recognise them.

'I'm asking you too many personal questions now,' I say, concerned that I'm using Prince and his pain as a means of liberating my own. 'It's bad of me.'

'No,' says Prince firmly. 'I've been in interviews where they didn't give a shit about me. How I felt. Nothing. I did a news program for somebody and they went right in. They wanted me to break down. They wanted emotion. It was good for TV. It was good for the news.'

The tension is broken when Prince tells me about his plan to write a children's book that he can take it to schools with him. And again I'm struck by the recurring patterns in boxing. So many boxers have found God and so many also express the desire to write. Perhaps this, more than anything, is what historically attracts the likes of Hazlitt, Hemingway, Mailer and Carol-Oates to the sport that isn't a sport: boxers are frustrated writers and writers are frustrated boxers.

We exchange ideas: I tell him what I think he should do. I tell him that he needs to find himself an agent and think about selling books at schools. As I speak he mumbles the word 'beautiful' two or three times, clearly unable to hide his joy at meeting someone who is prepared to take his ideas seriously. I tell him that I'm staggered by his strength.

'I've always been a leader,' he says. 'That's just my character. I know what I want to achieve. I look at what I was before this all happened, and how I used to think of myself and I think "what a twat". I wasn't evil. I wasn't a cold-hearted robber. I wasn't none of that. But put me in a situation where I didn't have and then you'll find out what I can do. When the heat of grief hit me I found out who I was.'

I suggest to him that this terrible experience has, perversely, made him a better person.

'Yeah. When I look back on my life I think I've always been on a steady growth. Making progress. Because before that happened my knee injury slammed me for six. I went from a guy who was looking at houses in good areas to thinking how do I even make a grand a month?'

'I done loads of different jobs. I did youth work because I had a passion for it. And I worked for a private ambulance service and used to get about £800 a month. It was ridiculous. That was half my mortgage.'

'And did you move out or are you still there?'

'Listen, that's another story. You'll believe in God if I tell you about it.'

'We'll see… That's a big claim.'

Prince laughs uproariously. It's a relief, the first time that either of us has laughed since I've been in this room. And then he launches into a long and elaborate anecdote about how solicitors and bailiffs knocked on his door one day but before he let them in he went on his knees and prayed to God, 'You enabled me to get this house… You are in control of everything… There's nowhere for my kids to go… Nothing… I need to stay here, God. Can you not let these people take my house?'

Prince tells me how he tried to reason with the bailiffs but was met with the resigned response of people who had seen it all before.

'They said, "Have you taken what you need out of the house? Because we're locking it off today." But then something strange happened: the men suddenly left the house and I could see them talking among themselves outside.

'And then they came back and said, "Mr. Prince, we're gonna go now." I was literally gobsmacked. And then everyone left and I was alone. I saw one car drive off. Then another. Nobody explained what had happened.

'They just went. So I went back on my knees and I was praising God.

'And no one ever came back to my house. When I tell my property developer mates about this, they're like, "Shut up!"'

'Praying never worked for me,' I say. 'When I was a kid I used to lie in bed saying, "Please God if you get me a new scooter tomorrow I promise I'll believe in you." It never happened.'

Prince laughs again and says, 'Hey look I prayed for my son. So what are you gonna say about that? They phoned me and said your son's been stabbed. I went in my car and prayed for my son's life.'

Prince goes into another lingering monologue about God again. Just like Michael Watson, the subject is never far from his lips.

'The wages of sin is death. We are all deserved of the same thing. The only way to eternal life is through Christ and doing and living how God made us to live is with a pure heart, to love each other.'

'I don't need a God, a deity for that.' I say. 'I've come to that conclusion on my own.'

'Because God's placed that within you.'

'Well you can't lose with that argument,' I laugh.

'But here's the thing: we've still got choice. We've got the choice to come away from what God has put in us.'

'You're a really intense guy,' I say breathlessly.

Prince goes quiet for a few moments and stares into space. Then he says, 'You know what? Something just came into my head. You said that and Noel Edmonds said that, too, after his show... How can you say this to a guy who's blubbering? With grief and tears beyond what he's probably ever seen from a strong man... He looked at me and said, "You are a powerful man." And then he said it again. I was a mess.'

In 2008 a visibly broken Prince appeared on a TV show entitled *Noel's HQ* in which the bearded Edmonds offered to help the fledgling charity. After a very long and emotional speech, Edmonds introduced Prince to specialists in clinical psychology, leadership and public relations who all offered their services to his charity free of charge. It was an immensely moving scene that apparently jammed the programme's switchboards.

It is at this point that the phone rings. It's my daughter wondering when I will be home. Prince takes the phone from me and speaks to her. At the other end of the line she politely feigns interest as the huge voice offers pleasantries.

I get to my feet and look into his. 'You know... It's been brilliant to meet you,' I say. I can barely get the words out. I'm choking with emotion. I just cannot comprehend what this man has been through.

'It's been great, man,' he says.

We climb to our feet and he hugs me like a big brother. I can feel the power coursing through his body like an electric charge.

'You're a fucking amazing guy,' I splutter.

'It's so nice to meet you, man.'

The hug continues until it almost begins to get embarrassing. It reminds me of that time in the hospital when I held Herol Graham's hand for what seemed an eternity. It's as if Prince is comforting me when I have no right to be comforted. If anybody in this world needs support it is Prince.

* * * * *

But he does love to talk and he's not finished yet. We go to the café next door to his office and I finally get the full story of how he injured the knee that led him to retiring from boxing back in 1999. When he'd been reluctant to tell me earlier I'd assumed that it had something to do with a criminal misdemeanour that he didn't want anyone to know about. As it happens it's nothing of the sort.

'The bone was sticking out of the side of my knee,' he says, cupping his hands when he describes the injury. 'There's still a metal pin in there that should have been taken out.'

'So how come you can fight now?' I ask.

He pauses for a moment. 'I haven't got a fucking clue!' he exclaims.

We both laugh.

* * * * *

Later that evening I locate that Noel Edmonds clip on YouTube. It's terrible to see Prince in such an dreadful state.

To his credit, the usually sanctimonious Edmonds handles the situation with a degree of taste and it's impossible not to feel your heart lifted by the acts of kindness on display.

When I've finished watching I text Prince and ask him if the specialists are still working with his charity.

He texts back, 'No! They just used my grief as a platform to get some exposure for themselves!'

I just hope I'm not doing the same.

Fury

I'M at my third press conference in a fortnight and feel no less an outsider. The boxing promoter Frank Warren mills around cheerfully massaging shoulders but even though we met long ago when I had hair and he didn't have scars on his chest from the bullets that almost killed him he doesn't have a clue who I am. He looks through me and I'm pleased that he does.

My third press conference in a quarter of a century and already there are faces that I am beginning to recognise as regulars. The silver-haired Colin Hart, erstwhile of *The Sun*, is again prowling the boards, eternally shaking hands, boxing's own Methuselah but, unlike last time around, I choose to avoid him. Also present once more is a tall dark-skinned man with a digital camera permanently strapped to his wrist, whom I'm told is called Kugan Cassius, something of a name in the boxing world but most probably anonymous in civvy street. He apparently conducts regular interviews for a YouTube channel he started a few years ago that has quickly grown to attract over one million hits.

Boxers and managers and promoters are understandably anxious to court his attention. In the old days newspaper men ruled the roost and could potentially make or break a fighter but nowadays the balance of power has shifted towards young black men toting iPhones, Nokias and Galaxies who film every second of any event that happens to make the slightest mention of boxing and then upload it on to different branches of social media while they still have battery power remaining.

I've come here today to kill several birds with one stone. Having contacted Warren's press office I am grateful to have been invited along to observe three prominent boxing figures strut their stuff. Two of them, Naseem Hamed and Ricky Hatton, are former world champion boxers at feather and light-welterweight respectively. The other is currently the undisputed heavyweight champion of the world, a controversial figure known as Tyson Fury.

Fury is probably the real reason I am here. For even in the modern era of boxing, possibly the most cynical, financially polluted epoch in boxing history – a chance to see the real, bona fide heavyweight champion of the world in the flesh[80] is an opportunity that even then most dilettante of boxing observers would be unwilling to turn down.

The press conference is being held in a large room called The Empire Suite in London's drippingly opulent Landmark Hotel. By coincidence I'd been here only a few months earlier after a former employer died and left a sum of money that was to be spent on a lavish bash in her memory. Unlike that night I stand innocently sipping mineral water and quietly watch as events unfold. Ricky Hatton, noticeably heavier than in his fighting days, is being interviewed on film by a heavy-browed young man whom I recognise from the last press conference I attended.

More film crews congregate around other fighters, discernible to me only by the stoop of the shoulders and their calcified fists. My eyes stalk Warren, impressed to witness him in action: silky smooth, effortlessly charming, a veteran

....

80 In boxing much kudos is attached to the 'linear' champion of the world. Such a boxer is often able to trace his lineage through generations of fighters.

of more of these type of events than his relatively youthful exterior would tend to suggest.

I think back to meeting Ambrose Mendy at the end of last year. And I remember him telling me misty-eyed how he and Warren discovered boxing together in the early 1980s and were entranced by the brutal spectacle. I also recollect him intimating on more than one occasion how the pair of them were close enough for the promoter to be nominated best man at his wedding. As always, however, there is more than one side to any tale in boxing. With even cursory background reading such blissful memoirs of friendship lost and found suggest themselves not to be taken at face value.

In Ben Dirs's 2013 book *The Hate Game*,[81] Warren claims not to have even invited Mendy to his own wedding three week's earlier and to have regretted agreeing to being Mendy's best man. The truth? Irrelevant. As always there is no truth in boxing. And there are no lies.

But I digress. The room is now filling up and people are starting to take their positions in the row of seats that have been placed before a large table at the back of the room on which rest name plates corresponding to the main protagonists of this occasion. One each for Warren, Hatton, Hamed, promoter Mick Hennessey, Fury and his father 'Big' John Fury.

I take a seat and find myself sitting close to Steve Lillis. Back in the day Steve was the racing correspondent of the *Sunday Sport* and I was that venerable organ's boxing writer.

....

81 *The Hate Game*, Ben Dirs, Simon & Schuster, 2013. 'He was working in our office at the time on sponsorship,' says Warren. 'And he asked me to be his best man. I got married about three months before him and he wasn't even invited. Anyway, it drifted on and on and suddenly I had to be up the church and I was thinking, "What on earth have I let myself in for?" My good friend Ernie Fossey [Warren's longtime matchmaker and right-hand man] said, "You're being stupid, you shouldn't do this."' Fossey was right: a week after Mendy's wedding, Warren sacked him.

Among the nipples and haunted fish fingers we tried our best to keep a straight face. If my memory serves me right, we've seen each other on two occasions since then and he greets me warmly, which I'm grateful for. He's older, as are we all, but slimmer and fitter than he used to be. When I left the *Sport* he effortlessly slipped into my moccasins and has been working in boxing ever since.

Unlike many of the people he writes about, Steve is completely without pretension and has done well for himself in the sport. He is now employed by BoxNation, the television channel that Warren set up in 2012, and spends his time interviewing figures from the boxing world in an honest and unthreatening manner that has won him many friends.

I find myself genuinely happy to be back in Steve's company, if only for a few brief moments. It's also something of a relief to be recognised by someone, to not be a complete stranger in a room full of people who all seem to know each other. As you would expect we swap anecdotes about the past and promise to meet up for a drink, which will very probably never happen.

There is a sudden commotion in the room and a looming figure descends upon the table. Tyson Fury is a staggering 6ft 9in tall but somehow seems shorter. He also looks a lot slimmer than I imagined him to be, a fact that is in direct contrast to stories of him being six stones overweight that are currently doing the rounds on social media. He issues a terse 'good afternoon, gentlemen' before lowering himself into a seat, where he is joined by the rest of the boxing ensemble with the perhaps inevitable exception of Hamed. Frank Warren makes a joke about 'Naz' never changing; that he's still late after all these years.

The press conference kicks off in pedestrian fashion. Also present at the table is Hughie Fury, cousin of Tyson and also a heavyweight boxer; the first part of the proceedings concerns his upcoming fight. But the watching press fidget as they wait for the real meat to be served. A few questions are gently aimed at Hughie, more through politeness than any real intent, and then it's on to the main event.

Tyson Fury has an adrenaline infused smile on his face as he speaks. A glint of madness in his eyes and the confrontational comportment of the habitually pursued. He murmurs something about being a gypsy and as such being used to ruining people's gardens. It's a throwaway remark that is greeted with a smattering of embarrassed laughter from the watching press. But there is also an unmistakable element of menace about his tone.

Like many people, I have seen the headlines about Fury since he unexpectedly relieved longstanding heavyweight champion Wladimir Klitschko[82] of his belts in Germany last year. Although he refutes the accusations of racism, homophobia and sexism that have blighted his reputation since that night, Fury's words and demeanour do nothing to underpin his claims of innocence.

An ill-fitting armour of belligerent indignation is worn by Fury and his brethren. They are angry: angry that Tyson is apparently gaining no respect from the press; angry that in their opinion travellers are universally viewed with contempt by the general public; angry with the questions that the press are *not* asking; angry that they have had to endure a five-hour drive from Manchester to get to this location when rightfully they should have been sitting in a chauffeur-driven limousine. They are angry with the whole world when in fact Fury should be having the time of his life.

Furious Fury is the heavyweight champion of the world, one of a very select breed of athlete who can trace his championship lineage back through the decades, through Muhammad Ali, Rocky Marciano, Joe Louis and Jack Dempsey all the way back to John L. Sullivan in the late 19th

82 **Wladimir Klitschko** born 25 March 1976, Kazakh SSR, Soviet Union. Former undisputed heavyweight champion of the world.

century. Fury is the man who beat the man who beat the man. He deserves to be a little pleased with himself. For surely this considerable achievement is more than he could ever have dreamed of?

Today Fury's anger is specifically related to the fact that one of the belts he won, the IBF belt, has recently been unceremoniously and patently unfairly snatched away from him after refusing to fight a nominated opponent. He is enraged that his former property is now strapped to the svelte waist of housewives' favourite Anthony Joshua, who won the title in a comedically one-sided performance the weekend before.

Fury calls Joshua's promoter Eddie Hearn a 'bitch' and a 'pussy'. He tells the press that Hearn is a 'daddy's boy' and promises to 'give him a slap' when they next meet. Veterans of the press conference genre will understand that such talk is usually best placed into the context for which it is intended: that of a vehicle by which to put buttocks on arena seats. Yet there is more than a touch of reality about Fury's performance. It appears to me that there is little apparent pretence contained within his outburst. Fury really does seem to mean what he says. His fixed smile is more a grimace of self-righteous indignation. And when Fury grunts 'next question!' after yet another abusive tirade it is not an invitation but an admonishment.

Because of this there are few in the press section willing to speak. Or perhaps there are other reasons: the fact that a *Mail* journalist named Oliver Holt was threatened with physical violence for publishing a taped interview with Fury. Or the fact that Fury's father has been to prison for gouging out a man's eye. Or the fact that his uncle, Peter Fury, manager and trainer of the heavyweight champion, is a convicted drugs baron who, according to *The Mirror*, allegedly ran a lucrative amphetamine distribution business from behind bars. Whatever the case there seems to be plenty of reasons for the attendant press to keep their heads firmly beneath the parapet. Their silence is more than a little awkward. And when questions do occasionally appear they are uncontroversial, vapid affairs that draw further scorn from the Fury ranks.

Although it is fully a quarter of a century since I last spoke at a press conference I decide to throw my hat into the ring.

I ask Fury about his assertion that a rematch of the fight in Germany will result in the loss of his belts. Although we are all fully aware that boxers who fight in an opponent's home territory traditionally run the very real risk of falling victim to outrageous mathematical errors in judges' scoring, Fury's performance in Düsseldorf last July clearly did not elicit any such arithmetical aberrations. I am interested to hear in Fury's own words why things might be different this time round.

'Listen,' he says, 'don't try and tempt fate twice. One's good enough and I'm happy with that. Let him come here.'

'But you've not heard anything to suggest that that would happen?' I ask.

'I've not heard anything. But let him come here, the German prick,' he replies in his thick Mancunian accent, immediately getting testy.

At this point Frank Warren interjects.

'It's very, very rare to get a win out there,' say the promoter diplomatically. 'Very few British fighters have done it. Why tempt fate?'

Although in terms of ring deportment any comparisons with Muhammad Ali end before they begin, when it comes to talking there are obvious similarities between boxing's greatest exponent and his most recent descendent. Despite the acrid mood that permeates all corners of the room I find myself chuckling at Fury's circus act. He's clearly intelligent. He's certainly articulate. And he does have charisma. Surely with only a few cosmetic tweaks he would stand a very real chance of gaining the respect from the press that he claims to covet?

'The only man who could beat Klitschko was me,' proclaims Fury, embarking upon a long and entertaining rap. 'I done it through unorthodox positions. That's how you beat them men. How you beat robots is do unorthodox things. Touch the floor – punch them in the face. Spin around in a circle, kick your leg up and hit him a one-two. What I've got can't be learned. You've either got it or you haven't. Him back there will tell you that!'

Heads in the room swivel to discover that Naseem Hamed has finally entered the building. It's the first time I have seen him in the flesh since he turned pro back in 1992 and the difference in his physical appearance is astonishing. Back then he was a talented skinny kid from Sheffield with a cocky attitude. Several world titles, worldwide fame, a spell in prison and countless millions later he is unrecognisable as that person. I've seen pictures in the papers, of course, but nothing prepares me for the transformation.

Hamed is wearing a loose fitting white shirt and is simply ENORMOUS. The peevish part of me is reminded of that episode of *The Simpsons* in which Homer purposefully gains weight as a means of avoiding work and ends up wearing a blouse in the style of Demis Roussos. It is as if the new Naseem Hamed has swallowed the old. And it is no exaggeration to say that Hamed could easily campaign at heavyweight these days if he were to consider a comeback. But then who am I to talk? Who is anybody?

[I can't help but think back to a day earlier, when I spoke on the telephone to the still recuperating Herol Graham and we mentioned his long-time friend. 'Next time I see Naz,' he had innocently announced. 'I'm going to have a word with him about his weight.']

'Come on Naz,' calls Fury. 'Don't be quiet at the back.'

'It's all right,' grins Hamed. 'You're doing really well.'

'Forget Anthony Joshua,' laughs Fury, casting an eye over Hamed's bulk. 'I'll give you a first defence.'

'I'd come unstuck,' says Hamed.

'This ain't the Prince show, this is the King show,' replies Fury. 'My son's called Prince. I named him after you because you're my favourite fighter, from England anyway.'

'Big respect.'

'I used to watch you. Try and do the things you do but about ten stone heavier. It might look a bit more awkward but it's effective still.'

The interchange provides welcome relief for everyone in the room. The toxic atmosphere begins to dissipate and shoulders noticeably relax. But then Fury's father begins to speak.

'Big' John Fury is an ex-fighter himself. His Twitter feed contains the undeniably factual boast, 'My bollocks produce heavyweight champions.' The facial resemblance he shares with his son is striking. Moreover, the vocal similarities are uncanny. You only have to listen to him speak for a few moments to understand the origins of Tyson's scattergun tirades.

'He's just toyed will all of ya,' says Fury Sr, in the sandpaper tones of an erstwhile Bernard Manning. 'He's got about as much respect for you lot as you have for him.

'Looking at all off youse laughing at bullshit, I'm astounded. You're supposed to be businessmen but you're playing games like school kids. Get real.

'I'll tell you what, people, show a bit more respect. I've done time back in my life and I know real people. Not paper, plastic people. You'll have to pull your socks up, all of you. All these interviews here are pointless because the paying public don't want bullshit like what's going on here. I was shocked when I come here today four hours in a car to watch this ping pong game. Ask some serious questions, show some serious respect and you'll get some back.'

The elder Fury's unfocused diatribe is endless and lacking in any punctuation. I once again find myself wondering why nobody from the press ranks is offering up any objections. Fury addresses the room in the manner of a headmaster reprimanding his assembly for spraying graffiti in the wrong colour paint.

'I don't think he is undervalued at all,' I pipe up, trying to reason with him. 'I think everyone here *does* respect him.'

'No they don't, mate,' says Fury Sr, dismissively. 'You're having a laugh.'

'I think you're talking about the mainstream press.'

'You're having a laugh! You know, there was not one genuine question asked today.'

'Well I certainly respect him,' I add. 'I think he's a great fighter.'

'Show it then!' demands Fury. 'Show the rest of the world. Cause I'm telling you now it's a joke from where I'm sitting!'

Therein follows a five-minute diatribe designed to illustrate the injustice and indignities that are gratuitously heaped upon his son. Even if it were possible to compete with the volume of the microphone, there is no point at all in trying to reason with this man. He only hears what he wants to hear; and that predominantly appears to be the sound of his own voice.

'I'm not fucking happy with that!' grumbles the white-haired journo seated next to me in a voice not so loud as to carry.

* * * * *

I spend a fitful night mulling things over and decide to try to continue my discussion with 'Big' John. I tweet to him but get no response. Finally, I contact the press agent of his promoter Hennessey Sports, who gives me the number of Tyson's manager, Peter, he of that alleged indoor candy floss business.

I call Peter and tell him that if John is willing I'd like to come up to Manchester and sit down with him for a cup of tea. I tell him that I'd be interested in speaking further with his brother because I think John's wrong and needs to be told so. Peter is friendly and laughs a lot. He tells me that John's opinions are not shared by the rest of the family. That John can sometimes get 'a bit carried away', and that the family's relationship with the boxing press is generally a good one.

We talk about Tyson's fight with Klitschko: I tell him that what impressed me most about his nephew's performance was not how he threw his punches, but more the way he threw the feint. We talk about what it's like living in the north and he laughs some more. And I tell him what a pity it is that Tyson's confrontational attitude yesterday ended up alienating people who are actually fans of boxing. My fear is that he runs the very real risk of making a sow's arse out of a silk purse.

We talk for about a quarter of an hour and as always I'm struck by how friendly and welcoming the boxing fraternity can often be, even to strangers. Peter's attitude towards me compared to what I experienced yesterday are as chalk is to cheese. As bacon is to eggs. How could the man I have just spoken to be in any way related to the angry apparition that confronted the press yesterday?

Love

I RECEIVE a text a few days later from Ross Minter. He asks me to sort out somewhere to eat so we can meet at 5pm. His father, Alan, is due to appear at a tribute night in Dagenham. Ross is accompanying him to the venue and the pair have a couple of hours to spare. By coincidence I am accidentally-on-purpose attending the same event.

Finding somewhere even quarter decent in Dagenham proves to be tricky. Mr Google doesn't help at all. Neither does Mr Yelp. Dagenham, it would appear, is to haute cuisine what North Korea is to haute libertarianism. As I methodically check out restaurant after restaurant it soon becomes apparent that dining out is obviously not a strong priority for the residents of this neck of the woods. They clearly prefer dining in, which is why almost every Dagenham eatery listed on the internet is of the pick-it-up-in-a-soiled-carrier-bag-and-stuff-it-down-your-face-on-the-sofa-while-watching-*Corrie* variety.

In truth I'd been hoping to spend a little money on the Minter clan. Take them somewhere nice. Somewhere that befits the former undisputed middleweight champion of the world and his dashing promoter son. But in the end all I can find is a bog-standard Pizza Express, which is situated a couple of miles from Dagenham's Roundhouse, location for 'AN EVENING OF CHAMPIONS'. I text this disappointing development to Ross but thankfully it doesn't seem to bother him.

I'm early when I get there. Naturally I'm early. But for once probably wisely so. When I arrive in Dagenham the sun is hot and the air is thin. But no amount of summer sunshine can bring a smile to the streets. Pound shops, charity shops and takeaways of every conceivable description are all that is on offer here. In the heat haze the dust of poverty clogs up the throat.

I trawl the pavements for several minutes but when I arrive at the location of the Pizza Express in question I am confused to discover it appears to have gone AWOL. I trudge onwards, thinking I must have made a mistake, checking my phone for directions as I go, only to be informed that I've apparently just walked past the restaurant. I frown and retrace my steps but once again I am instructed to turn back. It is then that I realise I've been hoodwinked. 'Expresso Pizza' proclaims a sign in big bold serif letters above a shop soiled takeaway. One can only admire the sleight of hand of the proprietor of this ramshackle dust bowl. I check my phone again and confirm that I am definitely standing outside the Dagenham branch of Pizza Express.

Now I'm growing concerned. The clock is ticking and I'm up and down the street several times before I can find an alternative venue. As it happens, it's a relatively well scrubbed looking Indian restaurant just across the road from the esteemed Expresso Pizza. I step inside to check that it really does sell Indian food and then text Ross to inform him that the venue has changed. 'Order poppadoms and water,' he cheerfully responds. Ever the optimist, I attempt take a picture of the restaurant so that I can send it to Ross but I'm immediately photobombed by a timeworn Dagenham native who has apparently never seen a mobile phone before, 'I couldn't resist that,' he cheerfully croaks in his 60-a-day voice.

I head back inside the restaurant and request a quiet table. The young Indian waiter looks at me as if I'm a madman. 'We don't have a quiet table,' he says.

'I beg your pardon?'

'We have a disco starting in 15 minutes and the DJ's just about to do his sound check. It's going to get very loud.'

'A disco? But it's only quarter to five.'

Now I'm panicking. Ross texts me to tell me that he's only minutes away and I have nowhere to take him and his iconic father. My only option is to stand outside the restaurant and grimly await the Minters' arrival. It's hot. I'm boiling. And I'm never coming to Dagenham again.

* * * * *

Fortunately Ross and Alan see the funny side when I describe my Dagenham-based restaurant booking misadventures to them. They are a lot more chilled than I as we decide to take a stroll and see what comes up. Ross is 38 years old but looks 20 years younger. He appears fit enough to don the gloves right now and talks as if conversation is going out of business. Alan is quieter and clearly fragile. He talks only when necessary and seems preoccupied. This is no surprise when I'm told that life has been no picnic for him in recent years. He is friendly but more subdued than his loquacious offspring.

Even though I've already decided not to do this I immediately find myself reminding the ex-champion of when our paths first crossed. About how I served his table back in 1980 when I was a wine waiter in Bristol and he was guest of honour. He says he remembers me talking about this at the Nigel Benn tribute in October.

We finally end up in an Afghanistan restaurant. None of us, it transpires, have ever partaken of this particular type of food but it's clear to us that in Dagenham beggars are seldom choosers. We giggle like naughty school kids as we negotiate an alien menu, the waiter unable to understand us, we unable to understand the waiter.

Spending time with Alan was not in my plans when I decided to retrace my steps in boxing. But the more I've thought about it the more apparent it has become to me that I really ought to. If Michael Watson is my boxing omega then Alan is my alpha. During my youth, boxing provided one of my very few points of connection with my father. Watching the sport together is one of only a handful of happy memories I have of spending time with him. And I have particularly clear memories of Alan. My dad was a voracious fan of the boxer and as such so was I.

Ross goes to the bathroom, leaving me alone with his father. I awkwardly ask him if he's going to be drinking wine with his meal, not sure if I'm saying the right thing. Alan's struggles with the bottle are well publicised. He tells me no and asks me if I drink. I say I unfortunately do.

'Why unfortunately?' He asks.

'Because I don't have an off-switch. If a bottle of wine is opened I have to drink it all. If I'm at the pub I'm likely to stay drinking until I fall over.'

Alan nods his head knowingly.

Ross returns and during our opening exchanges I discover that he has young children. I give him a copy of my most recent kids' book while the waiter heads off with our order. '*Johnny Nothing*,' he reads the title out loud. 'It looks very strange.'

'It is very strange,' I say. 'You're dealing with a very strange person.'

'Well you have to be strange to be involved in boxing,' says Ross.

Ross wastes no time in telling me how he became involved in the sport. It's nothing we haven't heard before: a toe dipped into water followed by a long period spent learning his trade in the amateurs. But in Ross's case his progress was further complicated by the fact that he came from a very well-known boxing dynasty. His grandfather was renowned manager and trainer Doug Bidwell who, along with Scotsman Bobby Neill, masterminded son-in-law Alan's not inconsiderable ring career.

'I loved boxing straight away,' Ross tells me with unashamed passion. 'I absolutely loved it.'

'How aware were you of your father's achievements?' I ask.

'I didn't really see dad too often as a child,' explains Ross. 'But when he used to come to my school it was a very big deal. And he'd sometimes take me to celebrity events so I knew he was something special.'

And what did Alan think of his son taking up the sport?

'I was pleased that he wanted to go ahead,' says Alan. 'There's a lot of kids who want to take up boxing and their parents won't let them. He phoned me first about it when he was getting married.'

'Not when I was getting married,' interrupts his son. 'Jesus, that was only seven years ago!'

'Sorry,' says Alan. 'I don't know what I'm talking about.'

'Do you want some water, Alan?' I ask.

'Yeah. Keep him quiet,' says Ross, the table erupting into laughter.

This exchange, I discover, is to set the tone for the evening: Ross doing most of the talking, Alan and I occasionally attempting to interject whenever permitted. And lots of laughter. Lots of laughter and lots of love.

'I phoned you when I was fighting at Chelsea football club,' Ross continues. 'I think that was the first show you came to.'

'That must have been your first fight then?' asks Alan.

'No. You didn't come to the early fights. I think that I was 17 then.'

'What age did you start fighting then?' Alan produces the question as if it's never occurred to him before to ask.

'Thirteen. You missed all that lot and I didn't really want to tell you at the time... I didn't really want you to be involved.

There were issues at the time and what have you. It was very much I didn't really want it then.'

I find myself trying to imagine what it must have been like for Ross to have endeavoured to make it as a boxer with such a famous father. And in Alan's case were are talking genuine fame at an entirely different level to the type that is experienced by the majority of today's boxers. When Alan defended his world middleweight title against Marvin Hagler in 1980, tens of millions routinely tuned in to watch the BBC highlights.

'Oh God! The pressure was terrible,' admits Ross.

'Did you get people who saw you as a scalp?'

'Listen, when people found out who they were fighting they trained doubly hard.'

'And how did your mother feel about you following in your father's footsteps?'

'Mum didn't want me to box. She'd been through it all obviously with dad. From 14 years old she followed dad all the way to 30. Seen all the heartaches. God mate!'

'That must have been some ride?'

'Jesus mate! He went through a lot. So here's me – her little baby – wanting to do the same thing. But she knew I needed something because I was a right pain in the arse. Hyperactive. I still am a little bit. So I need something to really challenge me.

'Then obviously she embraced my career and got involved. I think she could foresee the pressure because of the Minter name. It was bloody hard. There's been some horrible times.

'I can still remember my first ever amateur fight. I was 13 years old and walking out and everyone's whispering, "It's Alan Minter's son!" You could hear it. And I had that pressure on me as well as having the pressure of it being your first fight. For any kid that's hard work.

'I won the fight. I stopped the feller. But from then on the pressure grew and grew. How can you follow Alan Minter?'

Indeed. How can you follow Alan Minter? It's not that Alan was one of the greatest boxers ever to hail from this country, I think even he would agree that there have been plenty of other boxers with far more talent. In terms of iconic status, however, Alan was a towering figure in sport. Along with boxing contemporaries such as John Conteh, Dave 'Boy' Green, John H. Stracey and Henry Cooper, Minter was omnipresent during the 1970s on television and in the media.

Minter and his contemporaries were fortunate or unfortunate enough to grace a golden age of boxing – and celebrity in general, for that matter – in which television was a nascent commercial art form still finding its feet within the British psyche. The existence of only three television channels in this country had the effect of instantly bestowing fame of a stratospheric nature on anyone who happened to appear within the square box. This, it should be noted, was an era in which a dog that growled 'sausages' on Sunday evening TV would routinely experience celebrity on a par with any modern winner of *The X Factor*.

'I've met a lot of fighters over the years,' I tell the two men. 'And I don't generally get starstruck but your dad – I'm not just saying this – he's an all-time great. I mean, I've got vivid memories of sitting there in my parents' semi-detached with my old man shouting for "Boom Boom". That was what he'd call you.'

'That's right,' says Alan.

''Cos of the noise you made when you threw a punch.'

'Yeah, yeah.'

'And he used to swear his head off at you.'

'Yeah, "Move your 'ed!"' says Alan, getting excited.

'Massive wasn't it? It's hard to explain to people now,' agrees Ross. 'I was only two when he won the world title but to explain to people what he was in his day… To compare… He was like David Beckham or something… Well, maybe not David Beckham.'

'Did you ever get fed up of it?' I ask Minter senior. 'The fame? The people bothering you?'

'No. Not at all. But everyone always asked me the same questions. Yeah it was nice. It's funny, I was living in Crawley at the time and I was there only two days ago and no one recognised me at all.'

'I can remember vividly what I said to you when I served your table,' I interrupt, again recalling the occasion that I met Alan in Bristol. 'You still had the cuts on your face from the Hagler fight and I said, "Are you going to fight him again?" And you replied, "Yeah... I'll get the bastard next time!"'

'Did I say that?'

'Yes... But you obviously never did get him,' I say.

Alan thinks for a moment before speaking, 'Hagler was my last fight, wasn't it?' he says wistfully.

'No you had a few more,' I say, amazed that Alan is able to forget such key information; although he's by no means the only boxer I've met who has trouble recalling his career in detail. Contrast that with his fans, who can recite every aspect of his career in minute detail.

'Yes... That's right... I fought Ernie Singletary.'

'And Tony Sibson,' adds Ross.

'Why didn't you have an automatic rematch clause in your contract?'[83]

'To fight who?'

'Hagler... It's common practice now.'

'I don't know the reason.'

'Would you have liked to have fought him again?'

'Not really.'

More laughter.

'He hurt you didn't he?' says Ross.

'Yes, he was *dangerous*.'

'He sure was,' I say.

....

83 Nowadays it is common practice in boxing for a rematch clause to be incorporated into fight contracts. This gives the deposed champion an opportunity to quickly regain his title and the rich financial rewards that often come with it.

'The last time I saw him he asked me to come and stay with him.'

'Really? That's fantastic. Will you do it?'

'I don't know yet.'

* * * * *

Starters are served, which are unexpectedly spicy. Ross looks worried. He wipes his mouth with his hand and searches for water. In between gulps Ross explains that he seldom eats hot food. Even though he's no longer boxing he is ever watchful of what he puts into his body.

'My body is natural,' he says. 'I've not tried a drug of any sort whatsoever. I don't even like taking paracetamol. Even if it's not a banned drug it's cheating. If I was offered it I wouldn't do it. I've never touched a drop of alcohol in my life. Never even held a cigarette.'

'You want to live a bit,' I advise.

Minter Sr laughs.

'Boxing was your drug,' I say.

'Oh yeah. Definitely, The whole thing,' proclaims Ross, as the waiter comes to the table to take drinks orders.

'I can't get you a beer then?' I ask Ross but he misunderstands my attempt at wit and thinks that I saying this to his father.

'Dad don't drink,' he says warily. 'It's been a year now, hasn't it dad?'

'It's tough, isn't it?' I say.

'What?'

'Giving up alcohol.'

'No,' Alan says firmly, without elaborating.

The main course arrives and Ross climbs to his feet excitedly. 'We've got to have a picture,' he says, insisting that I'm in shot too.

* * * * *

We talk about comebacks and how boxers inevitably cannot resist the lure of the ring. I remark that at this table we have the unusual combination of a father and son who never returned. Alan's last fight was in 1981, when he lost to fellow Brit Tony Sibson; Ross's last fight was in 2008.

'You build your life around boxing. How do you then walk away from it? It is such a very tight knit community to suddenly just leave is so hard to do,' says Ross. 'I never watch boxing nowadays but being involved and being with the people, the old fighters, mate it's fantastic!'

'But would you consider fighting again?' I ask.

'I'm still fit. I'm still well, replies Ross. 'And it plays on your mind. I would like to come back, yeah. If I could get to that level. I mean fighters today, are they as good as they were in my day? That's what you was thinking weren't it?'

'These days it's easier to get the top and it's easier to fool the public into thinking you're a world champion,' says his father. 'Fighters like David Haye[84], they retire and the right money comes along, they come back.'

'Of course it's about money,' agrees Ross. 'And you miss it and you get drawn back into it. But when you start boxing it's not about money because you turn up to a gym, you train and you love it. You're not thinking about money when you walk into an amateur gym. You're thinking about fighting, about being the best. But any sensible person is going to try and reap the rewards.'

We talk about Alan's decision never to return to the ring.

'I suppose I was at that age when you've done enough. You've done what you had to do. You've won everything there

84 **David Haye** born 13 October 1980, London, England. Former EBU cruiserweight champion; WBA, WBC, WBO cruiserweight champion of the world; WBA heavyweight champion of the world.

was to win. I lost to Marvin Hagler and that was it – enough's enough.'

I tell Alan that prior to this meeting I had re-watched his fight with Hagler. One thing that surprised me was the disparity in size between the two fighters.

'Yes, he was a lot shorter than me with long, long arms. One thing I didn't realise was that he was a southpaw[85]. I decided to go forward and that was my downfall.'

'At one point you can almost visibly see you grit your teeth and get angry,' I say. 'And that was the moment you lost the fight.'

'Yeah… Yeah.'

Being a southpaw, I suggest, would obviously have given Alan a distinct advantage over other fighters. It must have been a shock to suddenly find himself fighting another.

'In what respect?'

We talk about how boxing is all about repetition. About how hours and hours of throwing and blocking punches in the gym enables these activities to become second nature. When you are suddenly faced with an opponent who delivers punches in a different manner you can find yourself relinquishing precious split seconds of reaction time.

'That's what made it so hard with dad's three fights with Kevin Finnegan[86],' says Ross. 'Because Finnegan was a southpaw. When he got in there dad didn't have that advantage. And it showed. Because suddenly dad's getting hit with shots that he normally wouldn't get hit with.

'It's such a hard thing boxing because everything's got to come good on that one night. Okay, it's the same for running and tennis, but in boxing you get punished for it. In tennis you don't get hit or put down. You don't get

---

85 A **southpaw** is a left-handed boxer. Southpaws traditionally enjoy a technical advantage over conventional right-handed boxers.

86 **Kevin Finnegan** 18 April 1948–23 October 2008, Buckingham-shire, England. Former British and EBU middleweight champion.

disgraced. Because as a boxer being beat is being disgraced. That's how you feel.'

I tell the pair about the former heavyweight champion Floyd Patterson. After losing his heavyweight title to Sonny Liston in 1962, the sensitive Patterson was so ashamed that he left the arena with his face disguised by a fake beard and glasses.

'I was a little bit embarrassed,' says Alan of the loss to Hagler. 'But if you've given your all you've just got to take it. You can't let it play on your mind as it did with me. Mentally it was very, very difficult.'

'Well Hagler was special and you were special,' I tell him. 'I'm sure you get bored with people saying that.'

'No it makes his head get bigger,' laughs Ross. 'There's a very, very fine line between love and hate in boxing. I didn't like getting hit. It bloody hurt. I didn't like the nerves beforehand and the build-up. I hated the weight loss. Feeling drained and ill. And most of the time I didn't like the day after, win lose or draw. It's such a massive anti-climax.

'Then you've got the good bits like the feeling you can just go and run whenever you wanted to run and you can beat people. The feeling you get when you're punching someone and not getting hit yourself. And then the adulation, the cheering.'

'Do you two ever talk about this when you're alone?' I ask them.

'Not really.'

'No,' concurs Alan.

'In the car you might have a discussion about, you know, "How did I look tonight?" Still worrying about how you looked.'

'But that's fathers and sons.' I say. 'I couldn't talk to my father either. It would take other people around me to make that happen.'

'Yeah.'

Ross asks if I want some more food. I tell him I'd better not because I've got to lose some weight.

'Give him that little bit because he'll enjoy that,' says Alan.

'He will enjoy that won't he? We've got to feed you up. You're looking skinny, mate.'

'You're kidding,' I say. 'Before I came out today I couldn't get any of my clothes to fit. When I put weight on even my shoes feel tighter. Have you ever noticed that?'

'No,' says Ross. 'It's because you've got elephantiasis.'

The three of us are laughing once again.

'The only way I can lose weight is by effectively starving myself,' I explain. 'I'll bet you've both had to starve for boxing.'

'For weeks,' says Ross.

'It's not eating but it's drinking water,' adds Alan. 'When you're training and training you're gasping for water. And when you get on the scales and you're 11st 6lb, have a drink of water and you're 11st 8lb. You can't eat but you want to drink.'

'I used to weigh myself probably eight times a day,' recalls Ross. 'I was very anal. It controls your life. I used to wake up in the morning with butterflies, worrying about what I would weigh.'

'I used to be 13 stone, maybe 14 stone and give myself eight weeks to get down to 11 stone six,' says Alan. 'And when you get nearer the weight that's when you're gasping.'

'And you still have to be ready to fight another man in the ring after weeks of starvation,' I say.

'Yeah, 'says Ross. 'I once pulled out of a fight because I was so weight drained that I could not go training. I couldn't even hit the pads.'

'It must have been particularly hard for you,' I say to Alan. 'Because you come from the drinking generation when all sportsmen seemed to celebrate by having a beer when in was all over.

'People like Bobby Moore and Rodney Marsh were all heavy drinkers. I bet you had a few with them.'

'All of them,' says Alan. 'Georgie Best… Bobby Moore… Oliver Reed.'

* * * * *

Alan climbs to his feet and heads off to the toilet, leaving Ross and I alone.

'I gotta say, I really like your dad,' I murmur.

'Yeah?'

'He's not at all like I expected. What's nice about him is he smiles an awful lot.'

'Well it's been a year that he's been off that,' he says, raising an imaginary glass to his lips.

'Oh really?'

'He's back with me now. Cause before that he was not with the family. He's been in a bad state. Real bad. But now he's training twice a week. He's hitting bags. Hitting pads. Doing weights. Running. He's changed: his face, his walk, the way he is. It's amazing. He's a different man.'

As if to demonstrate this Alan comes back to the table with a noticeable spring in his step. 'Watcha,' he chirps.

'He says he really likes ya,' says Ross.

'Thanks a lot!' I say in mock outrage.

'He fancies you!'

More laughter.

'He says you smile a lot.'

'I didn't used to do that.'

'His character's coming back.'

'So it's a rebirth for you as well?'

'Yeah,' says Ross.

'Well that's good. I mean I lost my father a year ago and you don't want to go through that.'

'Did he drink?' asks Alan.

'Yes. He did unfortunately.'

'He can talk can't he?' I say, pointing towards Ross.

'He don't stop,' says Alan.

'Well he obviously doesn't get it from you,' I say. 'You never used to talk like that.'

'No, I didn't. I was reserved wasn't I?'

'You're very reserved as it happens,' says his son.

Alan Minter laughs as I put away the iPad that I've been using to record our conversation. I thank the two men and tell them that they will probably think that I got nothing out of our afternoon but in actual fact it's quite the contrary.

'If you haven't you'll make something up,' grins Ross.

* * * * *

Outside the car, Ross theatrically changes his shirt. If I had a body like his I think I would also have no qualms about showing it off in public. He's clearly a lover of organisation. He picks his teeth in the rear view mirror, checks his nose for any source of potential embarrassment and sets off in search of Dagenham's world-renowned Roundhouse. His father sits quietly beside him, hardly saying a word. For a moment I think that his silence might be due to nerves but when I ask him what he intends to talk about later tonight he just shrugs, 'I haven't a clue,' he says like he hasn't got a care in the world.

'Do you do a lot of these events?' I ask

'A fair bit.'

'Do you like it?'

'It all depends on the audience. You can be saying a few things and they're not listening.'

'Yeah,' says Ross. 'We went to one the other day didn't we? And it was quiet in there no atmosphere.'

I'm guessing that a fair proportion of Alan's income must come from shows such as these. Indeed, there's a flourishing nostalgia circuit in boxing.

The format is generally the same wherever you go: a bit of dinner, an auction, handshakes and photos and then a Q&A.

'Except they all ask the same question,' Alan repeats his earlier statement.

'What's the question?'

'How good was Hagler?'

I tell him that I'm going to try and ask him a question he's never been asked before.

'Don't look so worried,' I say and the car fills with laughter.

* * * * *

Dagenham's Roundhouse turns out to be a large pub, on the back of which has been grafted a vast oblong extension. Affixed to the side of this structure is a giant billboard proclaiming 'AN EVENING WITH CHAMPIONS'. Black and white images of Alan Minter, Colin McMillan, Charlie Magri[87] and Dave 'Boy' Green[88] serve to add credence to this bold statement: three world champion boxers and one buccaneering European champion. It's quite a collection of talent on display here tonight, except that we happen to be several decades the wrong side of contemporary. People in their 20s or 30s might just about have fond enough memories of Colin McMillan to fork out the £15 entry fee. Most people, however, would have difficulty picking out his co-stars in an identity parade.

Except that I'm quite wrong to be thinking that: literally moments after climbing out of the car Alan is approached by a dog out walking its man. 'I know you,' says the newcomer. 'It's... You're... It's...'

....

87 **Charlie Magri** born 20 July 1956, Tunis, Tunisia. Former British and EBU flyweight champion; WBC flyweight champion of the world.

88 **Dave 'Boy' Green** born 2 June 1953, Cambridgeshire, England. Former British super-lightweight champion; EBU welterweight champion.

There's real affection in the stranger's eyes. Love maybe. He's past 70 but takes hold of the ex-fighter's hand in both of his and squeezes hard enough to turn Alan's knuckles white. The retired boxer smiles back at his unexpected admirer, genuinely pleased at being noticed. 'How are you?' he asks. 'You all right?'

'I used to watch you on the telly,' says the other man, a grin splitting his face in two. 'You were a great fighter.'

Inside, the pub is a subdued blend of danger and glitter. The two burly bouncers parked at the locked main door are certainly not there to keep the punters in. There's an edge to this place: the feeling that at any moment something could kick off. In an apparent attempt to offset the oppressive ambience silvery tinsel streamers flutter in the hot air at the entrance to the extension. Still more bouncers patrol the boundary.

I traverse the bar sandwiched between two generations of Minter. Young eyes follow our progress with curiosity, evidently it's unusual for people to be seen entering the premises with bashed up faces and broken noses. Not quite so uncommon for the reverse, one imagines. The extension to the pub and venue for tonight's festivities is huge. Someone tells me it was big enough to recently host a darts tournament with dozens of games running concurrently. This only makes the emptiness seem even more incongruous. In front of a small stage are four or five rows of wooden chairs, perhaps a hundred or so in total. Behind the chairs in the far distance can be seen the lights of an empty bar.

I follow the two ex-fighters into a dressing room behind the stage. Thirty or 40 people are sitting in small groups drinking lukewarm bottled water. I spot Dave 'Boy' Green, a two-time losing world welterweight title challenger, no longer so boyish. The sight of him sends a shiver down my spine and I'm instantly transported back to my parents' living room in Bristol, the summer of 1977, my dad drinking cider, yelling at the TV screen as a half-blinded Green is stretched out by a Carlos Palomino left hook. The disappointment afterwards. The pain of loss experienced that evening was a very real emotion to both father and son.

As if he reads my mind Green suddenly looks over at me and our eyes meet across this particular crowded room for several moments until I nod my head deferentially and smile, I presume shyly. Green nods back. Sitting next to him sharing a joke is former WBC world flyweight champion Charlie Magri. Head completely shaven, he seems to be even smaller than the last time I saw him face to face, which would have been some time at the end of the 1980s in the sports shop that he still runs in Bethnal Green.

Colin McMillan is also here: I shake his hand and exchange pleasantries. As always, he seems more interested in other people than himself. Since I last saw him he's celebrated his 50th birthday but is every bit as baby-faced and cute as he ever was. Ross and Alan, still standing next to me, are introduced to the promoter of this event, small in stature and not doing a very good job of hiding his financial concerns. 'Colin said that we'd get a lot of people coming in off the internet,' he pants. Colin smiles guiltily back at him.

I speak to Ross alone for maybe 20 minutes. He tells me about his post-pugilistic career as a boxing promoter. In common with others of his ilk that I've encountered, Ross sure can talk the talk. He has the energy of a younger Barry Hearn, patriarch of Matchroom Sport, arguably the most successful sports promotion company in the country today. And he has the blarney of the youthful Ambrose Mendy of 20 years ago. I tell Ross that he will do well. It's not going to be easy though; it never is.

Ross runs something called the Queensbury Boxing League, which is not affiliated which the BBBofC. He says he is attempting to do something different, 'Nowadays boxing's totally changed from when you was around. The pro scene is journeyman versus up-and-coming fighter. So you know the blue corner is going to win. The fighter's got music, the journeyman hasn't. Mine is 50-50. Every fight is 50-50. It's special. It's a night of entertainment.'

Ross is young and idealistic. Refreshing qualities in boxing that are seldom encouraged. He wants to change things, to shatter the status quo. I remind him that this was just how Frank Warren started: by promoting unlicensed shows until the board had no choice but to accept and eventually embrace him as a fully paid-up member of the boxing establishment. I tell him that his shows sound exciting.

'Come along next Saturday,' he says, immediately offering me two free VIP seats to the show. 'It will be the best thing you've ever done. It's totally different. I'm not being big-headed or anything.'

And then Ross is back on to his father. In hushed tones he gives me more detail about Alan's physical state prior to his rescue and rebirth. He talks about his father for a long time, his voice quavering with passion. The love and admiration is strong, too strong. Powerful enough to set me off thinking once again about my own father and the eternal gap left in my life by never having him and never being able to have him again.

Soon I'm struggling to hold back the tears. What a baby I've become. There was a time not so long ago when my heart was made of stone; I even used to boast that I hadn't shed a tear since junior school. But even though I'm aware that the spectacle of a middle aged man openly weeping in a dressing room full of ex-boxers would be, well, unthinkable, it's all I can do to stop myself from making an utter fool of myself.

Thankfully Ross doesn't notice and suddenly we're all being called into the main auditorium. Around 50 or so people have arrived and it's been decided that the show must go on despite the paucity in numbers. I perch myself on a padded bench to the side of the stage. I'm joined by Alan, Ross and Green. At my other side of me is Magri. In the semi-darkness an Australian comedian named Colin Cole hesitantly walks forward. He does a reasonably efficient job of warming things up, occasionally being heckled by Magri. Cole is followed by the powerful thighs of a glamorous young woman with a too loud backing track, who sings songs by Taylor Swift and Pharrell Williams.

As I sit and watch her attempt to entice an audience member up to dance to her version of 'Kiss' by Prince I'm struck for a moment by where I am. I can't help but wonder what my father would have made of me sitting here with the likes of Minter Sr and Green, the fighters we would cheer and swear and whoop and sometimes cry for. Unlike many people who earn a living by writing about boxing, I was never quite able to overlook the feeling of absolute privilege that I experienced whenever I was in the company of a boxer; and now that I'm into my 50s in the midst of semi-un-retirement nothing at all has changed – it's still an honour and an incalculable thrill for me.

There's an urgent tapping on my shoulder and I turn to see Charlie Magri yelling something at me. The music is too loud for me to catch every detail but it soon becomes apparent that he's telling me he remembers me from years ago. He hands me a piece of paper and motions for me to write my telephone number on it. He's looking to write another book about himself, he shouts. We should meet for a chat.

It's getting on for 9pm when I decide to make my exit. My daughter is alone at home and given her recent health problems I'm uncomfortable about leaving her on her own for too long. I'm not, after all, going to have the chance to ask Alan Minter a question that he's never before been asked. Knowing me it would have been something stupid. 'Calculate Pi to 14 decimal places,' I would probably have yelled. I lean over to shake Alan's hand. 'It's a real pleasure to meet you,' he says, and I can discern no insincerity in his words. My chest swells with love and pride.

Redemption

THE former light-welterweight boxing champion of Britain and Europe looks ridiculously good for his age. Thicker set maybe and the hair negligibly thinner but Clinton McKenzie is almost unaltered since our paths last crossed. That would probably have been during a business meeting some time in the early 1990s, if you can call it that. Like so many before us and since in boxing we'd been led up the garden path by a man who claimed to have money. Along with Michael Watson, who had also been ensnared, we'd agreed to add our names to a nonsensical sports management company that really was destined to go nowhere.

This is one of the first things we talk about after we've embraced. Such episodes are obviously part and parcel of boxing, a traditional magnet for the more libertine corners of society. I tell Clinton of how, long after I'd finished with boxing, I received an envelope out of the blue from the senior partner of said company demanding a large pile of money from me if I didn't return some anonymous documents to him. I returned them.

Clinton runs a gym in the bowels of Dulwich Hamlet Football Club. Like its proprietor it is neat and spotlessly clean. On the wall is a framed cover of the short-lived but celebrated 1980s style and music magazine *The Face*. Beneath its masthead, a boyish Clinton wears a chic flat cap and stares defiantly out at the world. Clinton tells me how a young Naomi Campbell was at that photo shoot. Inside the pages of the magazine the boxer shares top billing with the likes of Paul Weller, Vivienne Westwood, Harry Dean Stanton and the Pet Shop Boys. I had no idea that Clinton was once so famous.

Standing some way behind his father is the man that I've really come to see. Leon McKenzie and I met and talked a while ago at Herol Graham's bedside. You may remember me mentioning that it was the 12-year-old Leon, who back in 1990, had awoken Clinton, his boxer brother Duke and myself just in time to catch early hours television coverage of Mike Tyson losing for the very first time in a professional ring. Meeting Leon in that hospital had been a brief but undeniably intense experience for me: in common with the man he had come to visit, Leon seemed unable to prevent his demons from scrambling their way to the surface. In the brief time that we chatted I quickly learned that where Leon is concerned there is no such thing as a trivial conversation. And as such Leon seems disinterested in exchanging trivialities right now.

The first thing that I'm acutely aware of as we eye each other across the gym is that I may already have offended him in some way. Perhaps it is due to the amount of attention I have been giving his father; or maybe now that he's watched me operate for more than a few minutes he doesn't like what he sees. I really don't know. Whatever the case, Leon looks awkwardly at his watch and intimates that he won't after all be able to stay for the lunch we'd planned. He tells me that something's come up. That he has a meeting at three.

For a few moments there's an atmosphere. I shrug and tell Leon not to worry, that's it's not a problem. But inside I'm confused. Clinton exits the room, leaving me alone with his son. We talk. Sort of. I try to break the ice: I ask him when his next fight is. It's such a stupid question. Leon doesn't have a date.

At this juncture it's worth pointing out that in Leon we have no average individual standing before us. His story, even in the highly stratified world of boxing, is unusual in the extreme. A professional footballer with more than 100 goals to his name, Leon played in the upper echelons of the Football League for almost two decades. Upon his retirement Leon suffered well-publicised bouts of depression and eventually endured a six-month spell inside a prison cell for attempting to avoid speeding convictions.

With the best will in the world it's difficult to comprehend just what was going on inside the judge's head when he doled out such an impossibly severe and blatantly unjust sentence; particularly as in 2011 Leon had revealed that he had tried to commit suicide two years earlier while playing football for Charlton Athletic. Then in 2013 Leon made an unexpected debut as a professional boxer; not *that* unexpected you might think, given his boxing pedigree. However, Leon was 34 at the time – very late December in the career of most boxers.

It's the boxing that I find myself concentrating on. Naturally it is. As an ice-breaker I aim a torrent of studiously bland questions in his direction: Who's his manager? Who's his promoter? I don't really want to know any of this information but I'm just filling in the gaps that stifle the air and threaten to choke us. Maybe Leon is just a naturally shy person. Maybe not. I don't know. It's tricky.

Then for some reason I'm telling Leon about Frank Buglioni and the psychology behind his training methods. Now Leon is suddenly animated. He wants to know all about it, although it has to be said that he listens to my words with an unconvinced expression on his face. We flit from subject to subject. We talk about the economics of boxing and how difficult it is to earn any money from the sport. Leon tells me he's not doing it for the money. He's doing it for another reason.

Our voices reverberate around the empty gym. Leon keeps his distance, standing ten or 20 feet away from me; almost as if he's sizing up an opponent in the ring. We move on to the subject of depression in boxing. Leon's depression.

'I'm finding that it seems to be quite a common thing in the sport,' I say.

'Quite common but not really spoken about,' replies Leon. 'It's too much of a macho game to be spoken about.'

'I'm beginning to wonder if depression might be a physical thing,' I add. 'Yet another manifestation of all those punches that boxers take to the head.'

The boxer does not reply.

Leon's father returns to break the deadlock and the three of us agree to head off to a nearby pub for lunch. Leon drives while Clinton and I take a walk through the park. It's odd to be in Clinton's company after all these years but it also feels perfectly natural. Clinton was always one of boxing's nice guys: simple, straightforward, kind and steadfastly honest. I ask him how he felt when he learned that is son was going to take up boxing at such an advanced age.

'To be honest I was shitting myself,' he replies. 'I thought he was going to get hurt. But then I saw him sparring and I was reassured: I knew that he could handle himself.'

We reach the pub and Clinton surprises me by ordering lager. Unlike some ex-fighters Clinton has scarcely gained a pound since hanging up the gloves. He's the last person I'd expect to be drinking alcohol. When Leon arrives he asks for water. He tells me that he's a stone and a half over his fighting weight and even though he's not sure when he fighting next it has to go.

We find a table outside in the sunshine, father and son at one side, me at the other. I look at the two men and smile guiltily, 'Now that I've got you both here I don't know what to ask. I'm really rubbish at this interviewing business.'

'You've got to be natural,' Clinton gently encourages me.

'What struck me about you when we met in the hospital with Herol Graham,' I say to Leon. 'Was a common thread I'm encountering when I talk to fighters and ex-fighters: you do seem to wear your heart on your sleeve, as Herol does obviously.'

'Yes,' he says.

I remind Leon of the gift he presented to Herol, the framed poem. And of how I'd noticed the hurt in his eyes when Herol quickly passed it on to me.

'The reason I went to see him was to bring some sort of love or reality back to what he's achieved,' Leon tells me. 'But when I gave him the thing I don't think he knew how to take it.

'Yes, he passed it on to me,' I say.

'Yes.'

'Straight away.'

'He didn't know how to receive it. With a fighter's emotions there's no kidding me because I've walked every path. So just be yourself. You don't need to show me how tough you are.'

'Herol's really not like that though,' I say. 'I think A) he was pretty much not on this planet at the time; B) he was in real pain; and C) your gift was just so unexpected.'

'Well not really. I noticed straight away that he was appreciative but very much, "Oh, I'll read that later." He even said straight away, "I'm not good at reading things." So that's an emotional barrier already. Do you know what I mean? Maybe he doesn't want to go to a place where he's feeling a bit vulnerable and sad. I mean if I read certain things or listen to certain songs it can take you to a vulnerable place. The gift was just from the kindness of my heart.'

'I think it was just one of those things,' I say. 'I don't think he meant anything by it. Because Herol actually is a soft, gentle, emotional person. In many ways too emotional.'

'Yeah, he's always had that vulnerability about him,' agrees Clinton. 'Because of the way he acts. It was like he was happy all the time but it wasn't really him. He didn't really know how to be himself. You've got to have that sensitivity about you to understand that.'

'I'm the total opposite,' interrupts Leon. 'As you say, I wear my heart on my sleeve. So if I see my dad he can tell straight away if I'm going through something mentally.'

'And are you going through something mentally today?' I ask, remembering the brusque way he reacted to me earlier in the gym.

'Listen… I'm okay. It is what it is. Every man's got pressures within his lifestyle. I just do what I gotta do.'

'He takes it as it comes,' adds Clinton.

'When you decided to box it's obviously a bit of a family tradition,' I say to Leon. 'It's strange because you started at 34, which was a year older than your father was when he retired. It's almost as if you've carried on from where he left off.'

'Yes, I retired at 33,' says Clinton. 'I'd had a lot of hard fights so it was the right time because it was very hard for me to do at the end. I couldn't make the weight and still feel strong.'

'So tell me Leon,' I ask. 'When you decided to box was it purely for the sport or the money?'

'There's no money in boxing.'

'So what was the reason?'

'It's a spiritual thing for me. A personal journey. Boxing came into my life at a time when I'd lost everything. So boxing saved my life and brought me back again.'

'It made him believe in himself again,' says his father.

'Yes it did.'

'It made him believe that he could fight back,' says Clinton. 'That he could be this person he's always wanted to be.'

'And who *did* you want to be?' I ask.

'I've had two divorces. I don't wake up with my kids every day.

'There's a lot of guilt I've carried for a number of years. There's a lot of childhood stuff that I've carried with me. Only four years before this moment of faith I found myself behind prison bars. It all takes its toll.

'At 35 years of age I ended up in a place where I think, "What the hell's going on?" To be living with my baby sister at the age of 35, not many men could come back from that. I lost everything. All materialist things gone. Everything gone.

'I played football for 18 years. I was never really prepared to finish but I'd say for the last three years of my career I knew it was coming. And I couldn't handle that. So psychologically it was an uphill battle for me.'

'So you were at a very low point in your life and you decide, right… I'm going to box?' I ask.

'Yeah, pretty much. A few years before that I was at Charlton and lots of things happened and I was very depressed. The direction I had in my life was lost. I tried to take my own life.'

'Did you really mean to do it?'

'Yeah… 100 per cent I tried to take my life.'

'What did you do?'

'Pills… I tried to overdose. I took about 60 pills.'

'Do you remember what was going through your mind when you did that?'

'I'd just had enough.'

'My God, that's a terrible thing to do. That's just desperate, isn't it?

'I'd just had enough… I didn't succeed. That's why my story is a little bit different to most.'

Leon stops talking to me for a moment and stares at me intently. He suddenly asks, 'What are you trying to achieve by writing about boxing again?'

'I think you're a very serious young man, Leon, ' I say. 'If you don't mind me saying so.'

'I'm a serious young man? Why?'

'You're the first person I've met who asked me why I'm doing this, what's in it for me.'

'It's not so much what you're trying to get out of it. It's just that I've written a book myself and I'm just trying to see what you're trying to achieve. I wouldn't say that I'm a serious guy. I'm just very straightforward. And there's no pretence with me. Hopefully it's not found offensive.'

'Not at all. And you've got every right to offend me. It's not a problem.'

'So what *are* you trying to do?' he says again. 'Going around seeing former champions?'

'Well… That's a very interesting question because I'm not entirely sure myself yet. All I know is that my dad died a couple of years back and it hit me really badly. Unexpectedly badly. But one of the few happy memories I have of him is when we used to sit and watch boxing. He got me into boxing. For those brief moments when we watched it together we were actually father and son.'

'You bonded,' says Clinton.

'Yes. So when I left home I always had a love of boxing. So much so that I eventually became a boxing writer. Became the editor of a boxing magazine. Don't ask me how it happened. But when Michael Watson got injured I thought, "I can't do this anymore."

'It's friends of mine getting injured and I'm making money out of it. But in writing about it again I'm discovering what really attracted me to boxing in the first place, which is this fellowship thing.'

I tell them about what Steve Collins had said to me back in January when he had talked about the 'fellowship of boxing'.

'I think he's very right,' agrees Clinton. 'There's a bond in boxing that no one else can ever appreciate or understand. And I think we all have that element of the end of the world. You go into the ring and your life's at stake and we all face that fear, and we all know what fear is. You face that fear – and you do whether you like it or not – but we all face it in different ways.

'I was never a boxer,' I admit. 'The closest I got to it was my dad buying me one of those things you stand on and punch. And I had a couple of fights at school and I really didn't like being hit. I thought, "Why would anyone want to do this?" But even then I was aware that you face something completely unique in the ring.'

'Any man that walks into that ring to face another man, they face themselves,' says Clinton. 'It's very, very hard. Someone's gonna hit you in the face and you have to take that.'

'What do you recall of being hit in the face?' I ask. 'Can you remember the feeling?

'Well you have flashbacks,' says Clinton. 'There's nothing more dangerous than getting punched in the face.'

'Sometimes when I get hit it's more an element of shock,' says Leon. 'I feel very spiritual and I feel very, very powerful.'

'You're yet another boxer who obviously really enjoys it?' I ask.

"Oh, I love it. It's great. It's not gonna last much longer though.'

'You could make it last if you wanted it enough. You'd obviously have to sacrifice a lot.'

'Exactly.'

'And the human mind is very good at making you forget the sacrifices,' I say. 'What it seems to do is make you forget the bad things.'

'I could challenge that by saying that in my football career I've got many, many beautiful memories,' says Leon. 'But what I notice when I sometimes play charity games is when I walk on to a football pitch is little glimpses of certain injuries I've had.

'Things flash into my mind very quickly, very suddenly. I'm running towards a ball and I have a quick little flash of… No… Slow down… It's to do with the psychological damage that injuries caused to my football career.'

'What injuries did you have in football?'

'Too many: Ruptured Achilles… Ruptured my thigh… Broke both ankles… Three operations on my knee… Constant hamstring problems… Constant muscle problems.'

'I guess that means you can't run as fast as you used to?'

'Nowhere near as fast. I'm still very fit. I can still manage things. Obviously football training is a lot different to boxing training. Football is all about twisting and turning and jumping.'

'Stop/start. Stop/start. Stop/start.'

'Yeah. And I haven't got to really bring that into boxing.'

'So did you find that you received redemption in boxing?' I ask. 'Or did you rediscover yourself? What exactly did it give you?'

'It definitely gave me an inner strength and confidence. I always believed I could fight. I just didn't know if it was too late.'

'How good do you think you would you have been if you had started younger?'

'I would have been world champion.'

'When he spars with the pros in the gym he takes them apart,' agrees Clinton.

'I understand the highs of boxing and I understand the lows,' says Leon.

I tell Leon about what his father said to me earlier in the park. About how he was initially worried when he found out that Leon was about to take up boxing.

'I understand that now because my son is wanting to do a bit of white collar[89] and I don't really want him to if I'm honest,' explains Leon. 'But I can't take it away from him. So first and foremost I'm going to get him down for sparring and I might have to dig him a bit – not that I want to – but I need to let him know this ain't a joke.'

....
89 **White Collar Boxing** is a form of boxing in which men and women in white collar professions train like a professional boxer to fight at specially organised events.

'Inside somewhere I think he thinks that he can take out his dad,' says Clinton.

'I think we all do,' I agree.

'Like you did when you were 17,' laughs Clinton. 'He thought he could beat me up.'

'Yeah, and I never could.'

'I'll tell you what,' I suggest. 'It seems to me the best thing to do is not to get in the ring with him at all Leon. Let him fight Clinton instead. Let his granddad give him a dig!'

For the first time this afternoon there is laughter at the table.

'Look at you two,' I say. 'You just don't look like father and son. And your relationship isn't like father and son either. It's a nice one, I think. I bet he was a sweetie to grow up with – although I can imagine he was probably a bit strict.'

'Yes I was quite strict, wasn't I son?' agrees Clinton. 'I had my moments.'

'I'll try and explain my relationship with my dad,' says Leon. 'Like you just said, it doesn't seem like that kind of relationship but then maybe that's due to your own experiences. But the one thing that stands out is respect. And because I respect him – trust me – my dad's made many mistakes, and he's got many flaws but having respect was the crucial key to me having a healthy relationship with my dad.

'And it's obvious that you respect him too,' I say to Clinton.

'Oh yeah. Because I brought him up. I've told him off when he's had to be told off. And tried to get him to avoid making the mistakes I've made.

'Most boxers are nice people because they go through a very hard time. Boxing teaches them a lot about themselves. Also, they have feelings that normal people don't feel.'

'You obviously miss it as well?'

'Oh yeah!' Clinton exclaims, with real hunger in his voice. 'It's a special thing boxing. It's very solitary. It's being in that nowhere land with your back against the wall, fighting your way out. There's absolutely nothing like it.'

'I find that with me as well,' agrees Leon. 'One of the fights I always go back to was my third fight, which I drew. I had to bite on my gum shield in that fight and dig deep. So all the boxing went. Then I became a man. It was like, you're going to have to kill me… I'm going to have to die right now. And I felt it in that fight that I knew then I could fight.

'Every fight I've had has been hard. Because of my name everyone wants to be beat me. When I watch my dad fight on video it gives me goosebumps. I see him in another light. I see my dad basically prepare to die.'

* * * * *

My head is swimming by the time that Clinton McKenzie and I embrace outside the train station and say our farewells. *Boxing came into my life at a time when I'd lost everything. So boxing saved my life and brought me back again.* I can't forget what the troubled boxer said to me and I can't help but think that his words could equally apply to me. *Boxing saved my life and brought me back again.* It's melodramatic – I'm aware of that – because even at my lowest ebb I never considered suicide, although I certainly thought that my death was imminent. But now I've been given the germ of understanding: thanks to Leon McKenzie and people such Mark Prince I'm beginning to have an idea of why I might be doing what I'm doing. And I think I finally understand what I have to do next.

Boots

B UT before I can do what I have to do next I have a date that I shouldn't really cancel.

I'm in the Hilton in London's Park Lane because Chris Eubank and his son will soon be arriving here. It's uncomfortably opulent, the sort of place where the doorman speaks better English than you do, and I'm in two minds as to whether I really want to meet the man who recently – some might say absurdly – renamed himself 'English[90]'.

I barely knew Eubank at all when he was fighting; I must have actually been in his company on only a handful of occasions during the formative years of his career, when his profound eccentricities were generally perceived to outweigh whatever talent he might possess. I recall I once shook his hand at the end of a press conference given by his promoter Barry Hearn. Frankly, the only reason I want to see him today is because I'm realising that I'm coming to the end of this journey I've been on and it's somehow important that I speak to him.

Then there is the fact that I've already had encounters with his three main rivals: Nigel Benn, Steve Collins and Michael

....
90 **English** – In 2015 Chris Eubank renamed himself 'English' in an apparent attempt to avoid being confused with his son, who became a professional boxer four years earlier. Eubank also explained that English was his father's nickname.

Watson. What is becoming increasingly interesting to me is that all three have sons who have all chosen to follow in their fathers' footsteps. I sense a kind of pattern emerging.

As I enter the building I spot Johnny Nelson on his phone by the lifts. I wave to him but I'm studiously ignored. Again I'm not sure what I'm supposed to have done to him but I can't help thinking that it's in some way connected to Herol Graham and that hospital. As a matter of fact, his are not the only feathers that I might have ruffled lately. A well-known boxing trainer refused to meet me last week, telling an intermediary that I was 'too clever' (a double-edged insult if ever there was one) and that I was a 'spy'. A spy? I'm not. Really I'm not. But it's nice to be mentioned in the same breath as Daniel Craig.

Such comments, however, represent only a small measure of negativity that I've been encountering. Boxing has been too generous to me in the last few months and I feel privileged and grateful. The bad bits don't even leave a dent in the tranche of positivity that has been directed towards me recently. Moreover, I'm pretty sure that some philosopher or other must have already pointed out that in order to appreciate the good you must endure the bad.

And bad is precisely what I'm getting this morning: bad because of my hangover and bad because in Eubank's case I've already expended far too much energy attempting to snatch just a few moments in his company. My efforts have included countless emails to his manager wife, mostly unanswered, handwritten letters and Twitter messages by the hatful. But treating me mean has only succeeded in keeping me keen. I feel like Glenn Close in *Fatal Attraction*, the proverbial boxing bunny boiler no less. In reality, though, I'd actually given up on ever meeting him again; until yesterday morning that is, when I received an invitation to this press conference.

But he's already an hour late and it's a piss poor turn-out this morning. Evidently the news that Eubank's son, Chris Jr, has just signed a deal with Matchroom Sport is not floating too many boats in newsrooms across the thoroughfare. Not even the venerable Colin Hart has turned up for this one, nor has Kugan Cassius and his surgically attached video camera. All we have is a room full of mildly bored looking people. Even their jokes are a little crusty around the edges. The delicate China thimbles of tea being distributed are expensively lukewarm. But that's about the only thing going for this place.

I'm milling. I'm hob-bobbing. I'm suddenly a boxing socialite: I'm chatting to a very nice photographer I've just met named Adam. I'm having another very long conversation with Sky's Ed Robinson about children and the technical accomplishments of artist Stanley Spencer. I'm getting nodded at left, right and centre by people who are beginning, I suspect, to recognise me as a press conference regular, part of their gang. I'm grinning as promoter Eddie Hearn taunts a newspaperman by yelling a tuneless rendition of 'You'll Never Walk Alone' into his ear (it's the morning after Liverpool FC have just been taken to the cleaners by Sevilla in the Europa League Final). I'm shaking the hand of *Boxing News* editor Matt Christie. Good heavens. I'm a boxing writer again. I could get a taste for this.

And then I spot the Eubanks arrive. A pair of Eubanks: father and son. Boxer and ex-boxer. Whatever the collective noun for a Eubank is, it is among us (a *malaprop* of Eubanks? A *verbosity* of Eubanks? A *misnomer* of Eubanks?). They stand by the entrance to the room and have a heated exchange with somebody whose face I cannot see. Fingers are wagged and voices are raised. Presumably. Although as always one can't be entirely sure that any of this is really happening: After all, Eubank Sr knows all about putting on a show.

'English' breezes into the room wearing a dark green jacket, artfully distressed designer jeans halfway down his arse, and spectacular pointed boots that add a good couple of inches to his height. He looks sickeningly healthy. Baby-faced, skin shining like polished chrome, wrinkle free and clearly well-toned, he is another ex-boxer who looks like he could step into the ring at a moment's notice. I'm getting fed up of saying it and you're getting fed up of reading it. These people are just so annoying. What's immediately apparent, however, is that the elder Eubank never for one moment takes his eyes off his son. They follow his offspring with an intensity that might represent pride or concern. It's difficult to know which.

What everyone here *is* aware of, however, is that his son's last fight ended in near tragedy. Just as his father did almost 25 years earlier when he fought Michael Watson, the younger Eubank managed to put his opponent into intensive care. While defending his British middleweight title, Eubank Jr's young opponent Nick Blackwell suffered something that they're calling 'bleeding of the skull' and was placed into a medically induced coma. Although Blackwell is now out of danger he will never fight again. It's fair to say that our malaprop of Eubanks have since endured a perfect storm of negatively, bordering on abuse, both in the news and on social media. Small wonder then, that Eubank Sr is keeping a watchful eye on the fruit of his loins.

As press conferences go it's a pedestrian affair. Nobody present is *that* interested to hear about Eubank Jr's latest fancy promotional deal. Equally, no one seems particularly concerned about Eubank's next fight, not even it must be said, his next opponent, one Tom Doran of Wales. Like everybody else here Doran appears to be going through the motions when he is belatedly handed a microphone and asked to convince onlookers that he will not lose his unbeaten record.

While this is going on I find myself distracted by what the rest of the room is doing. People absent-mindedly pick noses and scrutinise earwax. I'm amused to see that Matt Christie appears to be so bored with proceedings that he is busily messaging somebody on his phone. It's only when it's all over that he tells me that he's actually been writing a piece for the

Boxing News website. More out of guilt than anything else I offer to check his spelling. And this is what I end up doing while the others are queuing for interviews with the Eubanks.

It's almost as if a part of me doesn't want to speak to Eubank Sr. Perhaps he intimidates me like Nigel Benn does but I don't think so. Or maybe it's the fact that because my allegiances were always with Michael Watson I still perceive him to be the enemy. I suppose that could possibly be the reason. Anyhow, when I eventually do spot an opportunity I half-heartedly sort of sidle up to him and extend a limp hand. I tell him that we met 25 years ago but he's not really listening. He's busy watching over his son like an eagle watches an errant eaglet.

'Why do you watch your son so intently?' I ask, as the seated younger Eubank is surrounded by a haggle of pressmen seeking quotes relating to the injured Blackwell. 'Are you looking to see if he's in trouble?'

'No,' says Eubank, his face turned away from me. 'He's handling the press more. And how he's doing it today, he'll be better tomorrow… And the day after that he'll be better.'

'And what will you do if he encounters a problem?' I ask. 'Will you dive in and save him?'

But 'English'/Eubank never gets the chance to answer my question. Because suddenly it's my turn to be a father and to dive in and save my own progeny. After more than seven months of trying to manoeuvre myself into a situation whereby I am finally standing face to face with The Artist Formerly Known As Eubank my mobile rings. And even though I'm aware that on an occasion such as this the proper etiquette would be to ignore such a rude intrusion, my eyes are drawn to the touch screen. It's my daughter's school. Of course it is. How could it not be?

In an instant my mind is making subconscious calculations. Organic processors are already reaching conclusions: Sofia: school: telephone: ill: hospital: lung: abscess: pneumonia. I turn away from Eubank and take the call. As I suspected, Sofia is unwell once again. I'm advised to go and get her.

In the taxi to the school I'm in philosophical mood. Fate, it seems, was never really going to let me spend any time with Chris Eubank. And I find myself questioning why I even wanted to do so in the first place. What was to be gained? Because, as always, there are more important things in life than talking to ex-boxers. Much more important things... Secrets. Secrets that have been kept hidden away for more than 40 years.

Ash

SO I do what I have to do. I do what spending all that time with a sick Herol Graham in that hospital and listening to Mark Prince and Leon McKenzie pour out their hearts to me has inevitably compelled me to do. What arguing with Tyson Fury's dad in that press conference was always destined to culminate in. What meeting one of my boyhood heroes, Alan Minter, and his son was somehow always going to lead me towards even if I didn't know it: I go and see my mother.

I've seen her only once since my father's funeral almost two years ago. On that occasion I travelled to Weston-super-Mare to attend a barbecue that was being held in my honour. It was my birthday. The first time that my birthday had been celebrated by my family since I was in my teens. Naturally, it very nearly ended in tears. The bickering began almost straight away as the secrets clawed away at us all, desperate to be released into the wild.

I turn up unannounced on a warm Saturday morning which obviously shocks her. It's not the sort of thing I usually do. Well actually I've never done this before. There is no sign of a friendly greeting coming from me when our eyes lock like strangers meeting for the first time. My gaze is icy cold. I'm spoiling for a fight. 'What are you doing here?' she asks in her still heavy northern accent, not aggressively. It's clear that she understands I have something important to say.

I lower myself into an easy chair close to the one in which he used to sit. Light streams in from the window behind me. On the window ledge is an emerald glass ashtray that casts a translucent green shadow. I remember it from the old house in Bristol. It's the one in which he used to stub out his Players No. 6. When I was a youngster I used to fish out those stubs and relight them when he wasn't around. Like all little boys, I so much wanted to be like my father. Like Leon and Ross and Tyson and Conor and Chris Jr and Eddie Hearn I wanted to do the things that he did. I run my fingers over it one more time, letting the memories soak into me.

I ask for silence. I demand it. I tell her to lock her dogs away in the kitchen, two tiny yapping terriers of indeterminate description that he used to treat like babies, almost as if he was trying to make up for treating his own babies like dogs. And then I blurt it out: the whole sorry story. For the first time ever I tell my mother everything.

I'm not going to go into detail here. Even though damaged people are eventually supposed to tell *everybody* there are still those around who would be hurt by specifics. Suffice to say he was a monster. A monster when I was child, who ruled by fear: psychological and physical. And still more of a monster when I became a teenager, who did things to me when we were alone that a father should never do to a son. A demon who stole my childhood from me in a manner that I've never really been able to get over.

And yet in spite of all this I still wanted him to be proud of me, to love me no less. It's absurd the lengths to which one will go to earn a father's approval. Even one who brutalised you. In retrospect it's certainly no accident that I ended up jettisoning the career in the arts that I'd always coveted and became a sportswriter, more specifically a boxing writer.

You don't need to visit a Chinese therapist to work out why I might have done this. Even though I could never admit it to myself it's clear that I did it for *him*. I did it because a part of me wanted him to be impressed by something that I had achieved. And I was prepared to mould my entire life around this silly little objective. Pathetic really, because he was never *that* impressed; or at least he didn't appear to be. And now that he's gone here I am doing it one more time: I'm a boxing writer again. Sort of. Except this time it's for me.

I spill out all the lurid details and her face remains expressionless as she listens. I explain that it's a secret that's been withheld from her for over 40 years because the worry was that the truth would be too much for her to take. But things are seldom as straightforward as they might appear: in the months since he died she has slowly turned from grieving widow to somebody who has difficulty hiding her resentment towards the man she was with for over half a century. What I have to tell her only adds to her loathing of him.

She calls him a bastard. She says that she hates him. She says it like he's still alive. She asks me why I never told her it was happening. I tell her that I tried to, at least I think I tried to. The memory plays tricks on you over the years so that you can never be completely sure of anything. 'Well you should have tried harder,' she says, too coldly, too callously. I remind her I was only 12 years old when it was happening, a year younger than Sofia is now. What did she expect me to do? Put in a formal complaint to HR?

On the journey down I had been telling myself that whatever happened this morning it was not going to be what I expected. Although, in truth I had no idea what to expect. Even so, I'm shocked and angry when she spots a neighbour walking past the window and cheerfully exclaims, *Oh, look there's Peter* – or whatever his name is – *he's a really nice man.*

It's an astonishing thing to say. Further exacerbated by her suggestion that we go for a walk on the pier, have a spot of lunch. Try to make the best of a bad day.

My voice is shaking. 'I'm not buying it,' I tell her. 'I just don't believe that you didn't know!'

Of course, later, when I think about it I will understand that I was being unfair. Here was a woman who had just been told a secret that no mother should ever have to hear. Frankly, no rule book has been written to outline the appropriate reaction in a situation such as this. You do what you can do. And clearly my mother is a woman in denial. Perhaps she always has been.

I get up and walk out. I don't say goodbye. I go back to London. Back to my real family. Back to Sofia, thankfully on the mend again after her recent relapse. Back from the past and into the present.

Session #6

'HOW could she *not* have known?' she asks.

'I know… It's hard to believe but I really don't think she did.'

I'm trembling as I look at her. Then at the clock with its unmoving fingers. Then at her again.

'I think there was a delayed reaction,' I say. 'Because apparently after I left she rushed around to my brother's house and was absolutely inconsolable. She couldn't stop crying.'

'People express their grief in different ways,' she says. I do wish she'd cut out the dial-a-clichés.

'Anyhow… I received a letter from her later on in the week. A handwritten letter. Can you believe that? Nobody writes handwritten letters these days. She said she's sorry and intends to try and make it up to me for not protecting me when I was a kid.'

Silence. Of course there's silence. She wants me to fill those spaces again. Crafty bitch.

'But I don't really see how she could do that. What's done is done. In fact, I almost regretting letting the cat out of the bag… Other than getting this thing off my chest I don't really see what good it's done.'

'How do you feel?'

'I dunno… I feel guilty I suppose, although I know that victims are always the ones made to feel guilty… Strangely enough I don't feel that an enormous weight has been lifted from my shoulders… I thought that's how I would feel but it kind of doesn't make a difference.'

Silence.

'I've decided to write this all down in a book. Well compile it for want of a better word. For the last seven months I've been going around interviewing ex-boxers and I really had no idea why I was doing it. I'd toyed with the idea of trying to sell the odd article to a newspaper but something's stopped me from bothering. Probably because nobody would really be interested in publishing anything I've written.'

'And do you know why now?'

Silence.

'Sorry… Do I know why what?'

'Do you know why you have been meeting boxers?'

'Good question,' I laugh. 'Very good question. Well naturally I've thought about it a lot. It was as if I'd set off down a ski slope and couldn't stop until I reached the bottom. I think that my father dying very obviously got me to thinking about the past… And unfortunately one of the only things we had in common with a love of boxing. A bit sad really.

'And the odd thing is that it only really struck me very recently that this journey I've been on has become all about fathers and sons. I'm not really into psychobabble but it was so obvious that I almost completely missed it.'

Silence.

'I mean I seem to have spent a lot of time recently in the company of boxers and their sons. I don't know if there was a subconscious reason for me doing this but I must have had a reason.'

'So what will you do now?'

'Well I've come to the end of my free sessions, so I think this will be it for me.'

'But I would really recommend that you seek further therapy.'

'I'm sorry but it's not for me… It's just not really my cup of tea… I think I'll stick to drowning my sorrows in the bottom of a glass in future.'

'The bottom of a glass?'

'You know… Having a drink… Drinking alcohol… I'm only joking.'

'You joke a lot.'

'Well I'm a funny guy… Like I told you before, *funny peculiar.*'

Carrying

G LENN McCrory walks me through the centre of Newcastle. A tall, good-looking man in a crumpled suit, he looks as if he carries the weight of the world on his shoulders. I soon find out that he's been doing that literally and metaphorically since he was a child.

Like others in boxing I've met during the last seven months, he doesn't recognise me. Although realistically there's no real reason for him to remember that just a month short of 25 years ago I was one of many celebrating in his dressing room after he defeated a Kenyan fighter named Patrick Lumumba[91] to win the IBF world cruiserweight championship. Indeed, after only a few moments in Glenn's company you get the impression that there are simply too many people in his life for him to take stock of them all. They are everywhere; and they all seem to want a little piece of him – myself included. In the space of a minute he is stopped three times in the street by well-wishers. His hand is duly shaken and his time is duly taken. Shaken and taken. But he gives of himself freely, liberally and without complaint.

'I can see how being a celebrity could really get on your nerves,' I say.

....
91 **Patrick Lumumba** born 27 July 1959, Busia, Kenya.

'Yeah… Well… You have to try and do the right thing,' he replies in his gravelly, clipped Geordie accent.

Glenn's buying me lunch today because he foolishly bet against my parenting skills. In the course of one of a number of very long and surprisingly intimate telephone conversations we've been having recently I told him about a technique he could use to get his troublesome one-year-old son Aidan to sleep at night. Yet even though I received a text from him in April saying, 'I did what you said!! 1st full night in 3 years! Legend!! Thank you!' Glenn still looks as if he could do with a good night's sleep. He's tired and distracted. Not really wanting to be here with me but too polite and too generous to let anybody down. And this reluctance to let anybody down, I will discover, seems to permeate every fibre of Glenn's being.

I've been interested to see Glenn again after all these years because I believe he has more in common with this 53-year-old former boxing writer than most. After his career in boxing finished, Glenn suffered from depression and is another who was prescribed the same anti-depressants as I. Like myself Glenn is also known to enjoy the odd sherbet or two. There is also the fact that Glenn's father died in February this year.

* * * * *

In the week before we meet, Glenn, who is also an actor as well as a long-standing boxing commentator for Sky TV, has been in rehearsal for a one-man play about his life. It focuses upon his relationship with his late step-brother, David. David suffered from a debilitating muscle-wasting disease known as Friedreich's Ataxia. I can recall his wheelchair-bound figure being an enduring presence at Glenn's training camp whenever I visited in the last 1980s. At the time I had no idea that they were brothers; they seemed to have nothing whatsoever in common. There is also a film in development and a book has just been published, entitled *Carrying David*.

'I didn't like him at first, frankly,' announces Glenn. We take a seat in a local restaurant and it doesn't take much prompting to get the ex-fighter talking about his late brother. He will do this a great deal over the next few hours. 'What we didn't realise is that David had an illness.'

'I suppose you must have seen him as an intruder?'

'Yeah... I got pulled out of the bottom bunk and had to go in with two brothers.'

Glenn fills in the details of his childhood: his father, a steelworker, his mother's side of the family all miners, too many siblings – the inevitable consequence of a fiercely Catholic upbringing. No money. 'As a kid I used to steal anything. We never had anything so I just used to forage. And that feeling of being lost in the day to day struggle of simply surviving.

'And then all of a sudden this kid came in and it's, "Now you've got more time for a stranger than me!"'

I shouldn't really be at all surprised by now, but I am: Another boxer, another open book of emotion. But in Glenn's case there is something innately disturbing about the combination of this strapping 6ft 4in man and the rawness, the unprotected vulnerability that leaps out at you. He's yet another ex-fighter who will reveal the most personal minutiae of his life to anybody willing to listen.

'David used to be slow. We'd go to school and he'd be slow,' recalls Glenn. 'He could walk but his feet started to twist in a bit. And the nuns would give me the strap for being late. One time I said, "Right, get on my back!" and I carried him. And he loved it. And we were running and laughing. From then I would carry him whether we were late or not.

'And then all of a sudden I had someone who wanted me. Somebody needed me. And that was our relationship. That was us. We had a special relationship.'

'Was carrying him the start of your boxing?' I ask. 'Did it build up your strength?'

'Yeah… He loved it… He lived for the boxing. When I was going to pack it when I lost five or six fights I was at my lowest ebb. But David just wouldn't give in: he'd fall off the toilet, he'd fall down the stairs but he'd just get back up.

'When he was 15 the doctor said, "Hasn't anyone ever explained his condition to you? He's got a muscle wasting disease." Normally the life expectancy is 15. So he was living on borrowed time.'

'That's awful,' I say.

'He died a month short of his 30th birthday. There were times when he was so bad that he'd be asleep and his breathing would start to drift. You'd lie next to him in the bed and think, "Should I stick a pillow over his face?"'

'Is this in your book?' I ask.

'No, I don't think it is.'

'Do you not want people to know this?'

'No it's okay… I loved him and I just couldn't… He fought for life right until the end… He fought every day to live.'

'Did you love him because he depended on you?'

'From that first moment we fell in love… You know… And when the kids at school called him a "spacker" I smashed the living daylights out of them… I got dragged off.'

Despite his size, it's hard to imagine Glenn using violence on anybody. Scarcely a sentence comes from his lips that doesn't contain the word 'love'. We've only been talking for about 20 minutes and he's already choking back the emotion. As am I. And then he suddenly changes the subject. Now he's asking me why I wanted to meet up with him.

For the very last time I tell a boxer *everything* about my father. About how we didn't get along in the worst way imaginable. But this time it's no longer a secret. Now that my mother finally knows it seems right, almost natural, that everyone should be aware of what happened.

'Why didn't you like your father?' asked Glenn, turning from confessor to therapist. 'How did that manifest itself?'

I tell Glenn about the abuse I endured as a child. I give him more detail than I afforded my mother when I met her the weekend before. Glenn doesn't seem remotely surprised.

'Did you have a dislike of your mum?' he asks.

'No… It's complicated.'

'She didn't help you, did she?' Glenn announces. 'You want your mum beside you, don't you?'

I tell Glenn about the unexpected effect that my father's death had on me. The strange dichotomy I experienced: about being utterly bereft by the loss of the man who was such a brute towards me and at the same time hating him more than I've ever hated anybody. I tell Glenn about the effect that the anti-depressants had on me: Me and Glenn and Herol *et al.*

'I came off them straight away,' admits Glenn. 'I just didn't have anything. It was as if I was walking in a mist. I kind of just decided to myself that without feeling pain you can't feel happiness. Without one you can't have the other.

'So I thought I'd just battle through. At the end of the day we're all going to the same place and we can just keep putting one foot in front of the other.'

'With me it was also the fact that I couldn't have sex any more,' I confess.

Glenn nods towards me knowingly.

'Was it the same for you?'

The ex-boxer laughs a little guiltily, 'Yeah… I'm saying all this shit but that was one of the main things.'

'I physically couldn't do it.'

'No… I couldn't… How did your depression manifest itself?' asks Glenn.

'Well it was weird,' I reply. 'Embarrassing. I'd be out and just start crying for no reason and not be able to stop. Or something would trigger it when I was at home alone and the tears would be pouring out of me.'

'I did a lot of crying too,' says Glenn. 'I still find it really hard because David is really, really raw… It never goes away.'

'I can see it's really raw, Glenn, I feel really bad about bringing all of this up.'

'After my first divorce I'd see a girl for a while and I'd start to cry and I'd think, "You don't want me." And I'd leave. And I went to see a therapist because I didn't know what was wrong. And I found myself flirting with her and her flirting back. And it wasn't doing any good whatsoever.'

'That's not really what's supposed to happen,' I agree.

'Yeah… I've never been to a therapist since but it's something I really should do… But then I just think, "I'll fix myself." But you never do.'

'There's times in my life when I thought I could quite happily die. I'd be sitting on a plane going "Please crash… Please come down."'

'Are you comfortable talking like this to strangers?' I ask.

'No… It's fine. I've done a lot of talking about David.'

'It really does sound like a case of classic clinical depression,' I say.

'Yes… I got diagnosed with long-term depression. It affected me really, really bad. I felt that nobody looked after me.

'It's very hard when you're in a difficult relationship… Your family's struggling. It got to the point where, honestly, every day was in a grey mist. I just could not lift the darkness… Everything was grey.' Glenn lets out a groan. 'Now when I look things are in colour.'

'Your public persona is very different to the real you,' I say. 'On TV you seem very confident… Well adjusted… Happy.'

'I'm a mess.'

'Well, we're all a bit of a mess really,' I agree. 'I used to take a lot of drugs to try to sort out that mess… Except of course you don't realise at the time that this is the reason you're doing it.'

'Mine was alcohol…' says Glenn. 'There's times when you drink too much and you think, "What did I do that for?" But it kind of takes away the pain a bit. And makes more pain at the end of it. But I never actually thought I was depressed. I just kind of thought that my glass was half full.'

'Same as me. That's exactly how my wife describes me.'

'But I think when David died it was one of those where… I prayed for him to die. To get him out of his misery. And then he went.'

Glenn issues an unintelligible grunt. He's still feeling the pain.

'I don't know whether it was guilt or whether I didn't want him to go… I didn't realise how much I loved him… And then combined with how my career was, and my marriage… Everything was horrendous.'

* * * * *

The conversation stalls for a moment. And once again I find myself astonished, humbled, overwhelmed by these incredible people who fight for their living inside a roped off square of canvas. Every single boxer I've met up with in the past few months seems to have been desperate to bare his soul. It's completely at odds with everything you might expect of these often brutally violent men.

I change the subject: I tell Glenn about Herol Graham and his near death experience. I flick on my phone and show him that picture of Herol's impressive scar. In doing so Glenn catches a glimpse of an old black and white photograph of me, taken a few years before he and I met. He stares at it for long time.

'Aah, I know that fellow,' he says eventually. 'I remember him 100 per cent.

'That's why I didn't remember you earlier – Jesus, you were just a kid then.'

'It's true,' I say. 'Now I'm an old man writing about boxing for the first time in an eternity.'

'What sort of pushed you away from the sport?' asks Glenn.

I launch into my well-trodden story, my apologies for having to do this one final time: about feeling complicit when boxers I knew were hurt. And about how I've now realised that I seem to have been using boxing as a means of getting over my dad.

'I know what you mean,' says Glenn. 'I wrote my book for the same reason – to try and get over my brother David.'

'He's obviously deeply entrenched in your life,' I say.

'Then I finished it and found out it was too angry.'

'Angry?' I say. 'Angry at who?'

'I was just angry at everybody: ex-wives… Management… It was just a case that I needed to get all that out.'

'Did you see the death of your brother as a metaphor for all of this?'

'Yeah… Probably… Yeah… Probably that just kind of summed up the whole of my life. It was just a struggle… Just hard… And in the end I thought, "I don't even want to put this out." And so I left it for two years. When I went back to it when I had kind of healed a bit.'

Like Derek Williams, whom I met up with what seems like a million years ago, Glenn is one of the few British fighters to have sparred with Mike Tyson. It's a welcome relief to move away from the dark subjects that have been occupying us and simply talk about boxing for a while. I like talking about boxing, I'm finally beginning to realise that more and more. So does Glenn.

'Larry Holmes[92] was my hero – I loved him,' he says. 'And I was sent over to spar with Mike Tyson in preparation for his fight with Holmes.'

'Who's idea was that? You were never really a heavyweight and hadn't you lost five times by then?'

92 **Larry Holmes** born 3 November 1949, Georgia, USA. Former WBC and IBF heavyweight champion of the world.

'It was my manager of the time. I remember Tyson's cornerman Matt Baranski befriended me because I didn't have a trainer. He said, "Who the fuck sent you out here? He's *loves* knocking people out... But a WHITE guy!"

'But Tyson never knocked me down. I did well with him. It was tough. It was a hard way to make money.'

'So how did you stop him from hurting you?'

'I never stopped moving. Tyson was unbeatable at that moment. I remember thinking that this guy's just got no weakness.

'And then I remember Robin Givens[93] walking in and he just turned into putty. And I was thinking, "For fuck's sake! No! No! No! No!" And I could tell... I could just see there and then that this was going to end badly.'

Strangely enough, Glenn was initially managed by Alan Minter's father-in-law, Doug Bidwell. Bidwell seemed to be willing to offer Glenn's services as sparring partner to anyone who could pay.

'When I sparred, Bonecrusher[94] tears were running down my eyes. I was only 19,' Glenn recalls. 'You're just a bit too young for that. My manager put me in sparring with anybody. And that's how I learned. Trevor Berbick[95] I sparred with, too. That was hard.'

Even harder for Glenn was the fact that he ended up being yet another victim of boxing's omnipresent financial predators. Although he won the IBF cruiserweight title Glenn, predictably, earned very little in the way of hard cash for his trouble.

93 **Robin Simone Givens** born 27 November 1964, New York, USA. Actress and first wife of Mike Tyson.

94 **James 'Bonecrusher' Smith** born 3 April 1953, North Carolina, USA. Former WBA heavyweight champion of the world.

95 **Trevor Berbick** 1 August 1954 – 28 October 2006, Port Antonio, Jamaica. Former WBC heavyweight champion of the world.

'I was on the dole when I won the world title,' he recalls. 'I signed off the night I won it. I somehow ended up having two managers. One manager took 33.5 per cent, the other took 25 per cent. I took home about £3,900 for that fight.'

'You read about this sort of thing all the time,' I say. 'But it's still shocking when you actually encounter it.'

'I don't think there was many as bad as mine,' Glenn agrees. 'After I retired I had to get a fight with Lennox Lewis to pay the taxman. I had nothing. I needed to get £80,000 and that's why I fought Lennox. I knew I was going to lose that fight.'

'It's such a terrible business!' I say.

'Yeah!'

'It's not the boxers… As we keep saying, the boxers are *lovely* people.'

'Yeah… That's why I was angry.'

'Is that another reason why you got depressed?' I ask.

'Yeah… Boxing had a lot to do with it. Because I found myself coming out of a career with no money. Nothing. I'd been world champion and got nothing. British and Commonwealth champion and got nothing.'

'How were you surviving?'

'I wasn't… I got two houses repossessed.'

'But everybody must have assumed that you had lots of money.'

'Yeah… They think you must be minted… But I had two divorces… One of them was an American – She's got my baby over there… She's seven.'

'Oh Glenn,' I say. 'That's terrible… I couldn't handle that.'

'No it's hard. Very hard.'

* * * * *

Almost inevitably the conversation turns to religion. I've been waiting for this to sooner or later happen. Once again, is there a boxer alive today who doesn't want to try to convert me to

God? But that's not entirely fair, because Glenn doesn't really try. He just looks genuinely concerned when I tell him that I am a non-believer.

'When people say that I really find it difficult to understand,' he says. 'I mean, why would you not want to believe in something?'

'I'm a pragmatist,' I tell him. 'It's not that I don't believe that there is some kind of underlying force that holds the universe together, it's more that fact that I find it hard to believe that it has a consciousness and wears a white beard.'

'But you must believe that there's something else after death?' he says.

I describe to Glenn my own lowest point. About the time a few years ago when my undiagnosed hypothyroidism had become so bad that my body had simply packed up. I could hardly walk, I was morbidly obese. I was depressed beyond human endurance. Writing was completely out of the question. Of how I lay in bed night after night trying to work how I could die in a way that would cause the least distress to my wife and daughter.

About how, ludicrously, I would spend hours pondering the nature of the universe, trying to unravel its beginning and end. Perhaps this was the closest I ever got to a religious experience.

'Am I talking nonsense here?' I ask, embarrassed. 'Is it the Guinness?'

'No... No... You're just speaking the truth.'

'Well boxing is all about truth, isn't it? Truth and lies.'

'I still occasionally have nightmares of fighting again and not being prepared,' says Glenn, his eyes far off in the distance. 'In my career I never pulled out of fight but in the dream you get to the point where you pull out. And the sense of relief is incredible. Because, you know, nowadays I'm not well enough to fight. I can't do it. So you've got that insecurity that you can't do it anymore.'

'That's your stress dream,' I say. 'How often do you have that?'

'Normally when I've bitten off more than I can chew.'

'I get a similar stress dream,' I say.

'All I ever wanted was to win the world title,' says Glenn. 'I'd been told my whole career that I'd never win a world title. Even my dad said that.'

'Your dad told you that?'

'Yeah… I think he didn't want to see me hurt. And when I won the world title that was it for me. My heart wasn't in it any more. I would have retired then. I'd had such a hard career.

'When I was a kid I loved Frank Sinatra and Richard Burton and the Brat Pack and all the hell-raisers. And I prayed that I could be like that. That's all I wanted. Because it was looking like I was either going to go down the mines or to work in the steel factory. And I had nightmares about the darkness. And I prayed to God saying I want to have every single experience. I want to live life… I want to live for two. I want to live for David as well. But careful what you wish for.'

Missing

ERIC Seccombe's daughter, Terry, finally gets back to me and we have a long telephone conversation. It's not good news. It transpires that Eric has developed a form of dementia known as vascular dementia. He's now 86 and is not expected to last long. I tell Terry about my reunion with Michael Watson, and of Michael's desire to once again see his former trainer. Her response is unexpectedly non-committal.

When I began this journey into my past more than eight months ago I was struggling to come to terms with the loss of my own father. And while that battle is far from over I believe that the impact of meeting up with so many faces from my past has been wholly positive. What it hasn't managed to do, however, is to make this old fool any less sentimental or idealistic or just plain stupid. In the back of my mind I had somehow imagined myself to be a hero: I'd gallop into view riding a white horse and magically reunite Michael with his one time mentor. Of course, as is usually the way in life: things never turn out quite the way you expect them to.

During the course of several recent meet-ups with Michael he'd begun to fill in a few details about Eric that I didn't already know. I had no idea, for example, that a short time before he became Michael's trainer Eric had tragically lost a son in a car crash. The son's name was Michael. And although I'd already sensed it, Watson had admitted to me that he used

281

to look upon Eric as a father to him. This formal declaration was confirmed on the telephone by Terry, who told me that her father in turn used to look upon Michael as a son. What better way, then, to make up for losing my own father than to give Michael back his father, and Eric his son? Wouldn't that be a fantastic thing to do?

The first indication that things might not turn out to be as straightforward as anticipated comes when Terry tells me that before she will allow Michael to meet Eric, she wants to first talk to Michael alone. The second indication comes via Michael's friend Lennie, who calls and tells me that Michael does not after all want to meet his ailing former trainer because he 'doesn't want to see him like that'.

* * * * *

So I go to visit Eric alone. Terry kindly comes and picks me up and it turns out that her father is currently staying in Holloway, literally a stone's throw from my own house. When I arrive he's sitting in a chair by the window watching television. I walk up to him and grasp his hand. He greets me with a beaming smile. He's older, naturally he is. Stouter. And the hair's gone. But he's still Eric. Still the nice, down to earth, ordinary bloke that you couldn't help but warm towards. I'm now more or less the age he was when I first met him all those years ago.

Ironically, of all the people from boxing whom I've met of late, Eric has the least trouble of all remembering me. It's obviously difficult for him to talk but he goes into great detail about a skinny bloke that 'used to write about boxing' who 'suddenly went missing'. And that statement, more than any that I've concocted to describe myself in the last couple of hundred or so pages, sums up best of all what I really am: I'm a bloke who used to write about boxing who suddenly went missing.

I stay for three or four hours and mainly listen to Eric talk. As the memories struggle to claw their way to the surface he tells me all about how he used to train Frank Buglioni, which I've never really discussed with Frank and comes as a bit of a surprise to me. Strange how all the threads disentangle themselves. We talk about the fights we used to attend together, about how Eric grew to genuinely like Nigel Benn. Perhaps I've got the former Dark Destroyer all wrong: everybody but me seems to have a good word for him.

We swap anecdotes about that wily old boxing manager Mickey Duff, now long gone, and other people no longer with us. Cuts man Dennie Mancini, who used to run a gym on Carnaby Street and also managed the Lonsdale Shop in Soho. He was frightening to look at but had a heart of pure gold. And we talk about boxers from the past such as Terry Downes[96] and Terry Spinks[97], the latter Eric boxed as an amateur. It's a pleasant if bittersweet way to spend an afternoon and Eric is in much better form than I'd been warned to expect. All the while Terry sits alongside us, filling in the gaps for her father when the memory fails, finishing off stories when the words run dry, refereeing our dialogue with unlimited patience and love.

One thing we don't talk much about is Michael Watson. His name barely comes up at all until finally, just as I'm just about to leave, I tell Eric all about my reconciliation with his former protégé, the man whom he was with from the amateurs all the way to a world title shot. He listens, seemingly unperturbed, his facial expression blank.

'Do you want to see Michael?' Terry asks him.

'Who?' says Eric.

'Michael… Michael Watson.'

....

96 **Terry Downes** born 9 May 1936. Former British and Commonwealth middleweight champion.

97 **Terry Spinks** 28 February 1938–26 April 2012. Former British featherweight champion.

'Michael Watson?' shrugs the old man. 'Why would I want to see *him*?'

* * * * *

We stop outside my house and I lean over close to Terry. We look into each other's eyes as she tells me how she and Eric 'nearly fell out' years ago when he encouraged her two sons to take up boxing. 'There's no way I was going to do that,' she says. 'It's too dangerous.'

I tell her that I can't help but suspect that Eric's dementia is linked to the number of punches that he took when he was a boxer. Just as the widespread depression that I've witnessed in more or less every ex-fighter I've come across in the last eight or so months has to have a physical connection with blows received to the head. We talk about the long-term damage that we've both seen in too many fighters whom we've known personally. Boxing's dangerous all right: if not today then tomorrow.

Later I receive a text from Terry. She tells me that her dad was 'full of chat' after seeing that bloke who used to write about boxing who suddenly went missing. And I think I may have just made another long-term commitment: I tell Terry I'll visit Eric again soon. 'Maybe we can both just sit and watch boxing,' I say.

Epilogue

HEROL has been out of hospital for a month or so now and I arrange to take him for something to eat in Muswell Hill. It's a beautiful sunny day and I catch a bus and then limp the rest of the way there. The house that Herol shares with Karen is about half a mile from the main street. It's a modest end of terrace property with a small garden. When I knock, the door is opened by his daughter Natasha. Powerful, lovely Natasha.

The living room is smartly decorated. And if it wasn't for the dozens of themed get well cards that take up every spare inch of shelf space you would never know that a once-famous boxer lived here. Natasha is pleased to see me and I her. We hug each other and talk happily for several minutes while Herol does whatever he's doing upstairs. It's a joyous atmosphere. So different to the last time we met.

Herol finally descends the stairs, freshly showered and dressed in jeans and a green sweatshirt. Before I have the chance to mouth a greeting he yells, 'Oh shaddup!' And the three of us giggle. He's looking good: fit and healthy. Hard to believe that it was touch and go not so long ago. 'The tests have come back and it wasn't Crohn's Disease after all,' he tells me. 'They don't really know what caused it.'

The 20-minute walk to the high street is entertaining: Herol seems to know everybody who passes by, and if he doesn't he will do by the time he's stopped and talked to them. He takes great delight in showing off his scar, a vicious and spectacular wound that vertically dissects his washboard stomach. The black woman pushing a pram along the street lets out a howl of shock when she sees it. As does the young muscled man in shades whom Herol tells me he used to train.

As we walk the sun sinks beneath the clouds and it begins to rain; it dawns on me again that Herol seems to be hard-wired into believing that everybody he meets must know who he is. It has to be a hangover from the days when this really was the case, when film crews pursued him through the Sheffield streets and 'Bomber' Graham was one of the most famous black men in the country.

Occasionally he will yell at a passer-by, offering to fight them and be greeted by a perplexed, sometimes worried expression. And every so often he will repeat his favourite saying to anybody willing to listen, 'He who fights and runs away lives to hunt another day.' In the boredom of that hospital I'd Googled the saying so at least Herol knew who it was by: Oliver Goldsmith.

This behaviour continues when we reach Chooks, an unassuming little restaurant on the high street that specialises in fried chicken. When the waiter comes to take his order he is also told to 'shaddup!' I shrug my shoulders helplessly as he looks over at me, not quite sure what he's dealing with. A healthy, fit Herol Graham is, it has to be said, incredibly good fun to be around. A stark contrast to the man who was howling in pain only a short while ago. I tell him that I had no idea he was such a laugh.

Even the ordering of food is a performance in itself, 'You shouldn't do this,' instructs Herol, pointing to a particular item on the menu. 'You should do it with a hot sauce. People will like that.'

'Good idea, sir,' says the waiter, already getting used to his unorthodox new customer. And unorthodox really is the best way to describe Herol's behaviour. On face value he seems to go through life in a similar manner as he did with boxing. Not for Herol anything so basic, so fundamental, as social convention.

When it comes to drinks nothing on the menu is quite enough to satisfy the ex-boxer. 'I want a hot chocolate,' he demands.

'We don't do hot chocolate,' says the manager upon being summoned to our table. By coincidence she is also Jamaican and seems familiar with the brand of person she is dealing with.

'Yes you do,' Herol earnestly insists.

'But we don't have a kettle,' she continues.

'That's okay. All you have to do is get a milkshake and put a chocolate brownie it and then microwave it.'

The waiter looks over at me and frowns. The manager gives me a sneaky wink.

'Well seeing as it's you,' she says, despite not having a clue who he is. 'But don't ever ask me again.'

We look on as Herol's concoction is prepared. Soon a steaming glass of white froth with a chocolate brownie floating in it which is marginally less appealing than a dog turd is brought to the table. Herol takes a sip and winces. 'I can't drink this,' he says. 'It's not very nice.'

* * * * *

So we talk. We eat and talk. And as always it's about boxing. This is what occurs to me about Herol and possibly everybody else I've spoken to from the sport during the past eight months. However hard you try *not* to talk about boxing, however hard you endeavour to find some other form of common ground, it's always boxing that wins out. This is not to say that it's all these special people know about – that would be patently untrue – but it's usually the best way that they can find to fill the silence in their lives that descends once the punches have stopped.

We talk about Sheffield and the working men's clubs where Herol used to invite people to hit him; we talk about other fighters; we talk about weigh-ins, press conferences and the other viscera that comes bundled with boxing. We laugh about Herol's habit of tapping his opponents on the buttocks in order to infuriate them. We talk about nothing new at all but despite this it's never anything but a joy to hear him chip away at his past.

We end the afternoon by indulging ourselves with a deep-fried Mars bar. Neither of us has ever tried this particular Scottish delicacy before and you will naturally have some trouble finding any boxing manual that recommends such a smorgasbord of fat and sugar. When we hug in the street afterwards and say our farewells Herol is already thinking about getting back to the gym. His wounds have scarcely healed, and his near brush with death might very possibly have given him a different perspective on a life that has been lived more than most. But he has calories to burn.